I0115329

i

Adaptive Society

Biology Supports Global Law, Consensual
Government, and Sustainable Technology

Ross Milburn

HONG KONG

Adaptive Society MEDIA

First Edition Published in Hong Kong by Adaptive Society Media

© Copyright 2015 Ross Milburn. All rights reserved. No part of this book may be reproduced or transmitted in any form or by any means, electronic or mechanical, including photocopying, recording, or by an information storage and retrieval system – with the exception of a reviewer who may quote brief passages in a review to be printed in a newspaper or magazine – without written permission from the publisher. For information, contact Adaptive Society Media, PO Box 34812, King's Road, Hong Kong.

Edited by Gillian Kew, WWW.GillianKew.org

LOC and British Library Alignment:
Publisher's Cataloging-in-Publication data
Milburn, Ross.
   Adaptive society : biology supports global law, consensual government, and sustainable technology / Ross Milburn.
   p. cm.
   ISBN 978-988-13110-5-4
   Includes bibliographical references and index.

1. Human evolution. 2. Technological innovations --Social aspects. 3. Free enterprise. 4. Technology --Social aspects. 5. Human ecology. 6. Social evolution. I. Title.

HM626 .M53 2014
303.4 --dc23

"The real problem of humanity is the following: we have Paleolithic emotions, medieval institutions and god-like technology"
E.O. Wilson

"As man advances in civilization, and small tribes are united into larger communities, the simplest reason would tell each individual that he ought to extend his social instincts and sympathies to all the members of the same nation, though personally unknown to him. This point being once reached, there is only an artificial barrier to prevent his sympathies extending to the men of all nations and races."
Charles Darwin

"Nationalism is an infantile disease. It is the measles of mankind."
Albert Einstein

"It is important to remember that government interference always means either violent action or the threat of such action. The funds that a government spends for whatever purposes are levied by taxation. And taxes are paid because the taxpayers are afraid of offering resistance to the tax gatherers. They know that any disobedience or resistance is hopeless." "The essential feature of government is enforcement of its decrees by beating, killing, and imprisoning. Those who are asking for more government interference are asking ultimately for more compulsion and less freedom."
Ludwig von Mises

"What is the basic, the essential, the crucial principle that differentiates freedom from slavery? It is the principle of voluntary action versus physical coercion or compulsion."
Ayn Rand

Table of Contents

Table of Illustrations

Preface

United Humans can Create Civilization Fit for All

*A*daptive Society is an explanation of the causes of the current partial failure of human adaptation to our technology-based home or "habitat," and a description of the minimal actions required for the human species to achieve satisfactory, long-term adaptation to a civilization built on rapidly-changing technologies.

In the past, attempts to discern the fundamental problems of civilization and prescribe remedies have often been ridiculed as utopian. Today, however, virtually the whole scientific community accepts that humans face major challenges and that sustainable ways of using technology must be found.

In the last 10,000 years, humans have created many powerful and valuable technologies, the side-effects of which have done them great harm. Problems such as warfare, unnatural hierarchy, the extreme wealth differentials that cause starvation, conflict between races and sexes, alienation caused by unsuitable and oppressive working conditions, pollution, unsustainable economic activities, and a general absence of the rights that are necessary for normal human development, are all ultimately the harmful side-effects of technologies that we all now depend upon.

Since we humans have created the causes of our own maladaptation, we have, as a species, the capacity to remedy them. I strongly urge all readers to consider the evidence I present in the following chapters and to commit themselves in whatever way they can to the coming struggle to legally unify the human species, a process that is essential to the achievement of a complete and lasting civilization that can handle technology without harming its members.

Ross Milburn, August 2014.

Introduction

The Greatest Adventure in Human History

A *daptive Society* explains how humans, who evolved to live in nature, can adapt themselves to live in an artificial civilization built
with technology. Successful adaptation, for the individual and for
the human species, will mean obtaining a good "fit" with every aspect
of the habitat, which is necessary for well-being. "Fitness" was first
given its biological meaning by Charles Darwin in his 1859 book, "The
Origin of Species," which showed us that, when individual members of
any species fail to adapt to changes in their habitat, their survival and
reproduction is jeopardized; if a whole species fails to adapt, it may become extinct.

When humans lived in nature, they were uniquely successful. The
first truly modern humans left Africa within the last 100,000 years, and
gradually migrated across the vast regions of Eurasia. Eventually, people reached the Australian continent, and others walked across the Bering straits to the Americas, and even up to the Arctic Circle, where they
became the ancestors of modern Eskimos and Inuit peoples. This ex
traordinary feat was achieved using human brainpower and early technologies such as stone weapons, clothing, and fire. No other species on
the planet (except, perhaps, human parasites such as head lice and fleas)
could have left their African home and lived comfortably in such diverse
worldwide habitats within such a short space of time.

Today, unfortunately, the fit between people and their artificial
habitat is failing, and that means a reduction in well-being for all humans. Almost every systematic human problem that arises – warfare,
starvation, great differences in wealth, unemployment, most diseases,
obesity, pollution and destruction of nature, to name a few – can be seen
as failures of fit between humans and their habitat.

3

It is widely perceived that evolution cannot adapt humans to the harmful side-effects of technology. Darwin showed us that evolution changes humans to adapt them to new conditions by the "natural selection" of individuals whose traits are best adapted to the habitat. But this biotic evolution is very slow and it cannot prepare people for the fast-changing conditions in industrial civilization that have never previously been encountered. Therefore, modern humans appear to be trapped – we cannot live without advanced technology, but neither can we fully adapt to living with it.

This popular explanation for the problems of modern society is often supported by scientists, but it is really only a fragment of the full explanation for the current human problems of maladaptation. At the same time that the general public has learned about the importance of Darwin's evolution of the species, scientists and thinkers have been piecing together a completely new and different kind of evolution. It is now being realized that many parts of human society, such as language, the learning process, economic markets, the dissemination of ideas, and the rapid advancement of technology, are subject to a "trial and error" process of evolution that has much in common with biological evolution based on genes.

For people in an industrial civilization, adaptation no longer depends upon biotic evolution, but rather upon the evolution of civilization itself. Most scientists call this "cultural evolution" but this description may mislead some people as to what it is that is evolving, and I therefore prefer to use a more inclusive term: "evolution of the artificial human habitat," or for short, "habitat evolution."

In Darwinian evolution, all species, including humans, are subject to genetic inheritance, variation, and natural selection, that result in adaptation to the habitat. In habitat evolution, the whole human habitat, comprising knowledge, learned behaviors and all the artifacts of civilization, evolve to create an adaptive relationship with the human population. This means that the evolution necessary to create adaptive "fit" between humans and their habitat has been inverted.

If the evolution of our habitat is allowed to operate naturally, it should rapidly remedy all maladaptive aspects of the environment, including not only major sources of injury and death, such as inequitable access to food and water, pollution and warfare, but also less tangible challenges to the quality of life, such as the psychological stresses of unemployment, repressive enforced schooling, excessive materialism and the increasing marginalization of family and community. All these "systematic" problems of civilization are, ultimately, harmful side-effects of technology, and humans who are clever enough to invent new technologies are also clever enough to remedy their defects.

But there is a problem. Modern government is itself a technology that has harmful side-effects, because it centralizes human society, transforming the social organization by imposing a monopoly of force, and thereby disrupting the evolution of the habitat. All current governments comprise elite groups that acquire a monopoly of force over their societies and are therefore parasitical in nature. Humans need to understand and to remedy this catastrophic accident of history in order to retrieve their normal social organization and to fully thrive as a species.

We know that the evolution of civilization is a powerful force that should support a thriving human community. In fact, during the evolutionary period, humans who lived in small bands of about 50 people did solve the problems of adaptation as they created early technologies. All the adult members of each band constantly discussed the problems facing their group and made consensual decisions to improve the fit between the group and its natural environment. Wise men and women were chosen as leaders, but they were not permitted to overrule the members of the group. In the rare cases when consensus proved impossible, and conflict was threatened, disaffiliated members could leave and join other bands, or form their own.

This form of government was much stronger and more "intelligent" than any government known today, for several reasons. First, decision-making by consensus meant that the brains of every man and woman contributed to decisions, so that more options could be explored and major blunders of judgment were less likely. Second, all members of the band would be motivated to support a consensus, ensuring that decisions would be implemented with enthusiasm, in great contrast to the political infighting that constitutes, for example, modern democracy. Third, hunter-gathers lived in communities based on the extended family, so that everyone took it for granted that decisions had to be compatible with the interests of the tribal elders and the infants, as well as the parental generation. Contrast that with modern societies, in which groups representing different generations greedily lobby to maximize their share of the state resources taken by force from productive individuals and companies. Fourth, human bands were small, so that the mistakes that each band made could only affect a few people. In contrast, when modern governments make mistakes, millions of people may become physically or psychologically ill, or be killed.

Humans need to live in small face-to-face communities and to govern their own affairs as they did in evolution. One reason for the persistence of religious communities in the scientific age is that most people wish to live in a small community with a strong moral system. Scientists constantly criticize religion, without realizing the powerful truth that religious groups reveal in their intuitive choice of lifestyle. Conversely, scientists can teach religious adherents about natural evolution and the unchanging laws that govern the universe. There is an opportunity for collaboration.

Even if humans re-created the small autonomous communities that supported their success in the past, could they really adapt to the modern technology-based city life? The answer is "yes," because evolution took care of that by helping humans to create an extremely sophisticated culture that supports collaborative behavior. In a human society without a coercive state, culture evolves alongside technology and continuously supports the adaptive fit between humans and their artificial societies. Natural human societies could easily handle the problem of achieving fitness within the technological habitat.

Currently, however, ordinary people, with their inherited morality and intelligence, supported by their families and their community, have been largely displaced as the source of government by the machinery of the nation state, based solely on conquest and the dictatorship of an elite that has achieved access to the social instruments that control monopoly force.

For 10,000 years, the governments of sovereign states have existed in mutual insecurity with one another. The ruling elites of each state have dominated their subjects with unnatural coercion and continually resorted to warfare. Rape, looting, torture and slavery – things that are mostly alien to normal human societies – became commonplace in most states. Today, sovereign states are still the norm, causing more warfare deaths in the 20th century than in previous history combined, more slavery in the 21st century than in 19th century Africa, and the greatest enforced hierarchies on Earth since our chimpanzee-like ancestors brutalized one another.

That is why it is essential that humans must muster the intelligence and the resolve to demand better government. We must move on from dictatorships, from communism, fascism, and democracy (which is "the dictatorship of the majority"). We must, above all, move on from the "sovereign state" which always yields absolute power to a tiny ruling elite. We need real civilization, so that humans can achieve an excellent fit with their artificial technology-based habitat. That is only possible if we have normal social organization that supports the cultural evolution that we inherited from nature, and that made early humans so magnificently successful.

Only Natural Government can Create fully Civilized societies

Most people, when asked to support the reform of government, tend to shake their heads in disbelief that such a large task can be achieved. Yet we have seen in the 20th century alone, the fall of great coercive governmental systems such as communism and fascism. Ultimately, such changes occur as a result of natural forces that are irresistible. If humans do not create an efficient and appropriate form of government, the natural laws of the universe will do the job for them, and the experience may be one of "tough love." The ultimate alternative to adopting proper government and social organization will finally be extinction; humans may disappear from the face of the Earth.

If you believe that I exaggerate, consider the fate of the Japanese and European communities, both of which have reproductive rates of little more than one child per family. As the populations of these great and successful human groups halve in size in each generation, they are threatened with rapid extinction, according to demographers. What could more clearly indicate that "natural selection" – the evolutionary process that made humans what they are and sustains them – has been massively damaged by the coercive, parasitic system of state power that emerged from the brutal conquest of early warfare?

In the 21st century, humans must restore the normal social organization of their species and extend it to encompass all peoples by the creation of global natural law that will outlaw the initiation of violence, and implement the "non-aggression principle" that is favored by all people who believe in peace and justice.

The re-creation of human autonomy, together with the creation of a great global free market and a universal system of law that will protect human rights for every member of the human species, is a breathtaking project, perhaps the most important ever conceived.

To realize this dream, the global population needs to study its own history and prehistory. Societies need to guarantee to every human the autonomy that evolved in nature, and thereby release the full intelligence of whole communities to express adaptive preferences and remedy the harmful side-effects of technology. In the 21st century, it will become a competitive necessity for human communities to re-create the habitat conditions to which all humans are adapted by evolution.

In *Adaptive Society*, I describe precisely how humans have arrived at their current precarious situation, and outline the educational task needed to galvanize the human species towards the great collaborative effort required to build a peaceful, and fully adaptive civilization. Enormous though this task is, it is well within the ability of the seven billion women and men on Earth. If you are a thinking person and you care for your fellow humans, prepare to take part in the "Greatest Adventure in Human History."

Chapter 1

Civilization is not Adapted to Human Needs

*A*ll the men and women who ever lived have walked a daily knife edge, straining their mental faculties and physical endurance to achieve an adaptive "fit" with the world around them. Individuals constantly adjust the food that they eat to fit their appetites and nutritional needs. They adjust their sleeping time to alleviate fatigue, and they may exercise to maintain bodily health. Some will consume alcohol or other mind-altering drugs, adjusting the dose to avoid embarrassment or legal problems. Relationships with spouses, children, friends, and workplace colleagues, are examined and re-examined to provoke the behavioral responses that support fitness. Clothing is adjusted to fit each wearer's body, current fashions, and the weather. Keys are cut to fit door locks, knives are sharpened to slice turkeys, cars are driven faster to get to work on time, or slower to avoid speeding fines. For humans, the whole of life is a conscious process of striving to optimize the individual's fit with that complex technology-based habitat we call "civilization."

This process of adaptation is vital to all the varied purposes of humans, because the fit between any organism and its habitat is the ultimate criterion for its well-being and survival. Therefore, the success or failure of every single aspect of human life is determined by whether or not satisfactory adaptation has been achieved.

For billions of years since the beginning of life on earth, all living things have been subject to adaptation as a product of biotic evolution, as described by Charles Darwin in his 1859 book: "On the Origin of Species." (Darwin 1999) Individuals of each species vary, in ways that influence the probability of their successful reproduction. Individuals whose fit with the habitat is above average will tend to have more offspring and thereby disseminate the traits that give rise to their fitness.

The attainment of good adaptive fit between people and their civilized habitat is vital for two reasons. First, fitness denotes that genetic traits are fulfilling their evolved function, which decreases disease, generates well-being, or happiness, and provides the opportunity to move towards genetic fulfillment or "self-actualization," which can be viewed as the goal of a well-lived human life. Second, in the long view, the evolution of fitness at the individual level becomes the successful adaptation of the human species, which reduces the probability of its extinction.

Darwinian or biotic evolution was responsible for creating the human body and the architecture of the human mind, including its morality. The full set of genes known as the human genome therefore determines the physical appearance of humans, many basic aspects of our behavior, and the broad outline of the human lifecycle, which typically runs from infancy through adolescence, to mating, reproduction, child-rearing, and old age.

The Inversion of Evolution

Darwinian evolution continues today, but it is a very slow process and it cannot help people in their daily struggle to achieve a fit with their civilized habitat that is based on rapidly-changing technologies. The process that enables modern humans to be adapted to their technology-based habitat is not Darwin's biotic evolution, but a spectacularly fast and relatively new kind of evolution that is unique to the human species. Let us start by calling it "cultural evolution," in which civilization changes rapidly, but human biology and genetics remain practically unchanged in the short term.

The term "cultural evolution" can be misleading, and is often attached to very specialized research dealing with particular aspects, such as the way in which ideas or beliefs are transmitted between people. In this book, I am concerned with the process of evolution that adapts *the whole human habitat*, including human-made artifacts, human knowledge, and learned behavior, to conform to the adaptive needs of the human species. The human habitat is the most appropriate domain to represent the subject of "cultural evolution" because the evolution of the habitat generates its "fit" with humans. Therefore, I am adopting the term "habitat evolution" and I explain this more fully in Chapter 3.

In the Paleolithic (Old Stone Age) period in which humans

evolved, the slow progression of Darwinian evolution was primarily responsible for the "fit" between humans and their habitat.

In today's complex technological culture, the primary engine of adaptive fit is evolution of civilization, which progresses hundreds of times faster than biotic evolution. In effect, evolution has been completely inverted so that, instead of humans evolving to adapt to their habitat in nature, the artificial, civilized habitat evolves to adapt itself to the human species.

Habitat evolution is fast because, unlike biotic evolution, it is driven by intelligence. The ability of the human brain to make decisions that will improve its owner's adaptive fit with the habitat is the subject of the discipline of evolutionary psychology. A primary source on this subject is *The Adapted Mind*, by Jerome Barkow and his fellow authors. (Barkow 1992) The authors describe the ability of humans to make adaptive decisions:

"The central premise of *The Adapted Mind* is that there is a universal human nature, but that this universality exists primarily at the level of evolved psychological mechanisms, not of expressed cultural behaviors." For example, humans inherit a capacity to learn language easily, but they do not inherit any specific language.

The authors continue: "A second premise is that these evolved psychological mechanisms are adaptations, constructed by natural selection over evolutionary time." Of course, as the brain resulted from natural selection, then we should expect it to serve the purpose of human adaptation and fitness.

"A third assumption made by most of the contributors is that the evolved structure of the human mind is adapted to the way of life of Pleistocene hunter-gatherers, and not necessarily to our modern circumstances." Here, the authors make the point that humans evolved in nature, and we can expect that human decisions are optimized to deal with the problems our ancestors encountered as hunter-gatherers in pre-agricultural societies.

This last point is crucial. If humans are adapted to live as hunter-gatherers, then how can their behavior be adapted to fit a technology based civilization? The solution is that the human habitat constantly evolves so as to maintain an adaptive fit with the human species, as I describe in Chapter 3.

Until recently, the evolution of civilization, including culture, has been a spectacular success in providing humans with the adaptive fit that has enabled them to live in new conditions. The unique intelligence and creativity of humans have catapulted the species to overwhelming biological dominance, with the global population exploding from about one million people at the end of the Paleolithic period, or Stone Age, 10,000 years ago, to seven billion people today. Thanks to the incomparable human brain, men and women have patiently discovered natural laws and then applied this scientific knowledge to numerous technologies, creating a great civilization on Earth, which may soon be extended to colonization of other planets.

There is a Cancer in the Heart of Civilization

Yet, in the 21st century, despite the incomparable achievements of the human species, people everywhere, especially the young, know that there is a cancer in the heart of their civilization. In the evolutionary era, human achievement was enabled by the success of first, Darwinian evolution, and then, evolution of the human habitat, which both maintained the fit, or adaptation, between humans and their environment. Yet, today, there is unmistakable evidence of a progressive failure of that adaptation. As technology continues to accelerate and transform human life, the signs of maladaptation are everywhere.

The human species has been divided by military conquest into nation states that exist in mutual insecurity. Despite the loathing of the general population for warfare, it continues, and approximately 231 million people died in wars and conflicts conducted by states in the twentieth century. (Leitenberg 2006)

Food production can now meet global needs, but almost half the population in some rich countries select a poor diet and adopt an unhealthy lifestyle that causes obesity and many related diseases. Yet, the UN reports that 870 million people are chronically under-nourished (FAO 2012) and six million children die of hunger each year. (FAO 2005)

Stone Age hunter-gatherers could obtain and prepare an excellent diet in four hours a day according to anthropologist, Marshall Sahlins. (Sahlins 1972) Yet, since the invention of non-sustainable agriculture, with its tiny selection of standardized crops, there have been many hundreds of serious famines. (Manning 2004)

When we evaluate the "fitness" of a species, the starting point is always reproduction. Living things that fail to reproduce simply disappear. Yet the Caucasian people of Europe, who led the world in science, culture and industrialization for 500 years, cannot raise enough children to maintain their population. The Caucasian population has shrunk from 25% to 12% of the global population in 100 years, and is expected to fall to around 7% by 2050, and perhaps disappear. The population of Japan, also among the most accomplished cultures on earth, is fast shrinking. (CIA 2013)

Archeologist Steven LeBlanc blames the decline of industrialized populations on cities, where space and food are expensive, and the fact that parents who stay at home for childcare cannot earn enough to cover their costs. (LeBlanc 2003) But if having children is the biological test of success and fitness, rejecting parenthood is failure, described by some observers as group "suicide."

Another indication that European government has damaged family life and reduced the will to live is the fact that Europeans aged 15 and above are the world's heaviest drinkers, consuming 12.5 liters of pure alcohol a year, more than double the world average. Alcohol is the third highest risk factor for mortality after tobacco and high blood pressure. (WHO 2012) Alcohol kills 195,000 people a year in Europe. (EU 2010)

In industrialized nations, 75 percent of mortality is due to diseases such as cancer, heart disease, strokes, diabetes, emphysema, hypertension, and cirrhosis, which are caused by the civilized lifestyle. (Boyd Eaton S.B.1988)

In the USA, hospital drugs kill about 106,000 people annually, nearly double the US deaths caused by the 20-year Vietnam War, according to research reported in the Journal of the American Medical Association. Nearly all medications have side-effects that kill small numbers of people, but this is omitted from death certificates, writes Dr. Bruce Pomeranz, at the University of Toronto. (Lazarou, 1998)

In the 19th century, the introduction of compulsory schooling began to separate children from parents. Compulsory schooling is an unearned punishment for children. At age 15 years, over 80 percent of OECD children say they do not like attending school. (WHO 2005) Children are born with a joyful disposition and a powerful drive to learn, yet in industrialized countries, they are locked up by law for the whole of their youth.

Children are now so expensive to raise that both parents usually have to work to support them. But it is biologically desirable for children to be close to their mothers for the first three years of life and to be breast-fed with human milk. Sadly, the high cost of raising children

Fig. 1. Obese man on beach. The epidemic of obesity in wealthy nations is one of many indications that the families and communities that once supported a healthy human lifestyle have been marginalized by the state. Photo: Tibor Végh (CC3.0).

forces mothers to work, so that infants have to be handed over to daycare, and fed with processed cow's milk. Young babies in daycare have higher stress hormone levels than those cared for by their mothers or another attentive person. Stress hormones have been linked with greater aggression and anxiety in older children in long-term day care, and they also affect the development of a range of neurotransmitters, whose pathways in the brain are still being built. (Biddulph 2006)

The richest countries are called "capitalist" but most of the population reject capitalism and feel economically powerless and manipulated. The top five percent of the US population own more wealth than the other 95 percent, and the bottom 20 percent have zero net wealth, or are in debt. Internationally, the wealth distribution is even more extreme. Very large wealth differentials make it impossible for some sections of a society to share in the common culture, and must contribute to poor economic performance, injustice and conflict.

It is widely recognized that current manufacturing, transportation, power generation, and agricultural technologies are unsustainable with regard to their use of resources and their pollution of the environment. Burning fossil fuels produces pollution that kills millions of people. In addition, the United Nations claims that it causes climate change, which could kill many species, impact human food production, and raise sea levels to threaten the homes of hundreds of millions of people.

Warning to Humanity

In 1992, the Union of Concerned Scientists, representing 1,700 of the world's leading scientists, including a majority of the Nobel Laureates in science, issued a *Warning to Humanity*. (Kendall 1992) The document stated that human beings and the natural world are on a collision course: "Human activities inflict harsh and often irreversible damage on the environment and on critical resources. If not checked, many of our current practices put at serious risk the future that we wish for human society and the plant and animal kingdoms, and may so alter the living world that it will be unable to sustain life in the manner that we know."

Warning to Humanity was directed at the people of the world, especially scientists, industrialists, and religious leaders. It called for action on stopping environmental damage, managing resources crucial to human welfare more effectively, stabilizing the population, eliminating poverty, ensuring sexual equality, and guaranteeing women control over their reproductive decisions.

Warning to Humanity urged scientists, industrial and religious leaders and other people to join the authors in caring for the Earth. But the document contained no recommendations on how to go about that task. Governments have so far clearly failed to deal with these issues.

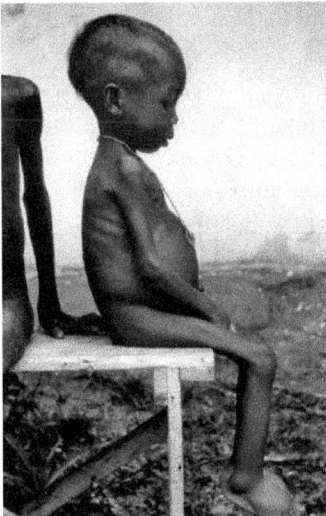

Fig. 2. Starving girl in a Nigerian relief camp. Starvation is avoidable, and its indirect cause is destructive economic and military competition between nations. Photo: Dr. Lyle Conrad, public domain via Wikimedia Commons.

These problems are a few of the massive shortcomings of civilization. Modern societies fail to support normal human life, while destroying much of nature. Civilization no longer "fits" humans and is a maladaptive habitat.

Solutions to the Problem of Adaptive Failure

The recent failure of adaptive fit between humans and industrialized societies is a potential catastrophe and many leading thinkers have sought to understand its causes.

The reduction in the quality of life triggered by industrialization has given rise to a significant social movement that is critical of the very idea of civilization. In 19th century America, David Thoreau advocated a rural lifestyle without much technology or government, in books such as *Walden* and *Against Civilization: Readings and Reflections.* In *Civil Disobedience*, he expressed condemnation of the state and of those whose acquiescence empowered it. Thoreau was a brilliant writer and his love of the natural world and of human freedom is still inspiring today. However, Thoreau did not offer a solution to the social abuses that resulted from the problem of state power over the individual.

In recent years, a movement sometimes called Anarcho-Primitivism has rejected the whole of the modern civilized lifestyle. The movement is vigorously led by writers such as John Zerzan, who illustrates how early farming was destructive to the ecology. "Deserts now occupy most of the areas where high civilization once flourished," writes Zerzan, "throughout the Mediterranean Basin and in the adjoining Near East and Asia, agriculture turned lush and hospitable lands into depleted, dry, and rocky terrain. In *Critias*, Greek philosopher Plato described Attica as, "a skeleton wasted by disease," referring to the deforestation of Greece and contrasting it to its earlier richness." (Zerzan, 1999)

Many writers now take the view that the hunter-gatherer lifestyle of prehistoric humans was healthier than that of societies based on early agriculture. Belfer-Cohen (Belfer-Cohen 1989) said that agriculture: "is not easier than hunting and gathering and does not provide a higher quality, more palatable, or more secure food base." Richard Lee (Lee 1968) shows that: "the diet of gathering peoples was far better than that of cultivators, that starvation was rare, that their health status was generally superior, and that there was a lower incidence of chronic disease."

Anarco-primitivists criticize just about every aspect of civilization, including those condemned in this book. However, participants in the anarcho-primitivist movement tend to believe that industrialization is *per se* antithetical to a thriving human society, and they fail to distinguish between the core adaptive effect of a technology and its unintended consequences, which are maladaptive. Consequently, the aims of such groups hinge mainly around restricting technology and adopting a more primitive and natural lifestyle.

Many scientists have pointed out the futility of desiring a more primitive lifestyle for a significant proportion of the human population. This population is now so large that it can be fed and supported only by advanced technologies, so there is no possibility of adopting a primitive lifestyle, even if more than a few people should desire it.

Are there Limits to the Growth of Civilization?

A very common explanation for all environmental problems is that the human population is too large and industrial society consumes too many raw materials, produces unneeded goods, and generates unnecessary waste. Among the many scientists who have supported this view was Professor Frank Fenner of the Australian National University, who played a leading role in the extinction in nature of the deadly smallpox disease. In June 2010, a few months before he died, Professor Fenner claimed that "Homo Sapiens will become extinct, perhaps within 100 years."

Fenner blames the population explosion and unbridled consumption, comparing modern humans with the people of a Pacific island that cut down its trees for religious reasons until they could not make fishing boats and starved. "We'll undergo the same fate as the people of Easter Island," he said. "Climate change is just the very beginning. But we're seeing remarkable changes in the weather already." Food is another critical issue. "As the population keeps growing to seven, eight or nine billion, there will be a lot more wars over food," he says "The grandchildren of today's generations will face a much more difficult world."

Most scientists are not quite so negative about human prospects, but all see ecological problems. In the 1970s, *The Limits to Growth*, a book commissioned by the Club of Rome think tank, examined five variables: world population, industrialization, pollution, food production, and resource depletion. (Meadows 1972)

The five variables were assumed to be growing exponentially, while the ability of technologies to create new resources could grow only linearly. Thus, catastrophe was predicted, in a similar to vein to Thomas

World Energy Consumption

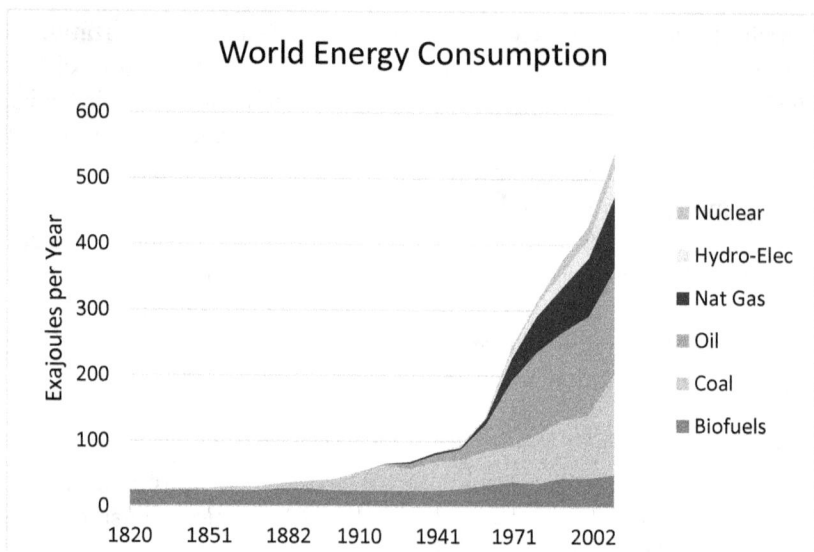

Fig. 3. World Energy Consumption. Energy consumption is the most fundamental requirement of living things. The remarkable growth in human energy production has been highly adaptive, but the maladaptive side-effects
of current energy technologies must be remedied. Source: Gail Tverberg,
www.ourfiniteworld.com, March 12, 2013.

Malthus' pessimistic 1798 essay on food production and the growth of
the poor. (Malthus 1993) And, as with Malthus, the Club of Rome has
proven to be, so far, quite wrong.

I believe that "over-population" is a paranoia that arises through a
simple mistake. People who live in cities mistake urban over-crowding
for excessive population. More than half the human population has migrated to cities, to access the jobs, business opportunities, and culture
that dense populations offer. But, while cities can be stressful, vast rural
areas are now denuded of people.

In fact, by far the most serious population problem facing humans
is the low urban birthrate. The absence of children to form the next generation of workers means that governments cannot raise enough revenue
to fund the pensions and medical care for retirees. "Statist solutions will
not solve the problem of the empty cradle, for it is the modern welfare
state itself that relentlessly suppresses fertility," writes sociologist Steven Mosher, president of the Population Research Institute. "By its very
existence, it discourages the formation of the very kind of strong and
independent families that are necessary for robust fertility, by fracturing

the intergenerational dependency of the family, by adopting "gender-neutral" policies that undermine the complementarity that is at the heart of successful marriage, by providing abortion on demand, by mandating sex education for children, by pushing state-funded contraception schemes on teenagers and young adults, and above all, by high tax rates." (Mosher 2008)

The United Nations population statistics show that global population growth is slowing and may be negative by the end of the century. And even if global population does continue to rise for several decades, it is unlikely to create scarcity of food resources. Science-based food productivity can grow much faster than the population. Researchers are developing many sustainable ways of producing food, ranging from types of organic farming that are integrated with nature's cycles, to industrial production of high quality food utilizing the biological processes associated with yeasts, fungi, or bacteria. And this can provide an adaptive diet, not the highly-processed "junk" food that dominates the diets of industrialized people.

Problem is Lack of Sustainability, Not Rapid Growth

Although many people believe that both the human population and economic production are growing too fast, this is not the critical factor. The major conflict caused by human society is that it is based on an industrialized farming system that ignores the natural sustainable cycles of nature, by destroying the soil, exhausting the water supply, cutting down the forests, and poisoning the air and the seas with fossil fuel-based fertilizers and pesticides.

Richard Manning makes a damming criticism of agriculture in *Against the grain*, a critique of modern agriculture and society. Manning claims that, in the year 2000, 85 percent of cropland in the USA was planted in four crops: corn, soybeans, wheat, and hay. "The effects of modern industrial agriculture range from pesticide pollution to freshwater depletion, energy consumption, erosion, and salinization," writes Manning. "Nitrogen figures in problems as diverse as red tides, fish kills, marine mammal deaths, shellfish poisoning, loss of seagrass habitats, destruction of coral reefs, and acid rain."

My argument is that the problem with industrialized society and agriculture based on chemicals is that they are not sustainable. If we create sustainable manufacturing and agriculture, then it is arguable that the fast rate of growth of the human population, or of manufacturing, would no longer disrupt the wilderness areas of nature or the quality of life.

Richard Manning does prescribe the kind of agricultural practice that might be sustainable: "This redesign will require something approaching permaculture... we need to focus on inventing a perennial polyculture, a system in which a variety of plants grow together permanently, performing services like fertilization and defense from insects for one another, as well as providing food. It is a vast undertaking that requires not so much a re-domestication of crop plants but rather a reinvention by selection, by breeding, by choice, by patient learning, by reexamining the genetic diversity that remains, by creating feral farming. Not back to the garden, back to the wild."

It is true that, if humans continue to behave in a maladaptive manner and abuse the Earth's resources, extinction is a real possibility. On the other hand, if the productive processes of civilization are reshaped to integrate them with the processes of nature, then they may be sustainable at much higher population levels that are needed today.

For example, this author lives in Hong Kong, which was judged the "best city in the world" in 2012, according to the Economist Intelligence Unit's ranking, which emphasized "liveability." Hong Kong has 7.072 million people living in 1,100 sq. km of land. If we copied that density over just half the Earth's total land area of 149 million sq. km, the population would be a gigantic 479 billion, against the tiny seven billion we have now. Too crowded? Well Hong Kong is only 25 percent developed and has over 40 percent protected areas, mainly country parks. Supposing that humans used half the Earth's land area, developing 25 percent of that half, and allocated 40% to country parks and the other 35 percent to sustainable agriculture, would that be so bad? And remember, under this plan, half the Earth's land area would remain as completely natural wilderness. When I hear scientists and environmentalists obsessing about over-population, I wonder if they have ever used their calculators.

Furthermore, predictions of doom based on human over-production have been around for hundreds of years, and the success rate of such predictions is abysmal. Growth can only be limited by the power of a centralized state and such action echoes the nature of communist societies, which actually generated more pollution and damage to nature than the decentralized market economies. The facts suggest that creating sustainable practices in agriculture and industry is the key to good living conditions, rather than any simplistic attempt at damage limitation through control of growth. Sustainable solutions arise quickly from science but, sadly, they are frequently blocked by political competition between states.

Scientists Who Believe Genes, Not Society, are the Problem

Surprisingly, many scientists seem to believe that the failure of adaptation between humans and the modern habitat is due not to our misuse of technology, but to the characteristics of human genes. These scientists do not blame the nature of civilization for human difficulties, but instead see limitations to evolution.

For example, leading ethologist, evolutionary biologist and renowned scientific author Richard Dawkins brought a radical new perspective to genetics by writing: "The argument of this book is that we, and all other animals, are machines created by our genes." But Dr. Dawkins goes on to compare genes to Chicago gangsters: "I shall argue that a predominant quality to be expected in a successful gene is ruthless selfishness. This gene selfishness will usually give rise to selfishness in individual behavior." (Dawkins 1976)

To be fair to Dr. Dawkins, his metaphor of the "selfish" gene is surely intended to emphasize that gene-based behavior can only be inherited if it permits or facilitates the survival of the relevant genes – an important scientific principle that he has championed.

But his metaphor seems to invite misunderstanding – after all, genes are made of a chemical called DNA Deoxyribonucleic Acid, and like any chemical substance, they have no moral attributes. Furthermore, we all know of humans who are habitually kind, and exhibit attributes such as honesty, integrity, compassion, justice, generosity, and honor. Such traits could not exist if the "ruthless selfishness" of genes mostly gave rise to similar characteristics in humans.

Fortunately, Dr. Dawkins explains further: "However, as we shall see, there are special circumstances in which a gene can achieve its own selfish goals best by fostering a limited form of altruism at the level of individual animals." But then, he adds: "Much as we might wish to believe otherwise, universal love and the welfare of the species as a whole are concepts that simply do not make evolutionary sense."

That raises the question of whether "universal love" is desirable from a moral point of view, or whether it is a religious concept. Why should we love serial killers or thieves? Morality is, in my view, a peer-to-peer behavioral control system. A "control system" for morality, by definition, must be equally capable of providing positive and negative feedback, but "universal love" would prevent that.

In this context, we must also be careful to avoid the religious myth of "original sin" which implies that the self-interest of individuals is somehow opposed to the interests of society as a whole. In an adaptive society – that is, a society such those that evolved in the Paleolithic period, and therefore any future "normal" human society – the interests of the individual are identical to the interests of the society as a whole. Biologists know that, in any social species, including humans, the behaviors of multiple individuals are highly interdependent, and they are genetically synchronized over millions of generations to optimize adaptive success. In such a process it is meaningless to try to separate the fitness of individuals from the adaptive success of the species as a whole.

Another scientist, Nobel Laureate biologist Christian de Duve (de Duve 2010), goes much further, blaming natural selection for many of the problems of modern life. "Natural selection, this all-powerful driving force of biological evolution, has privileged in our genes traits that were *immediately* favorable to the survival and proliferation of our ancestors, under the conditions that prevailed there and then, with no regard for later consequences." He lists the negative traits as: "selfishness, greed, cunning, and aggressiveness."

"On the other hand, natural selection has little favored qualities, as long-term pre-vision, prudence, a sense of responsibility, and wisdom, which would have proved advantageous only in the long run," continues de Duve. "Their fruits would have appeared too late for that." De Duve acknowledges the achievements of humanity, but says: "Human history, from the time records have become available, and probably before that, has been an endless succession of battles, wars, crusades, conquests, invasions, massacres, colonizations, and enslavements of various kinds." De Duve offers seven solutions to the problems raised by undesirable human genes, which include eugenics to modify those undesirable genes that are possessed by *all* humans, and subjecting children to a special education environment to "rewire" their brains, that may otherwise mature on a diet of political indoctrination or other anti-social attitudes.

Views such as these, which blame human nature and genes for the problems of modern society, ignore the central facts of human history. The large societies that arose with agriculture are fundamentally different from those that went before. Whatever challenges faced hunter gatherer bands – and they must have had their share of problems – they had virtually none of the diseases of civilization. Without industry: no pollution; without the centralized, coercive control of society: no institutionalized warfare; without agriculture: no division between work and leisure; without centralized control: no fixed hierarchy or social classes; without transportation to mix racial sub-groups: no racism; and without laws against victimless activities (e.g. drug distribution, prostitution, tax evasion): hardly any crime. And these claims have been repeatedly vindicated by the observations of anthropologists living with pre-industrial peoples. If we wish to know why humans cannot adapt to the modern habitat, then the one place where we will not find the answer is in the genes.

The Harmful Side-effects of Technology

I believe that it is self-evident that the failure of the adaptive fit between humans and their civilization is in some way connected with the use of technology. None of the problems we face today, from warfare to pollution, from obesity to drug addiction, from racism to wealth differentials and starvation, existed at all in the evolutionary environment.

What *is* technology? Let's define it as: "Any sustained change to the human habitat resulting from human learned behavior." When humans use their intelligence to create new ways of doing something, like making stone tools, wearing clothes or cooking, we can describe them as "technologies."

New technologies are adopted because they promise an adaptive advantage. Later, people often discover that harmful side-effects accompany a new technology, and scientists or engineers have to work to remedy or reduce the side-effects. But in some cases, the remedies are not applied, due to the cost, political obstacles, or even the fact that parasitic minorities within society may benefit from the harm done by technology's side-effects.

An early technology was the development of stone tools, which were first made about 2.5 million years ago. Stone weapons enabled people to hunt for meat to improve their plant-based diet and to kill predators. Other tools were used for cutting up prey animals and working with animal skins and timber.

When modern humans left Africa between 50,000 and 100,000 years ago they were able to make better weapons than earlier people, obtain more meat by hunting, and increase their population density. Many writers suggest that increased competition for resources triggered the first real warfare, which was therefore a harmful side-effect of the technologies of stone weapons and hunting.

Today, it is arguable that warfare resulting from food scarcity has already been remedied by property rights in farm animals and the global food market. Nevertheless, warfare continues as a discretionary, parasitic activity of the state, and I discuss this in later chapters.

Control of fire was an enormously important technology that enabled people to cook food, keep themselves warm, and scare away predators. But fire could also burn people, dwellings and artifacts. Today, industrial societies spend billions of dollars on fire stations, fire fighters, vehicles, hydrants, sprinklers, fire doors and extinguishers, to prevent fire destroying civilization.

Lead was among the earliest metals used by humans, because it was easy to melt and to shape. The Roman Empire used lead to make pipes for drinking water and containers for food, and they even colored food with lead salts. Lead accumulates in the body causing renal failure, hypertension, brain damage, anemia, and ultimately, death. As this powerful poison attacked the Roman population, from slaves to emperors, millions died and nobody knew the cause.

In the 20th century, lead was found to improve vehicle fuels and paints, from both of which it could enter the human bloodstream. It was particularly prone to damage the developing brains and internal organs of children, and was eventually banned. Sadly, lead is still used in many beauty products, along with other harmful chemicals, such as mercury nickel, and chromium.

Fossil fuels, including coal, gas and oil, powered the Industrial Revolution, have provided humans with powerful adaptive technologies, including prolific food production. Fossil fuels now create pollution that kills millions of people each year, destroys a significant part of nature, and play a role in the atmospheric gases that may be altering the climate in a potentially disastrous way. If the cost of the harm due to fossil fuels was charged to the users of such fuels, this would accelerate the development of alternatives, but inter-state politics prevent the application of market solutions.

In the late 1950s an anti-nausea drug called Thalidomide that was given to pregnant women as a treatment for morning sickness, caused serious birth defects in 10,000 children in 46 countries. When these deformities were linked with the drug, it was withdrawn from the market for use by pregnant women. Surprisingly, Thalidomide has recovered to find a successful niche market in the treatment of certain diseases, including leprosy and cancer.

Humans first built cities 6,000 years ago when agricultural production relieved people of the need to gather food or to hunt. Cities housed many specialized craftspeople, as well as the administrators, clerical workers, and traders necessary to support agriculture, manufacturing, and their associated distribution chains.

But cities attract mass populations, and crowding supports the transmission of diseases by viruses, bacteria and parasites, so that city-dwellers often live in fear of epidemics. Furthermore, city dwellers are more sedentary than, for example, farmers, and more subject to lifestyle trends such as poor diet, alcohol consumption, and the health risks of promiscuity. UN now estimates that 80% of all diseases are caused by lifestyle.

The above examples establish a basic pattern that is repeated thousands of times over: Humans adopt new technologies because they provide an adaptive advantage of some kind; then, later, they discover that the technologies have side-effects that are maladaptive.

Early Technologies Created Mostly Adaptive Conditions

Writers such as the Anarcho-Primitivists, who believe that it is impossible for humans to adapt fully to any industrialized society, fail to differentiate the basically adaptive nature of technology from its non-adaptive, harmful side-effects.

In reality, technologies provide humans with the most powerful means available to improve human adaptation, especially adaptation to inhospitable habitats. The most obvious example of this is the way that primitive human bands living more than 50,000 years ago used technology to migrate out of Africa and to populate most parts of the earth's surface, from the equator up to the Arctic Circle. These hardy and ingenious people, who survived by hunting animals and gathering plant foods, managed to travel thousands of miles and adapt to harsh environmental conditions vastly different from their ancestral, African homeland. This astounding achievement was made possible by simple technologies, such as weapons to hunt, tools to sew animal skins for warm clothing, cooking to pre-digest food, and the ability to construct protective dwellings.

So it is clear that primitive technologies were able to adapt early humans to habitats around the world that were completely different from their original African home. But supposing that we consider the challenge of extreme adaptation facing humans today, could our advanced technologies still provide an adaptive advantage? Let us examine an extreme adaptive challenge that humans may soon face – traveling to the planet Mars and setting up a major colony there.

Mars is a deadly, alien environment. First, all astronauts face loss of muscle tissue and calcium from their skeletons through low gravity in space, and this could be extreme during the long journey to Mars and life in Martian gravity, which is about one third of that on Earth. The Martian atmosphere is 95% carbon dioxide, which would kill humans within minutes if their blood had not already boiled due to the negligible atmospheric pressure. Because there is hardly any protective atmosphere, deadly ultraviolet radiation and high energy particles bombard the planet's surface. Finally, there is no plant or animal food. For primitive humans, Mars would be an immediate death sentence.

Within the next 20 years, an international expedition may set out to colonize Mars. Let's suppose that the plan is not merely to survive, but to create for the astronauts an environment that is as adaptive as the best environment on Earth. Could technology achieve this?

We can assume that the mission will be preceded by several robotic spacecraft that drop substantial supplies on the red planet, including pre-fabricated dwellings, foodstuffs and other essential items. Multiple manned spacecraft will follow, to provide assurance against failure of any single space vehicle. Scientists will naturally wish to enable a normal social organization among the Mars colonizers, similar to that which co-evolved with humans in the Stone Age, so the colonists will comprise two or more extended families, and all management of the project after take-off from Earth will be achieved by consensus among all the adult participants, to reflect the natural social relations of early hunter-gatherers.

In this scenario, technology will be used to negate all the health risks of space colonization. We can imagine that the space vehicles will rotate to create normal Earth gravity, as will the dwellings built on Mars. All buildings will be pressurized to emulate the Earth's atmosphere, and shielded from radiation. Artificial habitats will house livestock and other forms of food production, such as hydroponics, aquaculture, and fish farming. I believe that in such an artificial habitat, carefully designed to emulate the natural environment of their human ancestors, the Mars colonizers could have a wonderful life.

They would be physically much safer than their hunter-gatherer ancestors, with no danger from predators, and with advanced medicine to combat diseases. Their food supply would be nutritious and balanced and they could, in theory, grow a wide variety of food species, as existed for natural people in the past, which would be healthier than the restricted range of food from chemically grown plants and animals typical of the early 21st century. Perhaps a self-governing colony, with the lack of privacy in small communities, could exert peer pressure (not force) to almost eliminate consumption of alcohol and other damaging narcotic substances. Crime would be close to zero, as it often is among hunter-gatherer peoples, and warfare would be impossible under the rule of law and in the absence of rival groups.

The colonizers could enjoy sex lives much nearer to the normal behavior of hunter-gatherer peoples. In mass societies, sex is fraught with problems, because diseases including HIV make it medically risky, and religious dogma indoctrinates children to believe that sex is immoral. Properly used, science could easily eliminate sexually transmitted diseases from a small community. Scientifically educated people also know that, in nature, sexual relationships are primarily for bonding between individuals, and less than one percent of sex is related to reproduction.

The leisure activities of Mars colonizers could include not only most of the games that primitive humans played, but also the vast range of stimulating games and entertainment based on digital entertainment and education.

It is debatable whether such an artificial habitat could be as good as the best environment possible on Earth. But we can be sure that the colonizers would not suffer from the major maladies afflicting humans in the 21st century on Earth. For example, there would be no warfare, no starvation, no obesity or lifestyle diseases (because the adults controlling the society on Mars would have a strong desire to protect themselves and their children from such catastrophes). There would be no pollution, and food could be produced without antibiotics, pesticides or growth hormones that damage health on Earth. Autonomy of the individual colonists, and of the self-governing human band, could eliminate phenomena such as intensive advertising or non-adaptive lifestyle, protecting the group from excessive materialism or consumerism.

This insight into the potentiality of creating an adaptive Mars colony may help people understand that technology itself can be adaptive, and that the problems experienced by people in the early 21st century are due to human failings in utilizing technology safely and effectively.

How Is Our Social Organization Failing Us?

"Adaptation to the habitat" encompasses all the behaviors that constitute a human society and broadly defines its well-being: therefore the creation of an adaptive habitat is the most rational purpose for the management of human societies. This is already true for the self-management of the individual; all conscious decisions made by individuals emanate from the brain, which evolved solely to optimize the individual's physical and psychological "fit" with the habitat. Even decisions made by the unconscious mind are based on genetic traits that have been shaped by natural selection to support Darwinian fitness – psychologists refer to this as "the adaptive unconscious." (Wilson 2004)

However, in industrialized societies, there is clearly a major failure of social governance to create the best opportunity for members of society to achieve fit with their environments. This raises doubts about the priorities of human government.

The ultimate problem seems to be that human social organization has itself been corrupted as a harmful side-effect of technology. The prevailing system of centralized states, which exercise a monopoly of military power within their borders, and yet exist in constant mutual insecurity with other states, contrasts greatly with the traditional model of human social organization that evolved in the Stone Age.

Centralized states are mostly arbitrary divisions within the human species that utilize science and technology intensively for material competition and preparation for warfare with other states. This competition is executed by tiny, parasitic elites, leaving the vast majority of humans to survive by collaboration in which the range of choices has been greatly reduced. Human needs are addressed, too, but only in a secondary way.

Until recently, human societies were only discussed or recorded in history books as the passive tools of their rulers: the warriors, kings, and queens who determined the outcome of the constant competition between rival civilizations. The idea that centrally organized, hierarchical societies should provide satisfactory living conditions for the whole population was regarded as unfeasible. The general population only existed to provide the economic productivity and military power needed by the real actors on the world stage – political, military, and religious leaders.

The distortion caused by the coercive, parasitic state is much more serious when it is amplified by industrialization. The damage done by irrational government can no longer be restricted to the expendable social classes of slaves or serfs. Everybody is potentially affected by nuclear war, pollution, inappropriate food production, antibiotic-resistant bacteria and the 80 percent of diseases caused by industrial lifestyles. Everyone is subject to the generalized stress levels of living in a society where the adaptive nature of the human habitat is the very last thing to be considered by those with their hands on the levers of power.

Communication tools such as the Internet have provided a global view of the human species, and it is becoming clear that a common destiny unites every social class and racial group. Whatever the cultural differences between peoples, humans will sink or swim together in the challenge of co-existing with each other and with nature on planet Earth.

Therefore, a crucial decision now faces every man, woman and child on Earth – do we, or do we not, wish to support the creation of adaptive conditions for all humans? Do we wish to provide the opportunity for every individual to achieve self-actualization – the opportunity for fulfillment of their genetic potential?

If the answer is "yes," then humans must be committed to understanding how ancient societies based on natural social organization were able to generate adaptive conditions, and what aspect of technology has disrupted this process and caused the epidemic of maladaptation that we see today. The following chapters will deal with these basic cause-and-effect relationships.

If modern industrial civilization has major problems in creating adaptive conditions for humans, and if technology itself is not a fundamental problem, then the real problem must lie in social organization. In Chapter 2, we take a look at human social organization, to see if this could play a part in creating maladaptive conditions.

Chapter 2

The Adaptive Family versus the Parasitic State

*I*n the previous chapter, we discussed how the partial failure of adaptation, or "fit", between humans and the artificial habitat of civilization has resulted from the harmful side-effects of technology. Scientists and engineers can remedy all the harms caused by the side-effects of technology, but the abnormal organization of mass societies puts huge obstacles in their paths.

For several thousand years, all large, complex societies have given rise to two quite separate cultures that are constantly in conflict. The first culture is the natural, inherited culture of the general population, based on morality that has evolved over millions of years to support the human family and its birth-to-death lifecycle. The second culture is that of the state, which is the organization of centralized, sovereign (i.e. absolute) power over a specific population and the land it occupies. Sovereignty results from past military conquest, and is maintained by force.

The rulers of states can gain huge benefits of power, security and resources by conquering or even just dominating weaker states, and this tension creates permanent mutual insecurity. Insecurity affects the whole population of a state, making it easier for the government to control the subject population. The governments of states have an amoral relationship with one another and a parasitic relationship with their own populations. Centrally controlled states have divided the human species since the agricultural revolution, about 10,000 years ago. All complex societies arose after military conquest and were therefore byproducts of warfare. Warfare arose as a harmful side-effect of technology, as I explain in more detail in Chapter 5.

The culture of the general 21st century human population anywhere on Earth is based on family values inherited from the Paleolithic Period,

when groups of 50 or so humans lived as hunter-gatherers. Many anthropologists have attempted to determine how such people lived, by studying human groups that still have a pre-farming mode of subsistence.
They are aided by the archeological examination of early human
campsites.

Culture of the Natural Human Extended Family

For example, anthropologist James Woodburn has researched
some of the most egalitarian societies that survive, especially the Hadza
of Tanzania, and the !Kung Bushmen of Botswana. Simple hunter-gatherer bands obtain food by hunting, fishing, and gathering roots, fruits,
and the honey of wild bees. They collect food for immediate consumption and live in very small groups between which they can easily move.
Individuals are highly autonomous, with few commitments or depend-
encies. Such people rarely make war, preferring to move away from ad-
versaries to avoid conflicts.

Many other anthropologists have described hunter-gatherer cultures whose egalitarian relationships seem to be related to the simplicity
of their food production. It seems likely that all humans lived in this way
until about 10,000 years ago.

"In these societies, equalities of power, equalities of wealth and
equalities of prestige or rank are not merely sought, but are, with certain
limited exceptions, genuinely realized," writes Woodburn. "People are
well aware of the possibility that individuals or groups within their own
egalitarian societies may try to acquire more wealth, to assert more
power or to claim more status than other people, and are vigilant in seeking to prevent or limit this." (Woodburn 1982)

The most important attribute that enabled our ancestors to avoid
control by dominant individuals was their mobility. They lived in a cluster of bands, and individuals or family groups were free to leave one
band and join another without hindrance. Woodburn explains: "What it
(freedom of societal membership) also does is to allow people to segre-
gate themselves easily from those with whom they are in conflict, without economic penalty and without sacrificing any other vital interests.
Most important of all for the present discussion is the way that such arrangements are subversive for the development of authority."

No ruling elite could take over such a society. No leader could
make members pay a tax or fight a war, or obey laws with which they
disagreed because, unlike modern civilization, the membership of a

hunter-gathering band was voluntary. The freedom to move away from conflicts or dominant leaders not only prevented bullies from seeking coercive power, but also promoted self-discipline and autonomy in the general population. This was especially useful to the weaker or less productive families, who are the first to suffer under the hierarchical control of society.

Another factor supporting approximately equal human rights and opportunity was that simple hunter-gatherers all had access to deadly weapons, which made it very dangerous to abuse even the weakest of individuals. "Hunting weapons are lethal not just for game animals but also for people," writes Woodburn. "There are serious dangers in antagonizing someone: he might choose simply to move away but if he feels a strong sense of grievance that his rights have been encroached upon he could respond with violence." This was a very real threat. In the modern !Kung tribe, people can easily be ambushed or killed while asleep, for example, using deadly poisoned arrows. (Lee 1979)

Yet another factor that worked against strong dependence of one individual upon another was that all members of the tribe had free access to the resources of the territory that they occupied. As Woodburn explains: "Whatever the system of territorial rights, in practice in their own areas and in other areas with which they have ties, people had free and equal access to wild food and water; to all the various raw materials they needed for making shelters, tools, weapons and ornaments; to whatever wild resources they used, processed or unprocessed, for trade."

Even children had a high degree of autonomy because parents did not control their basic needs, especially food, as they do in complex societies. In simple hunting and gathering societies, "The household head has no comparable role as a real or symbolic provider, as the source of most good things," writes Lee. "It is, I am sure, not accidental that neither !Kung nor Hadza (African hunter-gathering peoples) usually place much emphasis on formal meal times. A great deal of food is eaten informally throughout the day." It appears that hunter-gatherer parents support their children but do not use this fact as leverage to impose their authority over them.

What happens when children are freed from parental authority? In hunter-gatherer societies, whole families are exposed to the threats and opportunities of the natural environment, so that consensus and collaboration arise spontaneously. As a result of sharing a single culture, autonomous self-interest and social needs continually converge.

Fig. 4. Simplified Timeline of Human Evolution

3,700,000,000 years ago - First Life on Earth

All living things are descended from single-celled life that existed nearly 4 billion years ago. Animals appeared 600 million years ago, and dinosaurs lived from 230 to 66 million years ago. Human ancestors split from those of chimpanzees 6 million years ago, becoming recognizably human 1.7 million years ago.

6,000,000 Years Ago – Common Ancestor

The probable common ancestor of humans and chimpanzees was Sahelanthropus tchadensis, which lived 6 million years ago. This species lived in African forests alongside the ancestors of chimpanzees, gorillas, orangutans, gibbons, and monkeys. Photo: Smithsonian Institution, John Gurche, artist/Don Hurlbert, photographer.

2,300,000 Years Ago – Homo habilis

Homo habilis walked on two legs, used stone tools, and ate some meat. Homo habilis had a brain capacity of 600 cc, compared with a chimpanzee's 375 cc and a human's 1,330 cc. Photo: Wikimedia Commons, from facial reconstruction at: Westfälisches Museum für Archäologie, Herne.

1,800,000 Years Ago – Homo erectus

The first humans to leave Africa had a 1,000 cc brain. The sexes had more equal body size, associated with monogamy. Loss of large canine teeth & erectile "threat" hair indicates more collaboration, less conflict. There is evidence of fire use and, later, purpose-built dwellings. Photo: Wikimedia Commons, from facial reconstruction at Westfälisches Landesmuseum, Herne.

195,000 Years Ago – Archaic Homo sapiens

The first anatomically modern humans, with a 1330cc brain capacity, evolved from archaic Homo sapiens. Cultural ability was limited compared with modern humans, perhaps due to an intelligence or language deficit.

Humans evolved to be less hierarchical and aggressive

The human brain increased rapidly in size and power during evolution because the behaviors generated by intelligence increased fitness. Most of the behaviors that benefitted from intelligence were collective activities such as child rearing, food gathering and preparation, hunting, defense against predators, and consensual governance. Therefore, collaboration was selected alongside intelligence, and human behavior altered radically. In particular, the dominance hierarchy typical of chimpanzees and other mammals, disappeared completely and was replaced by the contractual form of hierarchy we see in normal human societies outside of coercive government. (see Chapter 6)

60,000 Years Ago – Modern Humans

A second migration from Africa comprised Homo Sapiens with fully modern behavior. They made better tools and practiced a symbolic culture that included religion and art. Humans migrated from Africa to Europe, Asia and Oceania. By 14,500 years ago, they walked from Siberia across the Bering straits to the Americas. Modern people replaced earlier humans by competition or interbreeding. Adaptation to conditions in Africa, East Asia, South Asia and Europe produced four "racial" subgroups, with varying skin color, hair texture, and body shape.

Before 10,000 years ago - Warfare and Social Disruption

Modern humans had superior weapons and skills and could kill all the prey animals within a particular district, creating the conditions for conflict over resources. Warfare was invented and the insecurity of small societies at a time of increasing population density seems to have been the main driver for the emergence of larger societies such as tribes, chiefdoms and eventually, states.

10,000 Years Ago – Agriculture and Parasitic Government

Agriculture and population growth occurred in the Middle East, China, and the Americas. Agriculture yielded a narrow diet that caused poor health for thousands of years, and also resulted in continual famines that killed millions of people. But farming could feed more people, so the population expanded fast. City states had coercive governments, social classes, gender inequality and slavery. History began with the invention of writing about 5,000 years ago. Modern manufacture began with the use of metals, starting with bronze.

Present Time – Coercive State Triggers Maladaptation

Half of all humans live in cities, with intensive technology use. Parasitic state coercion disrupts social organization and prevents normal evolution of the habitat. Humans and their immediate communities are no longer autonomous. Adaptation between humans and their technology-based habitat is failing. Only a united human species can overcome these challenges by creating global laws that support the biologically normal egalitarian human culture that evolved in the Paleolithic periods.

In contrast, in a modern industrialized society, the state has a monopoly of power, and the self-interest of the ruling group generates parasitism, so that there is a constant conflict between the two cultures. One is based on "human nature," which is regarded as selfish (for example, in the Christian religious concept of "original sin") and the other is based on the interests of "society", which members are expected to serve. Thus, from an early age, children are pressurized to sacrifice their autonomy, intelligence and personality in favor of loyalty to the state and its agents in the hierarchy, who are parents, teachers and the legal system. When children choose to follow the dictates of natural behavior imprinted on them by evolution, they may be labeled as "juvenile delinquents" and punished, or diagnosed as suffering from invented diseases such as ADHD (Attention Deficiency Hyperactivity Disorder) and given drugs that may physically damage their brains.

One of the leading researchers on the prehistoric origins of political equality and inequality is Christopher Boehm, who writes: "But before twelve thousand years ago, humans basically were egalitarian. They lived in what might be called societies of equals, with minimal political centralization and no social classes. Everyone participated in group decisions, and outside the family there were no dominators."

Equality was mainly a product of suppressing the dominance of ambitious males, but females benefited as well, Beohm notes. "The egalitarianism of hunter-gatherers pertains more to males than to females, but the women enjoy far more political potency than did the women of Athens (A model for western society), and these mobile foragers keep no slaves. Their highly equalized version of political life goes far back into prehistory and, following Knauft (1991), I make the major assumption that humans were egalitarian for thousands of generations before hierarchical societies began to appear." (Boehm 2001)

Research into the genetic basis of collaboration has transformed the scientific viewpoint. As the authors of *The Adapted Mind* write: "Instead of the traditional view that selfishness is "natural" and altruism is only imposed socially against natural inclination, evolutionary biology has discovered that altruism and cooperation can be as natural as selfishness."

Translating Hunter-gatherer Culture into Modern Terms

For most of the evolutionary period, from the first humans 1.7 million years ago, until fully modern humans left Africa during the last

100,000 years, there was no warfare. Conflicts arise in any society, and people living in the self-governing bands of the Paleolithic would have discussed the best techniques for resolving disputes, as do the many foraging bands studied by anthropologists. This would have given rise to social rules that would be taught to children, to help them avoid disputes and resolve the disputes of others.

If small human bands co-operated to prevent their leaders acting like bullies, it is equally certain that they would not have tolerated aggressive behavior from ordinary members of the group. Non-violence is a natural behavior for an intelligent species, because violence, or the threat of it, blocks intelligent collaboration and reduces fitness. Today we call the basis of such behavior the "non-aggression principle."

The non-aggression principle evolved out of human experience. As an intelligent species, humans need to optimize collaboration, in order to optimize fitness. Collaboration between individuals with approximately equal intelligence can only be optimized if all members of the group are permitted to interact freely, exchange favors and other resources, and to participate in consensual self-government. This is not possible if some members of society initiate force to limit the free movement or speech of another person, or to commit theft or fraud or violent crimes such as assault, rape, or murder. Therefore, for two million years, the powerful biological force of natural selection acted in favor of the non-aggression principle.

The non-aggression principle is the basis of the most complete human liberty that can, in practice be provided to all members of society. This is because, if any person is permitted to initiate force against another person, that person's freedom is diminished and everyone's freedom is threatened. Many great thinkers, especially the English writers John Locke and John Stuart Mill, contributed to the emergence of this idea in formal terms, but it was only expressed with complete accuracy in the 20th century by writers such as US philosopher Ayn Rand and prominent US libertarian Murray Rothbard. Rothbard states:

"No one may threaten or commit violence ("aggress") against another man's person or property. Violence may be employed only against the man who commits such violence; that is, only defensively against the aggressive violence of another. In short, no violence may be employed against a non-aggressor." Rothbard also noted that: "Here is the fundamental rule from which can be deduced the entire corpus of libertarian theory." (Rothbard 1963)

In the *Adaptive Society*, the non-aggression principle is regarded as an essential element of human civilization and of the self-governance of all human societies, because it evolved as the central differentiating behavior that distinguished Homo sapiens from our nearest relative, Pan troglodytes, the chimpanzee, which initiates force as part of its normal social behavior.

Culture of the Coercive, Parasitical State

In great contrast to the culture of the general population is the culture of the state, which is based on the central control of society by a monopoly of force. Unlike the general population, governments have adopted the initiation of force and departed from the collaborative mode of interaction that was universal to the human species for millions of years before the emergence of the state. Apart from the state, only criminals employ force to obtain resources.

The practice of coercion by the state originated in the era of growing population density and intensive resource competition, when frequent warfare gradually amalgamated smaller societies into larger ones until the enormous nation states of today emerged. The growth of the size of states is reflected in the increasing severity of warfare. The colossal wars of the 20th century, in which tens of millions of people were sacrificed for no purpose, represent the logical outcome of social leaders exercising an illegitimate monopoly of power.

Warfare acts like a ratchet, because the struggle for survival in wartime is always used by political leaders to attempt to legitimize the expansion of parasitic state power over individuals and the economy. Propaganda is part of warfare, and governments adopt the habit of using outrageous lies as instruments of policy. Wartime police forces act like occupying armies and the habits linger when peace is resumed. States routinely employ espionage among the general population in the name of combating terrorists. In wartime, belligerent states copy one another's cruelties until they reach the lowest common denominator of depravity.

The process of maneuvering for advantage is inherent in human interaction, but the state's use of political persuasion is unique because sovereign power enables it to manipulate human rights and to confiscate resources directly, using force, rather than voluntary exchange. To illustrate this point, consider the widespread criticism of large corporations, especially those associated with fossil fuels and finance that power the economy. Corporations are described as "greedy" and "ruthless," and blamed for exploiting workers and creating harmful externalities, such as pollution.

But many of the harmful actions taken by corporations are legitimized and facilitated by laws passed by states. Corporations by their very nature as legal "persons" conceal the identity of individuals who cause harm, and limited liability actually legitimizes some kinds of harm, such as non-payments of debts. Corporations have zero ability to influence the law without bribery and state connivance. Just as states have an exclusive ability to create warfare, they have an exclusive ability to permit damage to others by corporations – both without public accountability. This combination caused US president Dwight Eisenhower to coin the term "Military-Industrial Complex."

All the harm created by businesses must necessarily be triggered by state policies, because, in a completely free and equal society without arbitrary state power, each business owner or employee would be responsible for his or her actions – there would be no separate "corporations" to blame.

Worst of all, the mutual insecurity that exists between states has locked the human species into this parasitic system. No individual state can abolish its armed posture unless it can persuade all other states to do the same. The whole of humanity has become temporarily imprisoned by armed groups, to the severe disadvantage of all.

A normal human society can only have voluntary governance. By using coercion to control society, the state has replaced the naturally evolved human social organization with a hierarchy more suited to chimpanzees or dogs.

State coercion is pathology like the coercion practiced by criminals, and for the same reason – both are parasites. To the extent that some religions have borrowed the power of the state, religion can often be a third system that practices coercion. Religions have been responsible for burning people alive and torturing them to death for failure to succumb to the supposed wishes of their particular magical gods. In current times, some religions are still regularly employing tortures such as whipping, and death by stoning for many activities that are biologically normal and harmless to others, such as homosexuality or refusing to comply with religious practices, or even with dress codes. Religious wars cause widespread deaths and homelessness purely because states and religious authorities indoctrinate people with conflicting religious myths and historical animosities.

If modern humans wish to live in adaptive conditions, they need to create a civilization based on voluntary governance, in which all forms of coercion are prohibited. However, some scientists mistakenly believe that the egalitarian social organization of the early human band has disappeared permanently, due to the different requirements of more complex societies, especially those based on agriculture, starting 10,000 years ago.

According to this view, the key changes that resulted from the coercion of centralized government, such as taxation, social classes, and employment, were *necessary* to coordinate the extra complexity of mass populations. This view is incorrect. Non-coercive social organization is a biological trait that arose from the unique intelligence of the human species and, even if it has been temporarily lost due to the harmful side-effect of technology, the damage can be reversed.

The Human Lifecycle Must be Protected from Technology

Until recently, scientists did not question the normalcy of modern societies, because moral values and human rights were regarded as being outside the province of scientific study. Today, that no longer holds, and biologists and anthropologists increasingly study human values and motivations as evolved genetic traits.

To understand why the social organization that evolved with humans is important, we can compare it to the human body. A doctor is trained to know the normal values of many parameters of the human physiology. When patients' bodies diverge excessively from these norms, a doctor may be able to diagnose a disease. Similarly, the social organization and lifecycle of people in industrialized nations has diverged far from the norm that evolved during the Paleolithic period, and this has resulted in a range of human diseases, as well as industrial pollution, unsustainable manufacturing, agriculture, and warfare. The diagnosis must be that the habitat built by humans is not adapted to support normal human life.

Technology itself is not a problem for any human community. Thus, in industrialized society, humans can happily adapt to the use of complex technologies that alter the physical form of foodstuffs, transportation, dwellings, communication, and other life-support resources.

However, humans cannot adapt to the harmful side-effects of technology that directly or indirectly alter internal metabolic variables. For example, the abnormalities in the nutritional balance of the human diet in industrialized societies result in a huge burden of disease. Similarly, the reduction in normal physical activity by most of the population due to the automation of physical work contributes to widespread obesity that reduces the quality and length of life.

Most important of all, the emergence of coercive, parasitical states with a monopoly of power must be regarded as a pathological stage of civilization. In contrast, the egalitarian social relationships, consensual government, and lack of warfare that typified humans (until population density and famine triggered warfare) form the *only natural structure for an adaptive society*, and should be adopted by modern humans as the basis of a technology-based adaptive civilization.

If we continue to accept the current industrialized civilization and all its maladaptive aspects as "normal," then we accept that human social organization should be subordinated to the indiscriminate and volatile course of human technology. Supposing that we applied that idea to the giant panda, the chimpanzee, or the leopard? Would the same scientists who acquiesce to the unnatural, centralized organization of human mass society regard it as equally acceptable for the social organization of animals in zoos or wildlife parks to be arbitrarily dictated by zookeepers, based on their convenience, or the buildings and technical equipment that happened to be at hand? Such a view would obliterate the scientific discipline of ethology, which is based upon studying the link between the genetic traits of a species and the habitat to which it has been adapted by evolution.

The social structure of any civilized human society, however complex, must support the individual autonomy and integrated face-to-face communities with which humans evolved, because they are as much a part of human biology as are the human physiology and the normal human lifecycle. A modern mass society incorporates a complex web of technologies that impinge upon every aspect of the human lifestyle, sometimes harmlessly, and sometimes lethally. But if we wish to avoid the likelihood of human extinction, then the utilization of technology must be ameliorated by feedback from the population at large. The only truly adaptive culture is the spontaneous order that emerges from the genetically shaped preferences of many individual humans, guided by natural selection. This is nature's system, and the idea that human politics or science has something better to offer is a delusion. In the first chapter, we established that nearly all human problems are aspects of a failure in the adaptation between humans and their artificial habitat of civilization. The obvious causes are the unintended consequences of technology, including industrialized warfare and unsustainable manufacturing and agriculture. But human intelligence and scientific knowledge could easily remedy these technical problems.

Humans are Awakening to the Crisis of Government

The underlying reason for human problems is the failure of social organization, which prevents the problems from being addressed. Human society is broken into two cultures with different purposes: the parasitic state culture of political leaders, and the natural family culture of the general population. Political leaders in the state culture may see failing adaptation as an advantage, because it weakens resistance to state control, enabling the parasitic elite to extract more resources in greater security.

The general public, forced to live within a state-imposed welfare culture, has mostly abdicated its responsibility and self-discipline for the future of the community. The state controls education and has a large influence over the mass media, and can easily mislead the public into blaming large wealth differentials, warfare, poor economic performance, and pollution on "capitalist freedom", or on foreign populations or aggressive overseas religions. If social conditions are highly maladaptive, people may consume more alcohol or mind-altering drugs but, with practically no help from the scientific community, they are not likely to make a correct diagnosis and demand the creation of more adaptive social conditions.

However, in the 21st century, international travel and global communications through the Internet have begun to provide a much clearer view of the human dilemma. Men, women, and children from every part of the world are able to talk to one another and to see videos of how others live. People compare their way of life and often find themselves disturbed by illogical disparities in wealth and freedom. This overview of the world is generating a huge change in the attitude of humans towards government.

Historically, there have been an uncountable number of conflicts between the general population and coercive governments, which have ruthlessly put down rebellions, killing and imprisoning innocent citizens at will, usually with only the remotest chance of being held accountable for their actions. In the European Enlightenment of the 17th century, progress was made towards defining the rights of people to overthrow bad governments. In post-industrial countries, the hungry are no longer hanged for stealing bread, and heretics are no longer burnt to death for rejecting the state religion. Nevertheless, the state has grown relentlessly larger and more powerful, creating a paradox.

Philosophers and some biologists are realizing that the coercive power of the state is merely the product of military conquest in the relatively recent past, after millions of years in which autonomy has been the natural state of men and women, and of the tiny family communities in which they lived. However, this realization has not alleviated the coercive control of the state. The actual power of the centralized state to exercise control over the lives of the mass populations has been relentlessly expanded.

Today, men and women the world over are wondering why they have such limited power over their own lives. For example, every day, the crews of the nuclear submarines of at least six countries rehearse the highly disciplined procedure for launching inter-continental ballistic missiles at all the major cities of the civilized world. If the missiles are ever actually launched, hundreds of millions of innocent people will be exterminated, and greater numbers will either die slowly or be permanently poisoned by nuclear radiation, just as the inhabitants of Hiroshima and Nagasaki were in 1945.

Politicians tell people that the missiles are unlikely to be launched, but experience has eroded the value of such promises. Ordinary people may wonder *in whose interests* they are taxed to pay for this preparation for war, when they have no reason whatever to attack the people of other cities, nor be attacked by them. Political leaders claim that such weapons of mass destruction are necessary for the security of their populations, but since the possession of such weapons makes the whole of humanity insecure, that cannot be the reason.

Why is warfare still practiced as a tool of state policy? In the 20th century, almost 300 million people, mostly civilians and innocent of any crime, were killed by warfare. In the 21st century, government elites continue to believe that they can use warfare as a tool to benefit themselves in some way. Whatever the varied motivation for warfare between states, it is always instigated by political leaders who are not, in practice, subject to the rule of civilized law. Why don't humans have effective global laws for their species? Why don't societies abolish the use of force by political leaders, and subject them to the *same laws* that restrain the mass of the people from murder or theft? Who is maintaining the right to make war and in whose interest is that right being maintained?

The technology of agriculture now provides more than enough food for the seven billion people on Earth, yet according to the United Nations, 13 percent of the world's population suffer from malnourishment and six million children die each year of starvation or related diseases. The ultimate cause of this horror is that millions of humans are caught between the destruction of their natural way of life in foraging or subsistence farming, and modern economic systems that would enable them to earn a living in global markets. Since all market transactions make both buyer and seller richer, why are both trade and technology controlled by governments in the name of militaristic competition? Since the majority of people in all countries do not want these people to starve, why are governments (as a group) acting to ensure their starvation? In whose interests are these governments acting?

At the same time, half the populations of industrialized countries eat artificially modified food of appalling quality, fail to exercise, and become obese. They tend to develop "metabolic syndrome" which is a combination of type 2 diabetes, hypertension, high cholesterol, and obesity. The unhealthy lifestyle also causes asthma, coronary heart disease, cancer of the colon, liver, and lungs, as well as alcoholism, gout, and many allergies. Unsurprisingly, depression and other mental health problems are common.

Such behavior is not only alien to normal human society; it has never arisen before in *any* species. There is no essential reason for such strange behavior in the super-intelligent human species, except that the social organization of modern societies is abnormal and does not provide an adaptive environment for the human lifecycle.

Another major issue is the global failure of governments to control the damage done by productive industries, through pollution of water, air, and food, even when they cause property damage, ill-health and even death to masses of people. This damage, which is labeled "externalities" by economists, is often seen as a collective cost of the community because governments that compete economically do not wish to impose costs on their own industries that might make them less competitive in international markets. Why don't humans prohibit all harmful externalities with global laws that would put all businesspeople on a level playing field? Would legitimate entrepreneurs object to being told by society: "You can run your business any way you want, unless it harms other people"?

In principle, all externalities should be part of the cost of production and in a civilized community, the owners of businesses should be held fully responsible for any harm that they do. Governments have used legislation such as the limited liability laws to create corporations and relieve their owners and directors of some of their accountability, perhaps in the service of ruthless international competition. Why don't we revert to a free market system in which all individuals are fully accountable for their actions?

Pollution, soil erosion, and deforestation are killing off much of the natural world and may be influencing global climate patterns, threatening life on Earth. If governments make laws against killing or injuring people using weapons such as guns or knives, why don't they make laws against externalities that achieve the same result? If the huge damage to the biosphere from economic activities is tolerated by governments, *in whose interest* is it tolerated?

The same question could be asked in relation to humanity's unfortunate consumption of mind-altering drugs and the irrational "war against drugs" that ostensibly attempts to control the problem. According to the World Health Organization, each year, over five million people die as a result of tobacco use and a further two-and-a-half million die from alcohol use, while only about 245,000 people, 3.2% of the total death-toll, die from the use of other illicit or prescribed drugs,.

The USA attempted alcohol prohibition for a few years in the 1930s, but this merely drove alcohol consumption underground and generated a national crime wave. The War on Drugs has similarly failed to reduce drug addiction after 70 years, but it has caused an immense crime wave with thousands of murders a year. Worldwide, taxpayers have to pay to imprison millions of drug traders and users, most of whom have harmed no-one.

Abolishing the War on Drugs would decriminalize consumption, allow addicts to be treated, and make it easier to educate young people on the dangers of drugs. A massive reduction in worldwide crime would follow the closing down of illegal drug production and sales. Legal drug vendors would be subject to safety standards and could not sell to young people below the age of autonomy, because that would be the initiation of force (or harm).

In addition, between one quarter and a half of prisons could close, freeing inmates to become productive members of their communities. Drug-related violence would disappear, and the high taxes that are spent on military-style weapons and SWAT teams to combat the drug trade could be saved.

If the War on Drugs was scrapped, the drug barons would be thrown out of business, and the police and judiciary would have less work. But the biggest losers might be crooked politicians. A thorough analysis of the economic factors supporting drug prohibition is *The Economics of Prohibition,* written by economist Mark Thornton, (Thornton 1991), who writes: "History reveals that prohibitions are indeed classic examples of the co-opting of public spirited intentions by rent-seekers within the political process thereby explaining the existence of what at first appears to be irrational policies."

In the field of human rights, why is suicide illegal in most countries? Some people with terminal illnesses may have a rational reason to prefer death. Once again, we have to ask *in whose interest* the state takes over ownership of our bodies.

The mutilation of children is widely practiced and implies the belief that they are the property of their parents or the state. In nearly 30 countries in the Middle East and Africa, girls are subjected to genital mutilation and about 140 million women are living with the consequences, which include pain, health problems, and sometimes death. There are also many lesser forms of mutilating the bodies of children, including male circumcision, brass coils worn that produce a long-neck appearance of women in certain parts of Asia, and the piercing of women's lips in some African tribes. Mutilation of a child contravenes the principle of ownership of one's own body. We should make global laws absolutely prohibiting the mutilation of young persons under the age at which they are able to take responsibility for their self-ownership.

How the State is Destroying the Family

In industrialized countries, the family has been undermined and fragmented by the state. Compared to the biologically natural family, the modern "nuclear" family (two parents and their children) is a cut-down version created by the huge mobility of labor demanded by the Industrial Revolution, as well as the loss of local community caused by the centralization of society. Whereas the original extended family integrated people of different ages and abilities, so that the strong could help the weak and the weak serve the strong, the nuclear family has no strong local community, and is therefore increasingly dependent on state welfare and other services.

It is true that the extended family has been maintained much longer in Asia and Africa than in Europe, but people everywhere are moving to cities and emulating the industrialized lifestyle of the West, which sacrifices the family to the centralized power of the coercive, parasitic state.

The family and reproduction are at the center of human life. Sexuality is one of life's greatest sources of happiness and bonding between humans. Yet, somehow, industrialized society has given us the worst of all possible worlds. Young people, especially, are threatened by sexually transmitted diseases. Marital disharmony means that children are seriously harmed by divorce that can entail years of hatred, legal conflict, and sudden separation. Increasingly, a significant proportion of men do not want to get married and many women do not want to have babies.

The number of children born to the average woman, measured as the Total Fertility Rate (TFR), ranges from eight in some African countries down to well under two in most industrialized countries. Clearly, the environment in which children are raised is utterly different and, some would say inferior, to the one nature gave to humans.

Typically, both parents now work for a living, and have little time to spend with their children, which has disastrous consequences. The divorce rate of 40-50% in the industrialized world often causes major psychological damage to both children and parents. In the USA, 28% of children live in "single-parent" families – in fact, they do not have a family at all by natural standards.

Children are forced into compulsory state schooling, and are likely to stay in an environment that they dislike for up to two decades. In the USA, nearly 5% of children resist schoolroom incarceration and demonstrate rebellious behavior, and they are likely to be labeled with supposed disorders that have no provable physical basis, such as ADHD (Attention Deficit Hyperactivity Disorder), and consequently given drugs.

In 2000, US psychiatrist Peter Breggin testified before the US Congress on ADHD. "It is important for the Education Committee to understand that the ADD/ADHD (ADD is Attention Deficit Disorder) diagnosis was developed specifically for the purpose of justifying the use of drugs to subdue the behaviors of children in the classroom," said Breggin. "By diagnosing the child with ADHD, blame for the conflict is placed on the child. Instead of examining the context of the child's life – why the child is restless or disobedient in the classroom or home – the problem is attributed to the child's faulty brain. Both the classroom and the family are exempt from criticism or from the need to improve, and instead the child is made the source of the problem" (Breggin 2000)

Dr Breggin also cites studies indicating that antidepressants frequently induce a manic reaction or severe emotional disturbance in young people, and can make children violent, depressed, psychotic, or suicidal. Stimulants cause especially severe adverse reactions in young children. Many of the drugs given to even pre-school children are highly addictive, and Breggin cites research showing that they may cause damage to brains, especially the growing brains of children.

In an editorial in the Journal of the American Medical Association, Harvard Medical School psychiatrist J.T. Coyle expressed concern that children aged 2 to 4 years were receiving stimulants, antidepressants, or antipsychotic medication. Coyle pointed out that psychiatric drugs bathe the brains of children with agents that threaten the normal development of the brain. "…there are valid concerns that such treatment could have deleterious effects on the developing brain of young children," said Coyle. (Coyle 2000)

ADHD is just one example of a proliferation of scientific labels for human behavior, which are controversial because they are based only on opinion, without any physical evidence that individuals are really ill and not merely in disagreement with the society around them.

Many concerned people lobby governments to alter laws that damage the family, but such protest is ineffective. A sovereign state is by definition a parasite that does not wish to tolerate real competition for leadership of the community, as we saw clearly when communist states destroyed all internal opposition. The family represents "integrated humanity" and was the natural source of leadership for millions of years. As long as the state exists, and makes laws, the family will be marginalized or destroyed. Humans can choose either to live as autonomous individuals, participating in the consensual management of the natural family, or they can be subordinated to the absolute power of the state, an alien entity created by military conquest.

Jennifer Roback Morse, President of the Ruth Institute, which promotes traditional man/woman marriage, pinpoints the underlying reason. "As state support becomes more significant, the mutual support of family members becomes less important. Parents no longer feel the need to marry each other, or even cooperate with each other. The state replaces the married couple as the primary support for children. And as a not-so-unintended consequence, state-funded child-care frees women from child-care responsibilities inside the home so they can work outside the home."(Morse 2008)

British Academic, Patricia Morgan, stresses the social value of the family: "…marriage performs critical social tasks and produces valuable social goods that are far harder or impossible to achieve through individual action, private enterprise or alternative civic institutions, and which cannot be replicated by public programs." But in her book *The War Between the State and the Family: How Government Divides and Impoverishes,* she highlights the enormous damage done to the family by the overwhelming power of the state to destroy the bonds of interdependence between family members by legislation and welfare.

"Human beings may well be a social species, but household trends suggest increasing fragmentation or atomization," writes Morgan. "Such trends impose pressures upon living standards and the environment, and are closely bound up with problems of poor child development, personal disadvantage, endemic welfare dependency and the increasing inequalities that have exercised researchers, policy-makers and politicians over the last decade or so. As individuals are disconnected from family, friends, neighbors, churches, clubs, associations and community networks, social capital is destroyed, trust evaporates, despoliation and predation spread."

Morgan is writing particularly about the damage done to the family in Britain, but the global trend is for the role of the family to be diminished by state controls and welfare policies. "These developments are not simply fortuitous or accidental, but are being created by government policies that are altering our demographics: policies that have progressively eradicated the links that bound families and communities together," writes Morgan. "Out of indifference or even hostility to human collaboration, by ignorance or design, these are subverting the formation of enduring bonds and furthering social dislocation." (Morgan 2008)

Alternative Views of the Parasite State

Massive intervention by the coercive, parasitical state has transformed human life. When modern humans evolved, they lived in small groups with no central government. Men, women, even children were free to carry on their lives, accomplish what they could and make their own mistakes, as long as they did not harm others.

Today, the state regulates almost the whole of human life. We are no longer the free human species that evolved, and many writers have produced novels warning people of the dehumanization that accompanies the growing centralized power of the state. Two of the most well-known are *Brave New World*, by Aldous Huxley and *1984* by George Orwell. Many more books and modern movies warn the general public about the potential abuses of state power. And, of course, in the 20th century, under regimes like the British Empire, Communism in Eastern Europe, and Fascism in Germany, Japan and Italy, the most awful tyrannies were conducted, with the genocide of millions in concentration camps from torture and starvation and the death of tens of millions in warfare.

Yet the general population has continued to live under this shadow with little review of the absolute power of the state. Almost every aspect of life is now controlled to some extent by the state, so that human behavior is forced into patterns far removed from those of the natural past. A human society controlled by a parasitic state can be compared to a 19th century zoo, because, like early zoos, the top priorities of those in control do not include the welfare of the captive residents.

In 1969, zoologist Desmond Morris published *The Human Zoo*, which detailed some of the problems. Writes Morris: "The modern human animal is no longer living in conditions natural for his species." Human social organization changed radically. Early hunter gatherers reached a delicate balance between competition and leadership, but in the super-tribes of the agricultural age: "The over-grown urban groups rapidly and repeatedly fell prey to exaggerated forms of tyranny, despotism and dictatorship."

Morris suggests that crime is not a natural behavior that has to be suppressed by law, but rather a behavior resulting from the change in social organization in large societies. "A member of a super-tribe (a mass society) is under pressure, suffering from all the stresses and strains of his artificial social conditions. Most people in his super-tribe are strangers to him; he has no personal, tribal bond with them. The typical thief is not stealing from one of his known companions. He is not breaking the old, biological tribal code. In his mind, he is simply setting his victim outside his tribe altogether." (Morris 1996)

One reason for the success of *The Human Zoo* was that it captured the fact that humans living in modern society feel trapped in a world over which they have no control. In early zoos, the animals were captured from the wild by ruthless hunters, who often killed many creatures for each one sold to zoo owners. Trapped in small cages, such animals had short, miserable lives. What such animals needed was identical to what humans need today – the freedom to prioritize their own survival needs in an adaptive habitat. Animals need their natural habitat, just as humans need an adaptive civilization. Scientific knowledge has greatly improved zoos, but the animal inmates are still subject to parasitism by humans, just as humans are subject to the parasitism of the state.

All over the world, many people have reason to feel quite a lot like zoo animals. The problem is not just that most humans are forced to put up with a huge range of technologies that are harmful to people; they have no practical say in the matter. Ideologies such as democracy may promise that people have control, but in practice they find that tiny elites have almost absolute sovereign power, which is beyond the reach of the majority of people. Instead of being used to provide an opportunity for self-actualization of all human individuals, social power is now used for military and economic competition between states, which also create super-rich corporations that are not legally accountable for the harms that they do.

Human populations living under the coercive control of states have been described by one prominent thinker as farm animals. Canadian philosopher, Stefan Molyneux, the host of Freedomain Radio (http://freedomainradio.com), describes the control of the coercive state as "tax farming," and the victims of this political control as "human livestock." (Molyneux 2012)

Molyneux describes how early rulers employed slavery and even cannibalism, but that brute force was gradually replaced with subtler means of control, especially indoctrination with religion and other ethical beliefs that enable non-conformity to be punished by peer pressure. Molyneux's description of modern governments as "tax farmers" expresses the parasitism of the state and its affiliated groups, and his explanation of the state's evolving methodologies for controlling the general population are very insightful.

Molyneux refers to the group that control the state as the "ruling class," and it is useful to consider who that might be. The expression "ruling class" is certainly appropriate to refer to the warlords who once assisted kings in the feudal system in Europe, China, and Japan. Military leaders who assisted kings in conquering a region were given lands, together with their inhabitants, to exploit. Regional lords could initiate family dynasties and join a class of aristocrats that could retain power over many generations, as the "ruling class."

For hundreds of years in the West, the Catholic Church was a close ally of the state and a source of ideology that could cower the population into accepting its subservience. In countries dominated by Islam, mullahs also capture the levers of power. In the few countries that are still nominally communist, the leaders claim to represent the workers. Today, people exercising political power may come from any social class, but they don't meaningfully represent anyone but themselves.

The fact that modern governments are socially heterogeneous is significant, because it shows that the historical analysis of Marx and other thinkers who attached importance to the struggle between social classes is incorrect. Social classes are transient phenomena that emerge from the wealth generated by particular technologies, combined with the hierarchy generated by the state, on top of the more modest differentials that result from natural economic competition.

The problem facing civilization is not one of class conflict, but the illegitimacy of sovereignty. As long as the public acquiesces to the state's initiation of force against it, the levers that control sovereign power will continue to be available, and ruthless individuals of every description will attempt to grasp them in order to exercise parasitic control over the public.

What would Happen in the Absence of the Coercive State?

We have seen that human civilization fails to provide a fully adaptive habitat for humans. The proximate (immediate) reason for this failure is the harmful side-effects of technologies that are otherwise adaptive. Yet we also know that the scientists and engineers who build the technologies on which civilization is based are quite capable of remedying or alleviating their unintended consequences. It is not technology itself that is the problem, but social organization that prioritizes values according to the needs of the parasitical state, instead of the general public.

The only way to retrieve normal social organization is for an international movement that will replace state coercion with absolute human equality under global law. But individual societies cannot unilaterally abolish their sovereignty. Worldwide, thousands of rebellions against state control have always failed, because the states together form a coercive parasitic system that will immediately recapture any communities that attempt to retrieve their natural, sustainable autonomous form.

Humans need to take a new approach to building civilization. All people of goodwill should support the creation of a worldwide movement to disseminate the scientific knowledge of human prehistory. Education will lead to a demand for sustainable government and adaptive conditions for all humans. Hopefully, the scientific community will learn to play a constructive role in recognizing and affirming the parasitic nature of the coercive state. Once the scientific basis for consensual government is recognized, global laws that prohibit the initiation of force by any human will be passed in one jurisdiction after another.

Individual autonomy under a social contract that supports the non-aggression principle (the prohibition of the initiation of force) is the biologically natural condition of human society. Once this is attained on a global level, the human species will never go back to the criminal government of the parasite state.

In Chapter 3, I will discuss how the natural state of *normal* human societies is supported by "spontaneous order" that provides stability without any governmental coercion.

Chapter 3

How the Artificial Human Habitat Evolves

*W*e have seen how the parasitic culture of the state is destroying the natural family and community. In Chapter 3, we will discuss how the rapid evolution of the human habitat that we call "civilization" generates adaptive solutions to human needs. The family and the community play a vital part in the process of creating adaptive fit between humans and their artificial habitat.

Darwinian evolution of the species was of overwhelming importance to our prehistoric ancestors, because it generated the "fit" between humans and their Paleolithic habitat that resulted in their well-being and biological success. Evolution altered human genes slowly by natural selection, and this enabled people to adapt to long-term changes in the environment, including severe climate change such as the ice ages, and later to adapt to the conditions in a range of different latitudes and ecologies, as people migrated across the planet.

In the 20th century, scientists recognized that industrial civilization is changing faster – perhaps a million times faster than the pace of biotic evolution, while maintaining a generally stable and adaptive habitat for humans. Instead of humans evolving to fit their habitat in nature, the artificial habitat that we call "civilization" is now evolving to fit human needs. Biotic evolution, as described by Charles Darwin, has not stopped, but it usually takes thousands of years to accomplish significant change, and so biotic evolution cannot maintain a fit between humans and their fast-changing technologies.

Understanding how the Artificial Habitat Changes

If human fitness depends upon the evolution of the artificial habitat that we call civilization, then it is vital that we understand how our habitat evolves. However, the evolution of the human habitat has not been described in a theory equivalent to Darwin's explanation of biotic evolution. Many scientists have created theories about the transmission of ideas between humans as the foundation for social evolution. But since the brain itself is not yet understood, such ideas may take decades to bear fruit.

Nevertheless, if we are to explain the failure of human adaptation at a time when the technology-based human habitat is evolving so fast, then we need to bear in mind at least a simple outline explaining how and why the habitat evolves Therefore, I am providing such a basic outline in this chapter. My hypothesis is down-to-earth, with references where it reflects the views of scientific researchers.

Nevertheless, I must warn readers to turn their skepticism up to full power. I suggest that you ask yourself whether the explanation provided in this chapter is based on evidence that can be falsified, or upon mere conjecture. Decide whether my theory fits your own knowledge about modern humans, and whether it helps you to understand the remarkable acceleration of the technology-based culture in which you live.

Now that you have been warned, let us start by deciding the precise scope of the evolution of civilization. If Darwin explained how the species of life are created and extinguished, what components of industrial society need explaining? The answer must be: those components that differentiate themselves from slow biotic evolution by evolving at an enormously faster rate. If we compare, for example, a modern city such as New York with the pre-agricultural tribal life of New Guinea, precisely what aspects of the former are evolving much faster than the latter?

The most obvious such feature of industrial societies stares us in the face: it is the artifacts. The skyscrapers, highways, vehicles and planes, televisions and computers. And changing just as rapidly are the intangible artifacts, such as music, literature, videos, and computer software.

The second component of the industrial society that alters rapidly is human behavior. But not all human behavior; we still perform the basic biological functions, such as walking, talking, swimming, eating, and sex, in a similar fashion to preindustrial peoples. So we can assume that that part of behavior is subject to slow, Darwinian biotic evolution.

But a large part of human behavior in industrialized societies is generated by the need to invent new artifacts, maintain them, and learn to use them. For example, the way that we work in offices and factories, our purchase of processed foods from shops, our travel in powered vehicles, and our reliance on electronic media such as TV and the Internet are all human behaviors that are subject to ultra-fast evolution.

The third component of modern society that is evolving rapidly is human knowledge. Although there may be some hard-wired knowledge associated with our biological functions that is subject to Darwinian evolution, much of our daily repertoire of behavior is clearly necessitated by the fast-changing technologies with which we have to deal. Scientific knowledge has already expanded far beyond any individual's comprehension. Education emphasizes mathematics, science and technology, to equip young humans to deal with their technology-based society.

To summarize, evolution of the habitat continually alters three components:

1).The artifacts that constitute civilization, both tangible and intangible;

2). The large part of human behavior that is associated with creating, maintaining and using artifacts, and therefore is not controlled by slow, Darwinian evolution;

3). The part of learned knowledge associated with the creation, maintenance and use of artifacts and of pure scientific research.

Note that these three fast-evolving elements of civilization cannot be directly encoded in DNA, but rather are subject to the laws of the natural world. For this reason, I describe learned knowledge, technology-related behaviors, and artifacts as "components" of the industrialized habitat.

Evolution of Civilization versus Biotic Evolution

In Fig. 5., we further clarify the distinction between humans, plus other parts of civilization that evolves slowly, through biotic or Darwinian evolution, and the human habitat, which evolves rapidly through evolution of civilization. The parts subject only to Darwinian evolution are the human physiology and that part of human culture that relates to what should be the unchanging functions of the human lifecycle, such as eating, reproduction, and nurturing children. The parts subject to rapid evolution of civilization are all the tangible and intangible artifacts, and that part of culture that is related to creating and maintaining new artifacts, and the teaching and learning related to their use.

The evolving habitat: Subject to fast, intelligently adaptive evolution		The human species: Subject to slow, biotic evolution	
Habitat of artifacts	Human Culture		Human physiology
All tangible and intangible artifacts made by humans, such as buildings, farms, transport, telecommunications, music, literature, computer programs.	Habitat maintenance. Creation of new artifacts and the education of populations in their use.	Lifecycle maintenance. "Homeostasis" of the lifecycle. Adaptive regulation of food, ambient conditions, social rank, reproduction.	Homeostasis of bodily parameters, such as blood pressure, pulse, respiration, enzyme levels, and hormones.

Fig. 5. Divisions between Darwinian and habitat evolution.

The human brain evolved to generate adaptive behaviors that result in human Darwinian "fitness." But there is a limit to what individuals can do to achieve "fit" with a habitat that is very maladaptive. Current human societies manifestly place a low priority on the provision of adaptive conditions for the general population.

So, now we have clarified the boundary between biotic evolution and evolution of the habitat. Biotic evolution explains the development of species of living organisms by changes in the inherited traits that enable them to survive and reproduce. Evolution of the habitat explains the development of learned knowledge, technology-related behaviors, and artifacts through changes created and selected by human intentionality.

The Mechanism of Habitat Evolution

We need to clarify the essential nature of "evolution." In order for something to evolve, whether it is a living organism or a component of the habitat, multiple instances of it must possess varied characteristics that differentiate their success within the environment. The successful individuals of each generation are more frequently copied, while the less copied forms tend to disappear. The most generic form of evolution, known as "Selectionism" and championed by Gary Cziko, comprises: 1. variation, 2. selection, and 3. transmission. Below we discuss how these three processes take place in the evolution of the human habitat.

The three components of the human habitat– knowledge, learned behaviors and artifacts – are created intentionally by human intelligence.

1. Variation in the Artificial Human Habitat

The great variety in the characteristics of the habitat compoents results in part from their being designed to fulfill different purposes, and also because of variation in the brains of their creators. People discover new knowledge, originate new behaviors and create new artifacts every day, but most of these creative solutions to adaptive needs are modest changes to personal lifestyles that will never be adopted by anyone else but the creator. However, human relations are dominated by reciprocity, which includes the exchange of value. In social life, the exchange of knowledge, adaptive behaviors and superior artifacts takes place continually. Where these created components are exchanged for monetary value, they form the innovations in what we call "the economy."

In high-trust communities such as the family, the two parts to each exchange of value may take place asynchronously without strict accounting while, in the marketplace, exchange is usually synchronous, guided by market pricing signals and strictly accounted.

It is useful to compare the variation in the components of the human habitat with the variation found in the evolution of life. In Darwinian evolution, the variation is created by blind chance, including the random mutations of genes, and genetic drift. Biotic evolution is completely blind, because there is no intelligence driving it. A major exponent of Darwinism, Donald T. Campbell, described Darwinian evolution as "Blind variation and selective retention."

The whole process of biotic evolution, from the random mutation of genes, to mitosis and recombination of the chromosomes, to the natural selection by differential survival of the adult organisms or phenotypes of each species, has evolved without any guiding intelligence, and therefore can be justifiably described as "blind." Richard Dawkin's 1986 book "The blind watchmaker" refutes the religious myth that complex living things could only be created by an intelligent god, just as we may feel that the examination of a watch may convince us of the existence of a watchmaker. Dawkins explains in detail how the "blind" forces of evolution may have evolved complex organs such as the human eye over a long period of time.

Surprisingly, human invention is also "blind" because there is no strictly logical way to identify the *completely new* solution that will solve a problem. Therefore, creators are forced to adopt the "trial and error" method of searching for a solution.

Nevertheless, humans have a powerful intelligence that can create a vision of the probable future and work towards it. Also, humans can use analogy to increase their efficiency at solving similar problems. Therefore, when humans participate in the evolution of their habitat, they are very much less "blind" than is nature in biotic evolution. Real watchmakers are not completely "blind," even though they must use trial and error to resolve the inherent uncertainty of nature's complexity.

Indeed, it is mainly the difference between the "uncertainty" of the intelligent human creator and the "blindness" of non-intelligent nature that enables humans to drive evolution of their habitat at millions of times the rate of biotic evolution.

2. Selection of Habitat Components

All evolutionary processes incorporate selection, but there is an important distinction between the "natural selection" of Darwinian evolution and the "human selection" of evolution of the human habitat.

In the evolution of any species, the process by which the "fittest" members of a generation would, on average, tend to survive and reproduce more successfully than the less fit member, was described by Charles Darwin as "natural selection." Darwin took pains to distinguish between natural selection in nature and "human selection" such as that used by farmers to breed new varieties of plants, or by pigeon breeders and racehorse breeders to create changes in the traits possessed by these creatures. It is therefore inappropriate to use the term "natural selection" in evolution of the human habitat to describe the purely human selection used to create the new knowledge, new behaviors, and new artifacts that comprise innovatory steps in the process.

The human mind has been superbly adapted during biotic evolution to monitor and maintain its owner's adaptive fit with the habitat, and this includes maintaining adaptive behavior throughout the phases of the whole human lifecycle.

A prominent scientist, and the founder of the discipline of sociobiology, Edward O. Wilson, emphasizes the central importance of maintaining the natural human lifecycle, and the brain's evolved capacity to do just this: "...the brain exists because it promotes the survival and multiplication of the genes that direct its assembly. The human mind is a device for survival and reproduction, and reason is just one of its various techniques…The reflective person knows that his life is in some incomprehensible sense guided through a biological ontogeny, a more or less fixed order of life stages. He senses that with all the drive, with, love, pride anger, hope and anxiety that characterize the species, he will in the end be sure only of helping to perpetuate the same cycle." (Wilson, Edward O., 2004)

In the 20th century, scientific ignorance and political expediency were combined in the view that the brain of a human child was a "blank slate" that could be reshaped through education. The human lifecycle was regarded as completely flexible, and able to adjust to whatever conditions were imposed on it by political ideologies such as communism, fascism, democracy, or religious fundamentalism. We now know that many human traits are genetically based and, therefore humans are genetically adapted to an evolved family-based lifecycle that cannot be manipulated to conform to political fashions without causing psychological or physical illness. The mistaken concept of the brain as a "blank slate" has been thoroughly examined and shown to be false by Steven Pinker (Pinker 2002), among others.

Unfortunately, both scientists and politicians have tended to underestimate the ability of the human brain to generate adaptive behaviors, at least in preindustrial societies. However, adherents of an important new discipline called evolutionary psychology research precisely what the brain evolved to achieve. The editors of a key book on this subject, *The Adapted Mind*, have established that the brain is a machine for adaptation: "The human mind consists of a set of evolved information-processing mechanisms… produced by natural selection over evolutionary time in ancestral environments," say the editors, "Many of these mechanisms are functionally specialized to produce behavior that solves particular adaptive problems." The nature of these adaptive problems is spelt out: "An *adaptive problem* is a problem whose solution can affect reproduction, however distally. Avoiding predation, choosing nutritious foods, finding a mate, and communicating with others are examples of adaptive problems that our hominid ancestors would have faced." (Barkow 1992)

Below, we discuss the three most central types of human selection that shape civilization.

Human Selection in the Creative Process: When individual humans struggle to generate new knowledge, behaviors or artifacts, they will always first conceive of multiple solutions and compare them, either in their imagination or by physical experimentation, to determine which constitutes the best "fit." The human mind is capable of envisaging the actual use of new knowledge, behavior, and artifacts and predicting their likely efficacy as components of the habitat.

Most innovations may only modify the habitat of an individual person. For example, individuals use variation and selection to find the optimum route to travel to work, the best way to cook their favorite recipe, or the best method to ask their boss for a pay rise. But, of course, only a small minority of such inventions prove worthy of widespread adoption.

The Selection of Habitat Components by the Community: When individuals discover new knowledge, practice new behaviors, or create new artifacts for their personal use, they may be imitated by their family members or acquaintances. Each person who encounters the innovation will at first carry out a preliminary appraisal of the innovation against the beliefs, behaviors, and artifacts that they already employ. If new concepts seems promising, they may try them out in their own lives, and then experiment with additional variation and selection to refine the adaptive fit with their personal lifestyle.

As the number of people that adopt a new or improved habitat component increases, its attractiveness is often enhanced by two mechanisms. (Richerson & Boyd 2005) The first is "conformity bias," which means that individuals tend to have a more favorable evaluation of an idea that is already widely adopted. This corresponds with the commonsense rule: "When in Rome, do as the Romans do."

The second factor that accelerates the adoption of an idea is "prestige bias," which is the more positive evaluation of innovations when they have been adopted by people considered to have high prestige. This might be equivalent to the preference for prestigious associations, known as "snobbery" or, alternatively, an evaluation that certain leading individuals have superior judgment. The commercial marketing of products, especially luxury goods, often utilizes prestige bias by associating them with celebrities or experts.

Selection of Habitat Components for Commercial Markets: Designers of new or modified habitat components for commercial sale may conduct market research and then attempt to match the requirements of a specific segment of users. Prototype products may be submitted to panels of potential customers to refine the match between product and market by initial variation and selection of features, prior to committing the product to mass production.

Once a product or service is supplied to the market, alongside many competing products, it becomes part of the process of variation and selection that determines which artifacts are adopted by millions of consumers or business purchasers.

The long-term evolution of a class of products is based on the accumulation of significant design features. Trivial variations in design may influence fashion in the short term, but may not play a significant part in evolution of civilization.

Products with different combinations of features and prices may vary greatly in their popularity and this will be reflected in their production volume. However, products that are produced in high volume – especially inexpensive products – do not necessarily have new design features, and therefore may not contribute to the evolution of that class of product.

The evolutionary process described above, applies to all habitat components, whether they are information products such as dictionaries, music, literature, sculptures, or software, behavioral products such as professional dancing, and product maintenance service, or artifacts produced for commercial distribution.

3. Transmission of Adaptive Change through the Habitat

When people discover new information, or create new behaviors or artifacts, their starting point is the previous generation of habitat components. So information is transmitted from generation to generation.

In Darwinian evolution, information about each generation of organisms is carried to the next generation by DNA in the form of genes. Darwin, who knew nothing of genes, called this process "descent with modification" which means that the offspring of all living things are similar to their parents, even though they may display adaptive changes.

Many researchers have assumed that "cultural" evolution, which I call habitat evolution, must include the copying of cultural ideas by a "replicator" equivalent to the gene, in which the copying errors create the variation upon which natural selection acts.

However, it seems that no replicator is required in habitat evolution. It is rather obvious that the transmission of information about a society's information, behaviors and artifacts is held in many kinds of media, including technical papers, computer databases, books and periodicals, patents, blueprints and other records, including the memories of inventors and other creative people.

The generalized copying of information, behaviors and artifacts does transmit evolutionary changes (innovations) through the general population, but this is much less important than copying in biotic evolution.

In biotic evolution, the genome acts as a "replicator", so that each new generation is an approximate copy of the preceding one. In habitat evolution, a clever inventor may create a new solution for a human need, that bears almost *no relationship* to previous solutions to the same need. This is because human intelligence can analyze *the need itself* and create a new solution using concepts from anywhere within the knowledge base available, so that no copying is required. Thus, there is no automatic Darwinian "inheritance" in habitat evolution, and no replicator to copy the previous generations.

Social Evolution is Unrelated to Copying

Scientists researching human cultural evolution have observed that humans spend a vast amount of time copying the information, behaviors and artifacts that constitute the civilized habitat. They have then sought to find an analogy between this copying process and the replication of living organisms by genes, which creates the continuity and variation in biotic evolution. The "meme" and the "culturgen" were invented as "replicators" that are analogous to genes.

English ethologist Richard Dawkins invented the "meme" and suggested that units of culture are copied from individual to individual, accumulating changes that create variety. The variants are subject to natural selection and the most successful ones proliferate and become steps in social evolution (Dawkins 1976). Two US scientists, biologist Edward O. Wilson and bio-mathematician Charles J. Lumsden, coined the term "Culturgen," a similar concept. (Lumsden 1981)

Note however, that genes that are subject to natural selection are those that materially improve the chances of organisms surviving and reproducing. It is quite unusual for genes that harm an organism to be "selected" and is a defect in the operation of evolution discovered by geneticists. In the case of memes or any other supposed "replicators," we are asked to believe that the human brain, the most complex machine in the known universe, that has evolved over millions of years specifically to make adaptive decisions, can somehow be misled by "units of culture" that are entirely passive.

In fact, since memes are merely ideas, and therefore passive, their evolution is only possible through human selection. We could examine the development of varieties of cereal crop by farmers, as an example of "human selection." Would it really help us to call the varieties of corn plant "replicators" and argue that they are competing to influence the farmer's brain to select them?

Or, we could say that there are memes for "consuming alcohol." One meme might be the idea that fine wines have subtle characteristics that confer a feeling of wellbeing and enhance social status, while protecting the consumer against heart attacks. Another meme may describe alcohol as a toxin that destroys human organs, especially the brain, and results in addiction and bad behavior. The intense competition between these viewpoints is a conflict between the people and the vested interests that support opposing views. If memes are "cultural ideas", they are absolutely passive and appear to shed little light on the conflict between humans.

Habits, Customs and Routines

In 2010, Geoffrey Hodgson and Thorbjorn Knudsen presented the idea that "habits, customs, and routines" are the elements of culture that are copied in such a way as to provide the continuity in evolution. (Hodgson 2010) The problem with this idea is that any theory of social evolution is about rapid change, and therefore it must be based on constant innovations. Habits, customs, and routines are generally based on ideas that are old enough to be well-proven. Human habits may last a lifetime, and customs include religious rituals that are thousands of years old. Even corporate routines (e.g. business processes) are based on reliable "best practices." In my view, habits, customs, and routines are forms of standardized behavior that increase human productivity and may serve other functions, but they are unrelated to social evolution.

It appears that the whole attempt to base cultural evolution on the same paradigm as Darwinian biotic evolution is mistaken. While it is true that humans constantly copy each other's beliefs, behaviors, and artifacts, it is also true that this copying minimizes variation. Only innovation maximizes variation and is therefore the foundation for evolution of the habitat.

The innovations that constitute the incremental steps in evolution of civilization arise only very rarely by accident from the process of human emulation; instead, they mostly arise through intelligent intention and are sourced from *anywhere in the universe of knowledge known to humans*.

For example, if ten trainee cooks attend a cooking class and make blueberry pies, the ten pies will incorporate many variations from the instructor's pie. Occasionally, one pie may incorporate some significant improvement over the model that was copied and it is conceivable that this could become part of the evolution of blueberry pies.

The reason why this does not explain cultural evolution is simply that the copying process contributed nothing to the innovation. An individual cook who makes a blueberry pie each week *without* any copying is perhaps more likely to generate a serendipitous innovation in the methodology or recipe. For example, an innovation could arise if the cook could not obtain enough blueberries and had to add another fruit to the mix; or if there was not enough butter, so that vegetable oil had to be used instead; or if the oven broke down and the pie had to be baked over a barbeque.

Consider the jet turbine engine, which now powers most airliners. Until World War II, aircraft were powered by piston engines. Obviously, the jet engine did not arise from a series of accidental modifications in copying piston engines. The jet engine is an alternative solution to an existing human need – the need for motive power for aircraft and air transport is a modern solution to a basic human lifecycle need for movement in pursuit of adaptive fit with the habitat. It was the genetically-based, *biological need* of humans to move that remained constant between the piston engine and the jet engine and the multiple inventors involved were addressing the biological need directly, not copying existing solutions.

Similarly, we can observe that the electric lamp is not a mutated copy of a candle, but an alternative source of light. Likewise, the use of coins as currency did not arise through making a poor copy of commodities such as salt or cattle that had previously been used for the same purpose.

We can conclude that the human brain has a capacity to identify the common adaptive needs that arise throughout the human lifecycle and to periodically create completely new solutions to meet them.

Evolution of the Habitat is not Darwinian

Evolution by definition comprises change which occurs in innovative steps that enhance fitness within a particular environment. Copying is the precise opposite of innovation. Humans copy in order to *reduce error and variety* in work processes, and to increase their productivity by adopting proven behaviors or designs instead of creating new ones. However, without variety, there can be no selection, and hence no evolution. Therefore copying certainly plays no part in cultural evolution.

There is a strong tendency in the English-language sector of biological science to regard all evolutionary processes as "Darwinian." However, the habitat evolution differs very substantially from biotic evolution. First, Darwin himself emphasized that natural selection was central to the evolution of species and was different in principle from the human selection used in creating new varieties of farm animals, crops, or racehorses.

Second, biotic evolution is based on genes as "replicators" that transmit information between generations of organism. As we have seen, habitat evolution does not require a replicator, because transmission of information is executed by humans and the records that they keep. Thirdly, the innovatory steps in biotic evolution arise randomly, mainly from mutations accompanying the copying of genes. In great contrast, the innovative steps in habitat evolution are created by the human brain, with its ability to predict the probable future, and to use analogy to simplify the trial and error process necessary to innovate. Richard Dawkins' "Blind Watchmaker" is replaced by a human watchmaker who has both eyesight and foresight, even though these senses are challenged by the great uncertainty associated with daring to innovate in a complex universe.

Evolution of Civilization is an Emergent Process

In studying the evolution of the artificial, technology-based human habitat that we call civilization, I have emphasized the importance of uncertainty. The uncertainty of the future means that each new habitat component (idea, behavior, or artifact) that is created by an intelligent person is likely to compete with other variants and will be subject to selection by the public for best "fit" with its purpose.

In managing their private lives, individuals create multiple potential solutions and then choose the best solution by what Darwin called "human selection." In biotic evolution, Darwin coined the term "natural selection" to describe the competition for fitness and reproduction. In the public domain we see many creative solutions for every human need, including commercial products, subjected to a third form of selection, which I call "social selection."

Darwin himself differentiated "natural selection" from "human selection." It is clear that habitat evolution (Or, "sociocultural evolution") employs "social selection" which is a non-Darwinian process. Nevertheless, in all evolutionary processes, the reason for variation and selection is to cope with the uncertainty of achieving "fit."

Habitat evolution and biotic evolution can both be described as "emergent" systems, because they enable "order" to emerge from the autonomous actions of many component parts. Emergence has not been fully explained by science yet, but at least two mechanisms seem prominent. The first is variation and selection, and the second is "self-organization" (or "spontaneous order"), the phenomenon that creates unique snowflakes, perfectly orderly and sustainable natural ecosystems, markets, and language.

Non-human Artificial Habitats in Nature

Many examples of emergence exist in nature. Most animals live in natural environments, but several species have created artificial habitats that invite comparison with humans. Beavers are large rodents that can cut down trees up to ten inches in diameter with their teeth, dam streams to create a pond, and build a lodge wherein they can store food and spend much of the winter. These animals even build canals to transport timber. Yet beavers have very limited intelligence and no apparent conscious ability to plan their ambitious construction projects.

Even more impressive are the habitats made by social insects like bees, wasps, and ants. A termite mound may be up to nine meters high, and house a queen, a king, and many offspring. The mound may be aligned with the sun, and have air ventilation shafts for thermal regulation. Some termites build and operate a fungi garden as a food source.

How do termites manage to collaborate in building their large, complex mounds without conscious intelligence, hierarchy, or centralized decision-making? A key activity is that each termite leaves a trail of chemicals called pheromones, which provides information to other termites. As termites move around their habitat, they can assess the proportion of their fellows doing specific tasks, such as fetching food, or building the mound, and use this information to switch to the task most needed.

This collaboration invites the perspective that termites are like neurons in a human brain – individually unintelligent but, thanks to natural selection, together able to make adaptive choices that contribute to their fitness. In his influential work, "The Extended Phenotype" Richard Dawkins explains how the genes of some species have evolved to control things outside their bodies, including beavers' dams, termite mounds, and spiders' webs.

Dawkins explains that the termite mound and the beaver dam are created under the control of DNA, like the embryos of animals' bodies. "Presumably an individual termite working on a little corner of a big mound is in a similar position to a cell in a developing embryo, or a single soldier tirelessly obeying orders whose purpose in the larger scheme of things he does not understand," writes Dawkins. "Nowhere in the single termite's nervous system is there anything remotely equivalent to a complete image of what the finished mound will look like."

If there is no plan, the termite mound "emerges" from the work of many termites which are individually carrying out simple tasks in response to simple environmental cues, especially pheromone signals. Dawkins explains:

"Each worker is equipped with a small toolkit of behavioral rules, and he/she is probably stimulated to choose an item of behavior by local stimuli emanating from the work already accomplished, no matter whether he/she or other workers accomplished it – stimuli emanating from the present state of the nest in the worker's immediate vicinity. For my purpose, it doesn't matter exactly what the behavioral rules are, but they would be something like: "If you come upon a heap of mud with a certain pheromone on it, put another dollop of mud on the top." The important point about such rules is that they have a purely local effect. The grand design of the whole mound emerges only as the summed consequences of thousands of (termites) obeying micro-rules."

Although the termite mound is produced by the distributed decisions of thousands of almost mindless insects, it is a precision-engineered habitat that results from millions of years of evolutionary natural selection. "It is entirely plausible, indeed almost inevitable, that both the shape and size of compass termite mounds have evolved by natural selection, just like any feature of bodily morphology," writes Dawkins.

"This can only have come about through the selection of mutations acting at the local level on the building behavior of individual worker termites."(Dawkins 1982)

The Lesson for Humans

There is no doubt that many aspects of civilization (such as language and markets, for example), are influenced by instinctual feedback from millions of people and exhibit the same kind of emergent stability and adaptation as is achieved by the social insects. Darwinian natural selection of humans in the past has, of course, played a part.

But the evolution of the human habitat cannot be understood without recognizing the central role of human intelligence. The termite mind is an example of Dawkins' "extended phenotype", but civilization is not.

Consider just one variable of an artificial habitat – the size of dwellings. Supposing that beaver colonies in a particular region can benefit from having a larger pond to protects them from predators and provide easy access to food and timber. Those beavers that create larger ponds will be favored by natural selection and tend to have more offspring, so that the genes that predispose them to cut down larger trees, or dam strong water flows, will be spread through the beaver population.

Now consider a parallel change: the height of a human dwelling. In Hong Kong, where I live, people built two-story houses in the 19th century. A hundred years later, the average residential building had 40 stories. Was that due to natural selection of those architects that were genetically predisposed to design higher buildings? Of course not – it was due to land prices and civil engineering principles that are not encoded in DNA.

A human architect may follow his genetic disposition to obtain remuneration and social rank by working for a client – but in performing the work, the architect must ignore predispositions and implement the rules of technology that determine the fulfillment of social need in an industrial society. Human fitness depends so greatly upon collaboration that people constantly suppress their genetically based short-term emotional dispositions in order to build and use a vast culture of learned information, behavior, and artifacts.

Prior to technology, natural selection planted within the human brain's reward centers the predispositions for behaviors that would promote their fitness in the natural habitat. For the present time, technology has rendered the habitat maladaptive, and that forces humans to ignore their Darwinian predispositions and utilize pure intelligence to obtain their desired biological rewards.

Only when humans can collaborate to restore the adaptive nature of their habitat will it be possible for the human species to regain its full humanity and live in harmony with nature and its own environment.

The evolution of the human habitat is different from biotic evolution, in that it uses quite different processes to achieve both variation and selection, and has no equivalent to the gene as a "replicator" to provide continuity between generations. However, as I show in Fig. 5., part of human behavior is Darwinian, and that includes the individual's constant monitoring and appraisal of the adaptiveness of the habitat. Social selection then utilizes the feedback of millions of people to guide society as a whole, maintaining adaptive and stable habitat conditions, just as natural selection does for termites. Therefore the *tendency* of evolution of civilization is to create adaptive conditions for humans by aggregating the input from human intelligence, with its instinctively adaptive behavioral output.

Why is Civilization no longer Completely Adaptive?

If scientists are correct in describing the adaptive nature of complex animal habitats as an emergent property that depends upon the unconsciously adaptive behavior of thousands of individual organisms, this raises a crucial issue for human societies.

It would appear that human collaboration will be most effective in creating adaptive social conditions when individuals act autonomously, rather than being centrally directed by a parasitic state. The adaptation between humans and their artificial habitat is failing, as we saw in Chapter 1. The civilized habitat is evolving, but currently, it is not being completely adapted to our biological needs.

At present, human governments attempt to deal with the many failures of human adaptation on a case-by-case basis. This action appears rational, but it is hopelessly inadequate, because the fundamental mechanism of evolution of civilization is failing. Science has already established that the evolution of complex systems such as civilization can be predicted only locally, for a short timeframe, and with uncertainty. Therefore, intervention in the course of social evolution is mostly counter-productive.

In the next chapter, we will see how the intervention of the parasitic state is likely to affect the evolution of the habitat.

Chapter 4

Parasitic Government Disrupts Habitat Evolution

*I*n earlier chapters, we discussed the partial failure of human adaptive fit with the habitat and pointed out that the immediate cause was the harmful side-effects of technology. However, humans have learned to live with technology, and remedy its harmful side-effects, over nearly two million years. We might have expected that social evolution would have coped with the challenges of changing technology and maintained adaptive habitat conditions for our species.

Why then is evolution of civilization faltering? I propose that the evolution of human society, and of its technology-based habitat, depends upon the normality of social organization. During the evolutionary period, as the human brain grew larger and more powerful, natural selection operated not only on human intelligence, but upon the autonomy and morality of the individual, and the consensual nature of human organization within the family and the band because these factors supported the expression of human intelligence.

We have noted that a catastrophic alteration in human social organization took place at the start of the agricultural age, when armed warriors took over the control of societies that had previously been governed by their own adult members for millions of years. Since then, humans have repeatedly attempted to shake off the burden of coercive, amoral government that follows military conquest, but without success.

In recent centuries, many new ideologies and political systems have been invented, in vain attempts to free humans from the burden of military conflict and the unnaturally large disparities in resources. Socialism, fascism, communism, religious fundamentalism, personality cult, democracy – all such systems have failed, because they are really variants of the original warrior-led despotism. The only system that has

ever worked well for humans has been the individual autonomy and equitable, consensual, power-sharing of communities that evolved in nature.

Only a huge effort of education and global collaboration can enable
humans to retrieve their biologically natural social organization and
thereby support the evolution of fully adaptive conditions in the artificial
habitat of civilization.

In this chapter, we examine some of the specific ways in which
coercive, parasitic government disrupts the process of habitat evolution.

First, let us take a brief look at the social insects, because we know
that their complex habitats, such as beehives, anthills and termite
mounds provide each species with the adaptive conditions that they require, which implies that the habitat and the species evolve together,
without any central governance. What would happen to termites, for example, if they were suddenly subjected to the intervention of a parasitic
form of centralized control, as happened to humans when agriculture
was developed?

Termites use mud to build air-conditioned "cities" that are oriented
towards the sunlight and contain a variety of chambers and facilities to
support the termite lifecycle from birth to death. It took millions of years
for evolution to shape the behavior of termites and their invisible communication system based on chemicals called pheromones. The termites
are highly adapted to their natural habitat, but any substantial change in
that habitat would destroy them.

Now suppose that a termite colony is suddenly controlled by an
intelligent, parasitic, force – perhaps some well-meaning scientists – that
claims to be benevolent. Supposing that the scientists believe that they
can make the termites more "efficient" by rearranging their behavior and
spraying pheromones on the termite trails to ensure compliance.

We can be sure of the outcome: the termite colony would fail to
thrive, even if the termites exhibited natural adaptive behavioral responses to attempt to remedy the situation. If the coercive "government"
maintained its intervention, the astonishing collaboration between thousands of termites would be disrupted and all the termites would quickly
die.

Modern human civilization is in the same situation as those termites: it is under constant attack from a self-interested, ignorant, but all-
powerful parasite called coercive "government." Almost all the human
misery on Earth is a consequence of intervention from the coercive state.

The corollary is also true: we sometimes observe groups of people with extraordinary low crime rates, a strong work ethic, and a healthy lifestyle that includes avoidance of narcotics or alcohol consumption. Such groups are always based around the strong family and community organization inherited from the Paleolithic period, which align the self-interest of diverse individuals into "collaboration," enabling the group to thrive. Paradoxically, religion often equips such groups to maintain their separation from the corrosive effects of the amoral state culture.

Humans are strongly guided by morality, which is a genetically-based, peer-to-peer control system for behavioral management. In the evolutionary habitat, our genetically based morality could control behavior very well. Technology has altered our habitat beyond recognition, and our genetic morality only operates properly through the agency of *culture*, which sustains adaptive behavior by prioritizing it over the utilization of technology. Culture is evolving rapidly as part of the human habitat, as I explained in Chapter 3.

But the coercive, parasitic state distorts human culture to serve its own selfish interests, and this reduces the human ability to act morally, or in an adaptive way with respect to new technologies. In this chapter, I will discuss the evolution of the habitat, including culture, and show the ways in which this evolution is disrupted by the state.

The Three Components of Habitat Evolution

In Chapter 3, I described the evolution of the human habitat that comprises knowledge, learned behaviors and artifacts. Like all evolution it comprises three processes:

Transmission. Transmission comprises the similarity between generations of habitat components that address the same biological functions for humans. Habitat components, such as food, musical compositions, and current courting practices may evolve to an extreme degree, yet we can still identify them as serving the same biological human needs.

Variation. Variation exists in the habitat components (ideas, behaviors, and artifacts) that are created to fulfill the same function. Millions of unique human brains create great variety and also demand great variety in the cultural components that they utilize.

Selection. In evolution of the habitat, selection comprises both individual and social selection of preferred habitat components. When individuals select an educational course, learn a new dance, or buy a piano, they hope to achieve the best adaptive solution for their purpose.

Note that the transmission, variation and selection that constitute cultural evolution are all generated by the intelligent volition of humans. The human judgments that drive social evolution are influenced not only by their adaptive preferences shaped by biotic evolution, but also by "scientific" knowledge based on causality operating in the environment, which is not encoded in DNA. So humans can potentially make adaptive decisions even in scientific and technical fields.

The technology-based "habitat," created by modern humans is subject to "emergent order," and should, in normal conditions, provide a fully adaptive habitat for humans. However, the future of cultural evolution is absolutely unknowable, and beyond the control of human individuals or groups; this is the fundamental reason why the imposition of the coercive, parasitical state is such a catastrophe for humans.

The rest of this chapter is devoted to examples of coercive intervention by the parasitic state and the effect of such intervention in blocking or reversing the effects of evolution of civilization and preventing the human species from thriving.

State Coercion and Hierarchy Negate Morality

In modern societies, the state replaces free market operations with a hierarchy based on privileges such as corporate law, limited liability, intellectual property monopolies, monopolies for professions, and rescue packages for banks and other companies deemed "too large to fail."

Democracy is built on the assumption of self-interest by social groups (pensioners, parents, the handicapped, industrialists, etc.) who lobby the government in order to maximize their share of resources confiscated by the tax authorities. The poor will always lose in such an amoral and unnatural system.

This parasitic morality contrasts with natural human bands that were highly integrated by consensus decision-making. All members of a band are so integrated that they take into account all members of the community in voicing their opinions.

State Coercion Makes the General Population Passive

State decision-making is based on the supremacy of groups that can muster the largest number of votes, a process that is hardly more likely than warfare to serve justice. When the state makes all key decisions about economic or social life on behalf of the whole population, the adult members of the population, who would normally be very active and highly involved in decisions about their lives, withdraw from their responsibilities and become much more passive towards the major decisions of their society.

The state declares war, taxes citizens, makes laws limiting human rights, and executes all the daily governance that should be carried out by the adult members of communities. The effect is to render the general adult population mentally impotent and relatively passive.

The public, realizing that it is powerless, simply resigns itself to being impotent, and ceases to think about the governmental subjects that are beyond its control. Humans become more like livestock, controlled by the state "farmer."

This passivity reduces the effectiveness of the three aspects of cultural evolution: continuity, variation and social selection. Passivity reduces the ability of the general population to create new habitat components. It also reduces the discrimination of the public, inhibiting its ability to practice social selection of new habitat components. Lastly, it reduces the general public's comprehension of society's biological needs, thus obstructing the continuity of the habitat that is necessary for its evolution.

Today, states have largely pre-empted local autonomy and adults can no longer select the policies that maintain the health of their community. As a consequence, adults also cease to demand the educational or entertainment content of the media that should support responsible decision making. Instead of intelligent investigation, the media focuses on trivia, and also becomes subservient to state power. Many observers consider that extreme violence featured in modern movies, television programs, and through the Internet, are degenerate and harmful, but since the general public is no longer in charge of society, its attitude to the morality that is taught to each new generation becomes passive. When we consider the degenerate nature of much modern entertainment, we can see that the emphasis on extreme violence serves the state, which has an interest in maintaining warfare as a policy tool.

State Schools Teach Obedience, not Creativity

Social evolution depends absolutely on variation and selection, and humans who create habitat components (new ideas, behaviors and artifacts) will always generate variety because of the genetic and cultural variation between creative individuals. In contrast, the state seeks to maximize its central control of society and this is facilitated by uniformity. All state-sponsored systems generate uniformity and reduce variety.

The global model for enforced schooling is one in which teachers have military-style authority over their pupils and are supposed to transmit knowledge to them by instruction. The model used for education is that of "filling containers." But in the 20th century, the scientific investigation of the learning process has shown that the direct transmission of new knowledge is simply not possible.

In his book, *Without Miracles*, Gary Cziko stresses at length that learning is a purposeful process driven by the student's mind. Individuals build on their existing knowledge by a process of "blind selection and selective retention" – the same trial-and-error process that enables evolution to achieve an adaptive fit between organisms and their environment. "...the twentieth century has seen the emergence of educational theories that have rejected the instructionist view of education," writes Cziko. "This has come about as more and more psychologists and educators dismiss the conception of students as passive buckets into which knowledge is poured by teachers and textbooks, and replace it with a view of students as active creators of their own knowledge."

Cziko refers to "...twentieth century theories that emphasize knowledge growth and reject the idea of education as the transmission of knowledge from teacher and textbook to student." As an example of more successful teaching, Cziko offers Montessori schools, which provide young children with a much higher degree of autonomy and responsibility, enabling them to learn by the trial-and-error execution of self-directed activities. (Cziko 1995)

In the evolutionary era, "education" involved constantly interacting with parents and adults who were themselves responsible for governing their own society by consensus. As adults surveyed the threats and opportunities that surrounded their tiny society, and considered how best to exploit the opportunities and avoid the threats, children actively helped their elders, and quickly came to understand the responsibility of adults in a fully integrated society guided by inherited morality.

In contrast, in post-industrial societies, the state forces children into compulsory schooling by threatening their parents with imprisonment. Public schooling is a mass system committed to serving, not the child, but the industrialists, government, and organized education trades, such as teachers, and textbook publishers. Compulsory mass education is deeply unnatural, and emphasizes obedience rather than self-actualization.

A major component of modern education is the electronic media, including television and the Internet. These media are powerful and could be used to help children become strong individuals, pursuing self-actualization by serving the community through free markets. In contrast, children are now the primary victims of violence in the media. I am not suggesting that the media should not depict violence or that it should be censored. I am merely pointing out that, in a healthy society in which parents were responsible for their own communities, the media would be much more likely to depict less conflict and violence, and depict it in a meaningful way, so that the media would act as an educational tool to improve the decision-making of society.

In a free society, there would be no coercive state to control the media. Adults in confederated self-governing communities would use their members' effective control of purchasing power to force vendors to comply with their customers' needs, as expressed by online voting of all community members.

State Coercion blocks Morality and Adaptive Judgment

The successful government of any human community depends upon the adoption of the natural system of morality that evolved in prehistoric bands. Morality is a peer-to-peer system for mutual regulation of behavior that evolved as part of human culture. Nearly all natural human behavior, especially in egalitarian hunter gatherer bands, is reciprocal in form. As individuals interact with one another, they also appraise one another for equitable reciprocation. They then provide feedback in the form of praise or criticism and, if necessary, reward or punishment.

Peer-to-peer morality is a powerful means of controlling behavior and minimizing delinquency. This morality automatically aligns the self-interest of ambitious individuals with the biological needs of the community. Family based culture in every human community is based on some version of this evolved morality.

In contrast, the state is generally amoral. Political relations are based on *realpolitik*, that is, the self-interest of each state, not on moral values. For example, in the democratic political system, individuals and groups are expected to pursue their selfish interests, to maximize their share of the resources taken from the community by state force as tax.

This greatly reduces the ability of the individual to judge social issues from the community's point of view – to speak and act with justice or honor.

When the state imposes amoral behavior on the population, and attempts to control delinquency by harsh sanctions, it also damages the "human selection" that is an essential element of cultural evolution. Just as "natural selection" is damaged by state coercion, and successful populations can no longer reproduce themselves, as I noted in Chapter 1, human selection is similarly damaged, and the artificial human habitat becomes maladaptive.

Democracy Replaces Responsibility with Greed

Much of the world's population considers that "democracy" represents the only obtainable standard of human freedom. In reality, democracy is a confidence trick that allows people to choose their sovereign master from two or three alternatives, a choice that prevents them either controlling their own lives or participating in the management of their own communities as adult humans evolved to do.

The members of a Stone Age band would have been habituated to viewing as a group the problems facing their community. Each individual, tightly integrated with other family members, would have been aware of the needs of infants, nursing mothers, children, active adults, and the older generation. Although these pre-industrial people were no less selfish than modern humans, their face-to-face relationships with other members of the community, and their deep knowledge of the problems arising both inside the community and from the natural world outside, would have lent wisdom to their viewpoints. In such a society, few people would, or could, choose to be irresponsible or excessively selfish, because such behavior would be interpreted as childish or delinquent and punished by loss of reputation and therefore loss of genetic "fitness." As a result, decisions made by consensus would have "fitted" the community better than any other solutions imaginable.

In contrast, a democratic government would have divided the community and appealed to the individual interests of each section, destroying the integration that is the main advantage of a small face-to-face community. We know from modern experience that democratic governments take by force about half the wealth earned by citizens, and then redistribute it to many groups, according to the power each has to lobby the state. Morality and social integration are completely bypassed by this process. In a democracy, it is regarded as legitimate for individuals to manipulate one another to maximize their share of the yield of state confiscation of wealth.

What would hunter-gatherers do if they were confronted with the threat of political democracy? They would first try to evict the coercive political group, and if that was not possible, they might try to kill the politicians. If all else failed, they would simply leave the group and join another, or set up a new community.

From a biological point of view, a healthy human society *must* be governed by a consensus of its adult members in order to pursue its purpose, which is to optimize the opportunity of all community members to pursue their fitness. Any initiation of force against any of the group members to alter the natural purpose of a human society is a pathology that should be eliminated.

Modern societies have millions of members but there is no reason why people should have any less autonomy than they had in pre-agricultural societies, and no reason why social decision-making should not be based on autonomous local communities in which members know each other on a face-to-face basis.

Reducing Social Variety Blocks Evolution

Evolution of civilization requires a large number of people in a mass society to select the most adaptive knowledge, behaviors, and artifacts. The selection of the most adaptive habitat components is made from a wide variety because, in a natural society, humans are free to create many alternative forms of knowledge, behavior, and artifacts.

But the coercive state tends to support uniformity, because that makes it easier to control the population and increases the short-term efficiency of military and economic operations. Uniformity is an obvious characteristic of disciplined services such as the military and police forces. But, more generally, all centralized decisions result in standardization and uniformity.

Standardization can certainly be a productive advantage in economic operations, but enforced standardization is entirely different from voluntary standardization. History is replete with examples of centralized state policies that have proven disastrous in the light of experience, thanks to their unintended consequences.

Variation and selection are necessary to achieve optimum values when different social pressures are balanced against one another. In the long term, enforced uniformity leads to social degeneration, as we have seen in all recent human societies, especially those described as "totalitarian." A reduction in social variation will generate a reduction in fitness.

Evolution of the habitat depends on variation and selection of knowledge, behaviors, and artifacts. Individuals always create variation, but natural heterogeneity is inhibited by the activities of the state in imposing coercive regulation on almost all aspects of life. The governments of industrialized countries make thousands of laws: so many that they are beyond the full comprehension even of lawyers. Each law takes away a little more freedom, decreasing the adaptive choices that enable evolution of civilization.

All over the world, states plan to bring pressure to bear on their citizens, to force them towards conformity. The pressures include incentives to adopt the dominant language and suppression of minority languages, supported by standard textbooks and curricula that offer only one version of history – the version that reinforces the state's current ideology. The irony is that, although all children within a state study the same version of history, every state has its own version, so an unadulterated version of human history simply does not exist. As children in each state are indoctrinated with different versions of the "truth," the ground is laid for the conflicts that give rise to warfare.

State Regulation Blocks Habitat Evolution

Overall, the effect of the state on cultural evolution is similar to that of pouring glue into a mechanical watch – it gums up the works. A watch can only keep good time if its components can move freely. Similarly, a human society can only be healthy and normal when all its members can express their genetically-based preferences freely.

Although I present the reduction of variety as an obstacle to social evolution based on variation and selection, it is interesting that the destructive effect of uniformity created by the state was noticed long ago. French historian Alexis de Tocqueville wrote about the wonders of US democracy and described the crippling effect of monarchy in 1840, at a time when all national governments were small and limited compared to their modern equivalents:

"The sovereign, after taking individuals one by one in his powerful hands and kneading them to his liking, reaches out to embrace society as a whole. Over society, he spreads a fine mesh of uniform, minute, and

complex rules, through which not even the most original minds and most vigorous souls can poke their heads above the crowd. He does not break men's wills but softens, bends, and guides them. He seldom forces anyone to act but consistently opposes action. He does not destroy things but prevents them from coming into being. Rather than tyrannize, he inhibits, represses, saps, stifles, and stultifies, and in the end he reduces each nation to nothing but a flock of timid and industrious animals, with the government as its shepherd."

Taxation is Theft to Maintain State Power

General taxation, in which the ruling elite decide how to spend money taken by force is clearly theft. Strictly speaking, the only legitimate part of state spending is for the maintenance of the basic laws against theft, fraud, and any kind of assault.

A significant element of taxation is expended on armaments and preparation for warfare. The existence of the state makes such defense expenditure unavoidable, because sovereign states always exist in mutual insecurity. We can expect that the human species will eventually come to a consensus to make warfare impossible by removing the special privileges of political leaders and holding them accountable for any harm they do.

All economic activities should be operated by autonomous organizations, mostly on a for-profit basis, to ensure their efficient use of social resources. However, some major services, such as roads, railways and post offices, will always be of great concern to the confederated but autonomous communities that negotiate on behalf of the general population. When Internet technology enables consumers to combine their resources instantly for any purpose, then major industries will be forced to operate their services in close compliance to customer needs. Thus the public will have the best of both worlds – the efficiency of for-profit operation, ownership by either private bodies or confederations of autonomous communities, and a high degree of control by customers represented by confederated communities.

The most corrupt practice is the sustaining of large corporations and banks that are "too large to fail." In a just and efficient society, there can be no case for using state force to extract money from taxpayers to compensate corporations for their failure in the market.

Welfare for the poor seems like a worthy cause. But governments are the primary force that creates poverty. For example, in the USA, it has been observed that that poverty was disappearing in the 1950s but, as part of President Johnson's "Great Society" initiative, socialist welfare policies expanded and the wealth differentials between rich and poor rapidly increased. Only a free market built on a free society delivers small wealth differentials.

Welfare in a free society will be carried out locally. Confederated, but autonomous communities will compete with one another, and will have a powerful incentive to manage their districts well, and that will include providing welfare services that will, where possible, assist people to become productive members of society.

States Prioritize Technology over the Quality of Life

Modern employment, in which millions of individuals commute to centralized places of work, is a product of the Industrial Revolution. In agricultural societies prior to the Industrial Revolution, people worked long hours, but they were mostly autonomous and could arrange the pattern of their lives according to the seasons and the needs of the crops or animals being cultivated.

Urban society is heavily engineered and the majority of people are subject to excessive control by technology based systems. For example, the system of product distribution through supermarkets involves not only the precisely engineered flow of products, the "supply chain," from worldwide manufacturers to the display shelves, but also the flow of customers through each retail outlet and the processes for car parking, circulation through the aisles between product displays, collection of price and product information, collection of selected products in baskets or trolleys, checkout queuing, payment, and home delivery.

It is easy to see that, as more and more social systems are engineered to control human behavior, humans are likely to be stressed because their intelligent, lively minds can no longer act spontaneously by using creation, variation, and selection to generate individually novel behavioral patterns.

However, it is equally important to realize that properly used technology is adaptive. Humans need to create systems to make their lifecycle efficient, including things such as eating and working. The problem is not that technology itself imposes a rigid system on human behavior but that state legislation has created an industrial hierarchy in which vast corporations impose standard systems that spread across states and even across the world. A free market economy would incorporate much more diversity, as nature itself does, and such a system would be self-regulating (by evolution of civilization and evolved human morals), so that humans lived within their comfort zone, combining sufficient efficiency with sufficient autonomy.

In a free society, in which the members of local communities set their priorities for the quality of life and way in which they would utilize their joint resources to build prosperity while protecting people, the "abuse by technology" that is commonplace today could not occur.

From a biological point of view, the state is a catastrophe for humans. Although some governments may be small compared with the societies that they control, their capacity to introduce centralized decision-making works against the human norm, which is decentralized, consensual decision-making. Consensus is at the core of social evolution and of the emergence of an adaptive society. Therefore, the abolition of the coercive state should be the highest priority of the human species.

Chapter 5

The Birth of Parasitic Government

*T*he seven billion people living today accept it as normal that the human species has been divided by military conquest into states, in each of which small elite groups have almost absolute sovereign power to regulate the lives of the majority. Yet this social arrangement is not only absolutely unnatural and extremely damaging, but it has existed for less than one half of one percent of the 1.7 million years during which our human ancestors have lived on earth. The coercive state is an unnatural, parasitic form of social organization that resulted from the unintended consequences of technology. We can expect it to disappear before the middle of the 21st century.

The general public worldwide, apart from small groups of libertarian intellectuals and a few radical philosophers, believes that the state is legitimate. A common, modern viewpoint is that the disparity between the original, non-coercive social organization of humans, and the coercive, hierarchical structure of modern mass societies, was an inevitable consequence of the complexity of mass society.

Many scientists in the biological disciplines are aware that humans are not well-adapted to modern civilization, and see behaviors such as warfare and ecological damage as being serious problems. What they have not generally recognized is that the coercive, parasitical government of the sovereign state is the most serious maladaptation of all, and that the state is a "harmful side-effect of technology" that can be remedied, just as lesser environmental problems are remedied, by purposeful human action. The normal social organization that evolved with human societies is an innate part of human biology that must be retrieved in order to recover adaptive conditions and human well-being.

In order for modern humans to begin the great task of retrieving their normal social organization, it is necessary to understand the history of our species and the origins of the state. Most important, it is necessary to understand how moral, civilized behavior evolved along with the human brain, and how it has been partly lost due to the harmful side-effects of technology.

Clarification of these issues is an essential basis of the platform for remedial measures. Below, I briefly describe the origins of the coercive, parasitical state.

Naturally Evolved Human Society

The earliest primate generally regarded as human was Homo erectus, who lived about 1.7 million years ago, had a brain twice as large as a chimpanzee, used stone tools, and walked on two legs. From that time until 10,000 years ago, humans lived in groups of several extended families, totaling about 50 people, by hunting, gathering, and periodically moving on in pursuit of new food resources.

Hunter-gatherers slowly improved their hunting prowess, obtained much more protein from meat, and learned to cook their food. As a result, natural selection shortened the human digestive tract, and re-shaped the body to make people more athletic and better able to hunt.

Several physical changes reflect a lowering of aggression between humans that can be associated with the change from the chimpanzee's dominance hierarchy to the egalitarian relations typical of humans in small natural communities. These include a reduction in body size, hair loss on the body, disappearance of the erectile hair used in threat displays, and smaller teeth, especially canines. Smaller teeth are mainly associated with the change of diet from plant food, which requires a lot of grinding action, to meat obtained from hunting, but it also signaled that humans no longer used teeth for fighting, as they had acquired weapons.

Evolutionary anthropologist Christopher Boehm believes that the improvement of weapons such as spears, by about 500,000 years ago may have equalized the fighting power of males and made it easier for the group to sanction violent individuals. "My hypothesis is that weapons appeared early enough to have affected dentition, body size, hair loss on the body, and display loss, and that they helped to ready humans for egalitarian society by making fights less predictable and by enabling groups collectively to intimidate or eliminate even a dominating serial killer."

Boehm proposes that the wooden hafted spear could cause this change. "Weapons were in a position to transform political behavior by 500,000 years ago, a figure that provides fully 20,000 generations for weapons to affect the genetic selection of body size and build, display behavior, canine size, distribution of hair on the body, and possibly bipedal efficiency." (Boehm 2001)

Most important of all, as the size and power of the human brain expanded, social behavior evolved from something like the dominance hierarchy of the chimpanzee, to a form of habitual collaboration that is the basis of all the behavior that we call "civilized."

Such bands initially lived in relatively isolated territories, surrounded by natural plant and animal food sources. Early hunter-gatherers, armed with primitive stone tools, lived among the bounty of nature in widely-spaced groups. Their only conceivable conflicts would have been personal disputes, such as competition for sexual mates. Therefore warfare between groups was almost impossible because it could have had no biological function.

Anthropologists have created a surprisingly detailed account of how stone age hunter-gatherers lived, mainly from the analysis of the lifestyles of pre-agricultural humans that survived into modern times. The conclusion is that they were egalitarian in structure, and men and women were approximately equal in authority. All the members of a group assembled in council to make decisions by consensus. The leaders of bands were individuals that had exceptional knowledge and wisdom, but they were prevented from acquiring coercive power over other members. Neither was leadership hereditary, because the band members selected their leaders.

Individuals were also prevented from achieving excessive personal status, perhaps because this could have led to coercive control of the group. Bands had no stratification into social classes. The territory occupied by a band was a shared resource until the invention of farming, 10,000 years ago.

The band was the political, economic, and social organization that humans and their ancestors adapted to over millions of years of evolutionary history. It follows that humans are genetically adapted to band society, and this kind of small, face-to-face society is the natural building block of any human society. The high degree of social integration that evolved between the members of a hunter-gatherer band could be expected to trigger appropriate behavior in each gender and age group that together support the normal human lifecycle. The corollary of this is that the absence of such social integration will fail to support the normal human lifecycle, as we know to our cost in the 21st century.

All modern societies are centrally controlled and the coercive rulers of each state seek to bolster the cultural unity of the mass population as a means of securing their obedience. Religion is one tool for this purpose, including the traditional romantic "creation myths" that claim that the first humans were created locally by a supernatural being with whom the people have a special relationship. Such beliefs can be used to justify an arbitrary moral code which then generates peer pressure to marginalize social dissidents and standardize mass beliefs. Also, the state tends to promote the racial or cultural superiority of the society, and emphasize that its policies support this superiority. In most cultures, other societies are denigrated and regarded as barbaric and unhealthy. This use of culture by the state facilitates the central control of society.

Natural Selection Drove Egalitarianism

Some people may therefore be surprised that humans attained equal rights and enjoyed autonomy long ago, during the latter part of the evolutionary period. But the prehistoric organization of society to optimize collaboration and harmony was simply the result of natural selection acting on human behavior and discriminating in favor of survival. The first "modern" humans from about 50,000 years ago all possessed razor-sharp weapons with which they could kill the largest animals. They dealt with one another face-to-face, so that any behavior perceived as inequitable could be challenged immediately. If any group attempted to conspire together to act coercively, the majority could easily muster a countervailing force that would challenge and, if necessary, expel or kill the delinquent members.

Even if a dominant group succeeded in bullying other members, it was relatively easy for the affected individuals to leave and join another band, or start a new one. Also, we should bear in mind that, long before the invention of agricultural "work", individual band members could not gather much more food that they themselves needed. This meant that slavery could serve no useful function and there was nothing tangible to gain from dominating other individuals, other than, perhaps, access to sexual mates.

Therefore, the driving force for egalitarianism and autonomy was natural selection. We have overwhelming evidence that intelligence is far more valuable than brute strength as an adaptive attribute. Furthermore, the biological value of intelligence is hugely amplified by collaboration, which must therefore have been simultaneously selected by evolution. We know that humans evolved to be more collaborative than any other species.

This prohibition of coercion in natural human communities is of extreme significance. It means that, in the uncompromising environment of human groups living in nature, human intelligence proved more valuable than fighting ability. Humans in primitive societies could live mostly by contract, because collaboration had more survival value than coercion. In effect, human culture was evolving to establish "contractual" behavior as the human norm, which we can now recognize as the "non-aggression principle."

The non-coercive leadership that became possible through voluntary collaboration enabled the full intelligence of all members to be available for consensual decision-making. This huge advantage for humans has been reduced in modern societies through the emergence of coercive government that uses hierarchy as the means of social control.

We can summarize the social organization natural to the human species by the principle that all individual men and women, including the leaders of any society, are "equal under the law." Although there was no formal law in primitive bands, there was an implicit social contract prohibiting coercion: such a prohibition is the natural basis for harmony and fitness in any human society.

Competition for Resources Triggered Warfare

Warfare was very unlikely in the early Paleolithic Period (Stone Age), because the relative abundance of natural food resources surrounding tiny, isolated human bands meant that there was nothing for communities to fight over. Males may have fought over access to females, and groups of males may even have raided other bands, as chimpanzee groups do, but this must be classified as "crime" rather than warfare.

Although there will probably always be some individual violence in society, warfare is a quite separate activity, because it involves the support of the leadership. In modern times, countries go to war because their parasitic governments dictate it, using conscription to force people into military roles, then using psychological techniques to overcome their natural reluctance to kill, and finally, enacting harsh punishments for those who desert their military units. Many writers have compared military service to slavery.

A key point is made by anthropologist Raymond Kelly, who distinguishes the group nature of warfare compared with crime. Kelly points out that family feuds, sometimes leading to murder, involve personal attacks, motivated by the desire for retribution against individuals who are perceived as having harmed the attacker. In contrast, warfare comprises the random killing of members of one group by another. "The principle that one group member is substitutable for another in these contexts underwrites the interrelated concepts of injury to the group, group responsibility for the infliction of injury, and group liability with respect to retribution," says Kelly.

Nationalism is a powerful driver of war. Warfare "entails an ideology of the group, but also the kind of internalization of a group identity illustrated by the statement, "I am an American" (as opposed to "I live in America" or even "I am a citizen of the United States of America."),"" says Kelly. (Kelly 2000)

Nationalism, or the extreme loyalty seen in feuding families, only makes sense when groups are involved in competition for territory, food, or other key resources. For small, widely-spaced hunter-gathering bands in the early Paleolithic period, warfare seems almost inconceivable.

However, in the Upper Paleolithic period, things changed. From 50,000 years ago, modern humans developed far superior weapons and learned to kill even the largest animals. (Martin 1967) It is easy to believe that efficient hunting enabled populations to rise rapidly in the most favored river valleys, where bands would have come to depend heavily on meat consumption.

But high population density and high meat consumption created a lethal risk. When the population density was high, it meant that, if the plant or animal food supply dropped in a bad year, people could starve. Previously, when food became scarce, human bands could split into smaller groups and move to new areas, but as the population density grew within a particular region, the land and resources available to sustain each person declined. There was no global market to provide resources and no regional communication to enable food sharing solutions to be sought.

Human experience within the historical record shows a direct connection between warfare and the high population density that causes competition for territory and resources. Another unmistakable lesson is that, once societies live in mutual insecurity, it is virtually impossible to turn back the clock and eliminate periodic warfare.

During the evolutionary era, the technology of weapons and hunting increased human fitness but the unintended consequence of these technologies was warfare. Initially, people may have been forced into warfare, as they faced two options: watch their group, including their children die, or attack their neighbors, killing the males and taking their food resources. Since it is biologically natural for people to value themselves and their own children more than their neighbors, warfare was inevitable, and this kind of warfare could be called "moral" warfare.

Mutual Insecurity Triggered Larger Societies

Once warfare becomes endemic in competing human groups, then preparation for warfare became necessary to the survival of every society. Virtually all societies since that time have expended resources on weapons and planning for warfare. Preparation for warfare greatly increased the probability that warfare would take place. The growing population density further reduced the size of the "buffer zones" between rival societies, increasing mutual insecurity and making warfare even more likely. This was despite the fact that almost all humans would have preferred to avoid it.

Obviously, warfare favored the survival of large societies over smaller ones, and this must have forced groups to amalgamate, by violent coercion, or by protective alliance, into larger societies. The first such transformation was the tribe, which comprised at least hundreds of people, and usually a fixed settlement, unless the groups were seasonal herders. Tribes comprised many kinship groups that exchanged marriage partners and collectively owned their own land. People were still able to know one another by name in the smallest tribes.

These tribes retained an informal "egalitarian" system of government. Sometimes, the tribe had a "big-man" which is an informal position with limited power. There was no class system in a tribe and no member of a tribe or band could become disproportionately wealthy by his or her own efforts, as each individual had debts and obligations to many others. In present-day tribes it is almost impossible for an outsider to guess who the village big-man is, because his dress and dwelling-place are unexceptional.

Once human bands had begun to amalgamate into tribes, the insecurity generated between large and small societies intensified and provided a strong motivation for further amalgamation. As population growth and warfare between tribes progressed, the process continued to reinforce the survival advantage of the larger human communities that could defeat or absorb smaller ones. In time, and especially where the practice of agriculture had started, tribes gave way to a larger form of organization called, "chiefdoms."

The Chiefdom

Chiefdoms had populations of several thousands, up to several tens of thousands. The large size of such groups must have given rise to problems over the resolution of conflicts between members, because the vast majority of the people in the chiefdom were neither closely related to each other by blood or marriage, nor known by name. The potential for conflict in a chiefdom was greater than that in a band. In a band, there were separate family groups who were probably related genetically and certainly very familiar with one another, and such groups could pacify family members who were in conflict and help to negotiate a resolution. In a chiefdom the families were less familiar with each other, so that conflict between individuals was similar to conflict between strangers in a modern city. That was one reason why chiefdoms had leaders with coercive authority who were able to adjudicate in disputes. The chief often had a hereditary position that could be passed on to the holder's sons or daughters.

In addition to the monopoly on the right to use force, the chief had the final say on many of the major social decisions and effective control over critical information relating to relations with other chieftains or the gods. Chiefs wore special costumes and the common people might have shown respect, for example, by prostrating themselves.

In order to feed the large population, most chiefdoms developed agricultural food production. Also, there might have been centralized distribution of crops from farm production, in which some would be retained for the chief and his elite supporters, a system that was a forerunner of taxation.

It is easy to understand how the land, which had previously been a collective resource, would have been controlled by the chief. Coercive government requires a hierarchy, and the chief's favorite warriors and counselors would surely tend to initiate families regarded as "noble" over time. Once an aristocracy is created, it is natural that it should control the land. The people who actually farmed the land would have to pay tribute to the chief and other noble families, in the form of crop sharing.

Some chiefdoms commissioned public architecture, such as temples, and grander settlements for the chiefs. For the first time, society was stratified, with manual labor and menial roles at the bottom for slaves captured in battle.

Again, I would emphasize that we cannot have direct knowledge of how the growing size of primitive societies affected the social organization. However, anthropologists have studied modern bands, tribes, and chiefdoms, and found that larger, more complex societies tend to have more coercive leadership, and we know that human nature has not altered much in 10,000 years.

The Birth of the State by Force

The final transition of human communities was from chiefdoms to states, which had populations of about 50,000 or upwards. The first states included those in Mesopotamia, the Indus Valley Civilization, Ancient Egypt, and the Government of the Han Dynasty of China.

States are not just larger, but have a more complex structure, enabling extensive human specialization as a foundation for a powerful economic and military organization. Humans living in chiefdoms may have been conquered by states or forced to adopt the state pattern of life in order to survive the challenge of generalized warfare. States are involved in redistributing goods and withholding a proportion for the ruling elite, as a kind of tribute or taxation.

The complex transaction of life in states necessitated the invention of money as a token for value. A merchant class arose, and differences in mercantile ability soon increased the stratification of society into social classes. Note that the same differences in ability in a hunter-gatherer society would have been absorbed in the familial and inter-familial relationships, in which a relatively egalitarian society and welfare for the old, the very young, and less capable are primary purposes, supported by the functional integration and close relationships of a small community.

Under the coercive state, women lost their equality with men. Warfare, primarily a male province, became the business of government. Farming, and the production of numerous artifacts, provided not only the tribute demanded by the state, but also the means of funding warfare. Therefore, most forms of work became the province of males. Major landowners controlled their workers in a relationship that foreshadowed feudalism. The idea of "noble" families demanded that lands should pass from each generation to a single offspring, preferably a warrior son, rather than being split up among the offspring. Primogeniture (inheritance, especially of land, by males) diminished the power of women, and made husbands keen to control their wives' sexuality, in order to guarantee the paternity of their children.

The Catastrophe of the Parasitic State

The technology of agriculture eventually created efficient food production that supported a much larger human population. But this advantage was accompanied by a wide array of harmful unintended consequences. A primary consequence was that people who had previously eaten an extremely diverse and nutritious diet of gathered wild plants and animal protein from hunting switched to a diet mainly based on a few species of crops, especially cereals developed from grass seeds. The result was that humans became about six inches shorter in stature, with poor bones and teeth, and a multitude of new diseases. Scientists believe that, 10,000 years later, in the 20th century, humans were still recovering from this inferior diet. A global review of the literature on stature and health during the agricultural transition concluded: "Early agriculturalists experienced nutritional deficiencies and had a harder time adapting to stress, probably because they became dependent on particular food crops, rather than having a more significantly diverse diet." Eventually, modern food production increased human height once more. "The trend is especially notable in the developed world during the past 75 years, following the industrialization of food systems." (Mummert 2011)

Research by the Commission on Behavioral and Social Sciences and Education (CBASSE) indicates that members of the hunter gatherer tribes such as the !Kung, the Aché and the Hiwi have about a one third probability of exceeding the age of 60. This compares favorably with people in early industrial societies, and it takes account of the very high rate of infant death and hunting accidents among hunter-gatherers. It supports the view that Paleolithic people had much better dietary health than modern humans, at least until the 20th century. (Kaplan 1997)

Before farming, hunter gatherers spent only three or four hours a day obtaining the food they needed, but farming created a class system in which most members of the population were obliged to work for long hours to support the whole society. The productivity of agriculture eventually enabled the specialization of labor, so that many other kinds of artifact could be made. The average amount of property owned by individuals greatly increased.

The fact that people could be profitably employed to work on farms greatly increased the advantages of slavery. The enslavement of criminals or enemies captured in warfare started a practice that lasted for thousands of years and evolved into the organized capture of people, especially Africans, and their mass transportation to work as cheap labor. Also, the existence of diverse kinds of personal property enabled thieves to make a living; people found it much easier to be dishonest in a large society in which they could rob strangers.

When people lived by hunting and gathering from nature, the only motive for one society to attack another was if they were starving and wanted to obtain their rivals' food resources. But when the first states were formed, with a social hierarchy and property ownership, there were suddenly powerful new reasons for the leaders of states to attack one another.

If the ruler of one state could conquer another state and put to death its leaders, he or she could take over the tribute, or taxation, claimed from the workers and attain a higher standard of living. The combined state would be more powerful, providing greater security against external attack. The people of the victim state could be enslaved and females could be taken as concubines, and the soldiers of the victorious army rewarded with stolen property and positions of authority over the expanded state.

The state thus created a great potential for warfare and this was reflected in the emphasis placed on making superior weapons and the training of soldiers in the techniques of battle. In a world of warring states, preparation for defense or attack required meticulous planning, mastery of weapons, and a degree of coordination that can only be achieved by coercion in a disciplined military hierarchy.

The creation of disciplined military hierarchies was in direct contrast to the egalitarian way of life of the small, itinerant bands of earlier periods. Previously, in small tribes, the acceptance of discipline may have arisen naturally in times of intense conflict. However, in order to turn men armed for hunting into disciplined soldiers who would obey a leader without question, such men had to be subject to a special kind of employment contract. In large agricultural communities, it could become a permanent arrangement, thus creating a new caste of young warriors with a formal type of hierarchy previously alien to humans.

Bear in mind that large societies lived in constant mutual insecurity. They had to prepare to defend themselves; and such preparation for warfare was self-fulfilling because it increased the insecurity of neighboring societies. The constant rearranging of alliances and the frequent use of pre-emptive attacks completed the subjugation of humans by a system of warring states. Even today, states continue to exist in mutual insecurity and therefore people have come to regard preparation for warfare as a normal part of life.

Humans were trapped into warfare by the very success of their technologies. The evolutionary trend for the previous two million years had been away from aggression and towards collaboration, but now this was reversed. Sovereign states were created solely by military conquest, and through that capacity for warfare, the governments of sovereign states acquired their universal, but illegitimate, monopoly of power.

For 10,000 long years, an increasing number of humans have fallen victim to the coercive parasitism of the state. People worldwide feared their own state and at times when its tyranny was most acute, they would have preferred to abolish it. Unfortunately, as long as humans in each state lived in fear of the leaders of other states, the continuation of their slavery was inevitable. This continuation would mean not only an absence of social justice, but the increasing failure of cultural adaptation to the artificial habitat and the associated likelihood of human extinction.

The Legitimate Aspects of the First State Leaders

An early function of coercive government was to provide a service of resolution and reconciliation of parties to disputes about murder, theft, fraud, property, and rape. The emergence of these crimes and disputes gave rise to the creation of the legitimate law that is common to nearly all human societies. Today, we still consider that the most important function of government is to protect the person and the property of citizens against criminals within the society and enemies outside it, by employing the "second use of force" against those responsible.

This fundamental task of protecting every individual and his or her property against the first use of force is a basic requirement of civilization. Only by combining in the defense of their persons and property can citizens implement the non-aggression principle, and live exclusively by contract, which is the real meaning of civilized behavior. It appears that all modern societies, even technically backward ones in the developing world, have implemented formal versions of this law against the initiation of force, which has coevolved with humans for at least two million years in the form of informal taboos.

However, although systems of law arose within states, there was no equivalent system of law to resolve disputes between whole societies, so every state had to defend itself. Political leadership became enmeshed in power struggles, because every sovereign state existed in mutual insecurity with its neighbors. The leaders of such societies had to constantly prepare for possible warfare, and make alliances against their most dangerous rivals.

The invention of the parasitic state transformed human culture, so that all human children from 10,000 years ago until the present time have grown up believing that warfare is a normal activity and that killing humans from "enemy" societies is morally acceptable.

The Creation of Parasitic Government

Before the invention of farming, hunting and gathering yielded only enough food for daily requirements, and this demanded that virtually everyone should work. This provided a strong platform for human equality. When agriculture began to produce a food surplus, and especially when the specialization of labor created other craft skills for production of artifacts such as pottery, tools, clothing and jewelry, the ruling elite, who already controlled the warriors, were able to stop working and concentrate on ruling. This change marks the start of the 10,000-year tradition of the parasitic, coercive governments running their societies like tax farmers with human livestock.

Nearly all states were dominated by military rulers who were likely to become parasites, provided that they had the military power to suppress rebellion. For this purpose, they needed to "buy off" the leading groups of citizens with suitable privileges, in order to make them fellow parasites.

Coercive, parasitical government was born! The wealth, security, and standard of living of the ruling elite no longer depended upon how much they served their fellows in society. Instead, it depended upon how they could use military power to exploit the host population and how they could use warfare to extend the size of their host community by conquering neighboring societies.

In hunter-gatherer bands of the late Paleolithic period, warfare was a tragic side-effect of otherwise adaptive technology, and it could easily have been abolished by inter-group collaboration at a later date. Under the state, warfare became a more discretionary activity that rewarded the victors. Nothing can be so closely tied to state coercion as warfare, the greatest curse of the human species. The coercive state was created, directly or indirectly, as a result of warfare, and the killing of large numbers of innocent people by governments has become so commonplace that many people regard this kind of murder as a normal part of human behavior.

In the 20th century, coercive states killed between three and four hundred million people, including both warfare and other large-scale murder. In the 21st century, the killing goes on. Progress towards peace is hardly worth reporting, for the most advanced industrial countries, including the democracies, have been the main instigators in the major warfare of the 20th and 21st centuries.

As we have seen in Chapter 4, the coercive, parasitical state disrupts human adaptation, striking at the very heart of human life and reducing the well-being of the global population in ways too numerous to count.

The State Was a Harmful Side-effect of Technology

The most important thing to understand about the coercive, parasitic state is that it was not intentionally created to serve society but was an unintended consequence of technology, like lead poisoning, air pollution, or lung cancer. Like these other misuses of technology, it must be recognized as an evil and abolished.

The lives of billions of people are blighted by parasitic government but they have not recognized that such government is a dreadful anachronism that resulted from the misuse of technology, because it has existed for 10,000 years and during that period, no humans, except a fast-diminishing minority of hunter-gatherers, have lived in fully normal societies.

It is easy for both scientists and non-scientists to recognize that pollution, deforestation, soil erosion, or habitat destruction are unintended consequences of technology, because these phenomena are manifestly destroying nature and threatening the quality and even the existence of human life. Parasitic government also has a terrible effect on human society but people have come to believe that warfare, wide wealth differentials, social classes, irrational laws about victimless crimes, and many other abuses of government are difficult social problems that cannot be solved. In fact, such problems are merely the symptoms of abnormal social organization, generated by sovereign power.

Only when the general population understands human prehistory and the harmful side-effects of technology will it recognize coercive parasitic government for what it is – the greatest tragedy ever to befall the human species. Only today, for the first time in 10,000 years, can we begin to perceive the means by which normal human social organization may be resumed. For today, humans are able to communicate globally to agree on the project to retrieve the natural autonomy that humans evolved with during the Paleolithic period.

We can, in the early 21st century, create formal global laws to enact the implicit rules against the use of force, to implement the non-aggression principle, and for the protection of property rights that evolved in small human bands. Modern humans can create a federated global civilization in which diverse individuals and communities can live in peaceful harmony and trade freely. We can also almost completely suppress the harmful side-effects of technology. Modern humans can do what was impossible 10,000 years ago in the Paleolithic period, build a complete civilization.

Although the parasitic state does terrible damage to the human species, and now threatens its very existence, coercive government is actually highly unstable, constantly divided by futile political conflicts, prone to constant vacillation, and fundamentally opposed to the moral predispositions that evolved with the human species.

In contrast, consensual government controlled by tightly integrated communities with face-to-face relations, is much more powerful, being aligned with both human nature and the natural environment. In the adaptive civilization that lies ahead, both government and law will be stronger and all people will be as free as it is possible to be, and as equal in opportunity as it is possible to be.

It is crucial to realize that all humans alive today have inherited the capacity to live peacefully and collaboratively, provided that their social organization is normal. Although humans also have the capacity for warfare, this is a behavior triggered only by the pathological relations between social groups subject to unnatural coercion. The much deadly harm caused by the coercive, parasitic state can easily be avoided in modern times by human action at the level of the species.

Chapter 6

State Ideology, Hierarchy, and Force are Unsustainable

*I*n the 21st century, about four billion people in China, India, and Africa will demand a postindustrial standard of living that people in the developed nations take for granted. Hitherto, the industrialized countries have attempted to "pull up the castle drawbridge" by using their military and economic power to manage trade by force and prevent the developing countries from achieving parity. The excuse offered for this egregious policy is that the Earth's resources are insufficient to provide the whole global population with the high standard of living achieved by rich countries.

As I pointed out in Chapter 1, the myth of over-population arose from the global migration of people to cities, which causes observers to equate "crowded cities" with "a crowded planet." The human carrying capacity of the Earth is not fixed: it depends upon the sustainability of the technologies employed by humans.

As hunter-gatherers, the Earth could only support about two and a half people per square kilometer (Hamilton 2007), whereas Hong Kong alone now supports 7,000 people per square kilometer. It may not be a good idea to copy Hong Kong's population density everywhere, but it is surely worth bearing in mind that a population 14,000 times greater than that accommodated by nature can live rather comfortably when supported by today's technology.

I could add that, if the urban area of the beautiful city of Paris were transplanted to Mexico, and then copied repeatedly until it filled that country completely, the enormous city that resulted could very comfortably house the 7,113,000,00 global population. The rest of the world would be free for wilderness, industry, transport, and the farms needed to produce croissants and champagne for the lucky people in Mexico.

If humans develop sustainable technologies for agriculture, manufacturing, and transportation, current environmental degradation could be completely prevented. In that case, the Earth could certainly carry human populations tens, or even hundreds of times higher than the present level without major disadvantages. And, as I have pointed out, in a future, well-integrated civilization governed by communities whose primary concern is the quality of life, we can expect families to revert to the "normal" size that will achieve replacement level for the population.

Future societies that retrieve the normal social organization that evolved with humans will be able to adapt their technology-based habitat, and their own behavior, to greatly increase their own fitness. This will eliminate the stresses that have previously caused unnatural rapid growth or contraction of populations. These stresses have included, for example, traditional farming, which encouraged fecundity, because parents valued children as labor. The opposite stress is imposed by social democracy, in which the state fragments the family structure and segregates children in enforced schooling, thus making parenting both expensive and less rewarding. Without such distortions, there are rational grounds for believing that population growth will fall to zero, making the population issue irrelevant.

Current "Civilization" is Unsustainable

Humans have arrived at a crossroads in their use, and misuse, of technology. The harmful side-effects of technology are seriously damaging the natural ecology and the quality of human life.

It is widely accepted that modern agriculture, with its dependence on fossil fuel fertilizers and the depletion of water and soil resources, is unsustainable. It must be replaced by a new agriculture that is integrated with the natural ecology, so that the soil, the insect and fungal populations, and other species present are protected by nature's ecological cycles.

Manufacturing is currently based on the one-way flow of natural resources, from mineral ores, timber, and oil-based plastics that are processed into products and buildings. These materials end their lives in landfills and incinerators, accompanied by the unsustainable pollution of water, air, and food. We must move towards 100% recycled manufacturing processes that are compatible with the natural cycles of the ecology. Transportation and other large industries must similarly be transformed.

But much more urgent than the case for sustainable agriculture, manufacturing, or transportation is the case for sustainable government. Sustainable government means self-government by small communities of extended families in which the sexes and the generations are socially integrated and which support natural evolved morality, and which can contribute on a federal basis to adaptive policies. Unfortunately, the global public does not understand that the failure of adaptation is due to the prevailing coercive, parasitic model of human governance, even though the biological case against it is overwhelming and it is more damaging than any other misused technology.

The global scientific community should be lobbying hard to support the vital interests of the human species. The coercive, parasitical state must be replaced by scientifically coherent based global law, based on the evolved morality of our species.

Unfortunately, the state has thousands of years of experience in suppressing human rights, and that now includes subordinating scientists to its parasitic practices. For example, the state ensures that it is the largest investor in scientific research, that it controls education and therefore the credentials of scientists. The state, through public sector procurement, directly or indirectly employs a huge proportion of scientists, effectively gagging much of the scientific community.

In the military sphere, the state may often be the sole customers for ships, planes vehicles, weaponry and ammunition designed to kill people. Scientific expertise is also extensively used for the tools and expertise of espionage, surveillance of the domestic and overseas populations, and the medical expertise associated with modern forms of torture routinely used by state intelligence agencies. Therefore, a scientist wishing to speak up for human liberty, or a more natural form of human society, requires exceptional integrity and courage.

The Three Tools of the Coercive, Parasitic State

In order to combat the parasitic activities of coercive states, we must be constantly vigilant to recognize the tools utilized to suppress human rights. The three major characteristics of the state that damage human societies are:

Force. The use of arbitrary force which prevents the contractual relationships on which civilization must be exclusively based.

Ideology. The indoctrination of the general public by fraudulent ideologies that may create conflict and even war.

Hierarchy. The creation of unnatural hierarchies that hinder the application of intelligence to human problems.

Below, we discuss in turn the three tools utilized by the parasitic state to manipulate its host population: coercion, hierarchy and ideology.

Coercion Fundamentally Conflicts with Human Intelligence

All the disputed political philosophies of human government can be resolved down to a single fundamental issue: whether human action should be instigated by the voluntary collaboration of free individuals, which we call "contract," or by the top-down control of parasitic elites, using "force."

It is this issue – "contract versus coercion" – that determines whether humans blossom and grow organically to their true destiny as noble and enlightened guardians of the beautiful planet Earth, or whether they continue to pollute and degrade the whole of nature, eliminate thousands of species, wage wars over resources, starve a quarter of the world's human population, operate a hierarchical work environment based on disguised slavery, and possibly, render all humans extinct.

In a society based on the sovereign (all-powerful) state, political leaders have the privilege of doing many things that would earn severe punishment if they were undertaken by members of the public. These include the right to declare war (to initiate force), to make arbitrary laws (to take away others' freedom), to raise taxes (to steal), to regulate social or economic behavior (to employ force against others' property rights), and to enforce state schooling (to indoctrinate helpless young people into ideologies demanding self-sacrifice and obedience).

In a completely civilized society – the only society that can provide a fully adaptive habitat for all its members – all individuals, including political leaders, must be *absolutely* equal under the law. Once humans take their own rights seriously, and switch to fully contractual interaction, the population will become extremely sensitive to any deviations from equal rights, because such deviation represents privilege and privilege is by definition a crime in a society of equals.

We already know the verdict of nature: contract should displace coercion. For 99.5 percent of the 1.7 million years of human biological history, until 10,000 years ago, our ancestors lived as autonomous individuals in small bands organized around the extended family, without any coercive leadership. Even the relationships between parents and children were mostly non-coercive. That contrasts with the widespread modern practice of spanking children, forcing them into schoolrooms, and administering pacifying drugs to those who are "restless."

All Sovereignty is Incompatible with Human Rights

We frequently use the word "sovereignty" to denote the independence of a nation from control by another nation and we assume that that is a good thing. But the word "sovereignty" literally refers to the power of a conqueror or monarch to reign, that is, to have absolute ownership of a nation of people and their land, which is identical to dictatorship. Modern politicians avoid this connotation by talking of the "sovereignty of the people," which suggests that the people collectively dictate the policy of a nation.

Supposing the people did literally rule over their nation by voting on every issue: would that be a good thing? It would actually be a form of dictatorship, for the majority could take away the rights of any individual or group, imprison people unfairly, oppress minorities and do all the things that individual dictators do.

In practice, our actual situation is even worse, because the sovereignty of the people is always delegated to a political leadership, which makes all the decisions. Consequently, elite groups that control parliaments, congresses and other forms of government always control sovereign power, and oppress the citizens of their nation, proving repeatedly that sovereign power of any kind cannot coexist with unalienable human rights of any kind. Civilization depends upon people recognizing the rights of the individual person and protecting those rights by law.

Libertarians sometimes refer to the "sovereignty of the individual," but even this would be a great evil, because a sovereign individual would have unlimited power to act. In a completely civilized society, individuals cannot have "sovereign" rights, even over their own bodies, because the right to move one's body is necessarily constrained by the equal rights of others. Individuals may have property rights to their own homes, which permit them to exclude others. Property rights, including the right to our own bodies, are essential to freedom. Without property rights, we would live in a jungle, in which "might was right."

The only legitimate role of centralized power is to implement, under the direct consensual control of the community, the institution of biologically natural law. Natural law is the explicit form of the "civilization" that evolved in pre-industrial societies, based on the implicit social contract of members to forebear from harming their

Fig. 6. Russian Delta II nuclear-powered ballistic missile submarine in 1997. Six countries have spent trillions of dollars on submarines that can destroy all major world cities with nuclear missiles. This constant threat of "species suicide" results from a simple absence of global laws against coercion. Photo: US Navy.

fellows and to jointly defend the rights of members of the society. In other words, the non-aggression principle.

If each state has sovereignty, or "absolute" power, as it has today, the liberty of individual citizens and their right to their own property depends upon the goodwill of the state, which can be withdrawn at any time. Therefore true human "rights" can exist only if all forms of sovereignty are abolished. In practice, this means abolishing the coercive nature of all governments, which means abolishing the state.

Note that abolishing the state does not abolish regions, countries, districts or communities. In a civilization based on the non-aggression principle, any community can be maintained, but its relationships with other groups is based on contract, rather than warfare or unfree trade managed by the state. Note also, that abolishing the state does not abolish government. Rather, coercive government, backed by military force, is abolished in favor of much more powerful, efficient, and natural, self-government.

Dealing with Major Threats to Society

History shows clearly that free collaboration between individuals that we call the "free market" produces more goods, and generates more justice, than does communism, or other collectivist social arrangements. But many people still cling to the idea of the state as a benevolent father figure. One reason is that most people find it difficult to accept that free collaboration can deal with crises, such as warfare or great threats that affect a society. The main problem is that people living under the coercive, parasitic state find it difficult to imagine how the institutions for voluntary governance would arise in a free society.

Arguments for the superiority of state power to deal with major threats to society were put forward by a leading legal scholar, Carl Schmitt. (Schmitt 2005) Schmitt accepts human freedom for routine matters, but argued that, in the face of threats that would render humans extinct – perhaps a lethal version of climate change – state coordination, with its capacity to make a universally enforceable decision, would be the best means of overcoming the threat.

An effective rebuttal of Schmitt's claims is provided in a recent paper by scholar and educator, Michael McConkey. (McConkey 2013) According to McConkey, the state is too incompetent and corrupt to rise to the challenge of a major extinction threat to society. "... even to assume state actors' good intentions one has to willfully ignore a long history of rent-seeking, regulatory capture, discretionary bailouts, and general cronyism that is endemic to any rent-generating opportunity." McConkey offers US examples, including the creation of and response to the 2008 housing finance crisis, the pharmaceutical industry's support for the US health-care reforms, and the military industrial complex that distorts the domestic economy and foreign relations in scores of countries, including the USA.

McConkey references Ludwig von Mises (Mises 1935) and Friedrich Hayek (Hayek 1945) for their descriptions of the calculation and knowledge problems that make even the best-intended central-state planning impossible as a rational undertaking. Regulatory failure includes outcomes diametrically opposed to stated aims, a phenomenon called the Peltzman Effect. (Peltzman 1975) The coercive power of the state is inherently evil and is aptly summed up in the proverb: "The road to hell is paved with good intentions."

The corrupt special interests that benefit from any regulatory initiative are already embedded in the process, notes McConkey, explaining: "sovereign regulation by the state does not and never was intended to serve the ostensible public good but rather it has been part of the collaborative pilfering by the rulers' capitalist cronies...."

Continues McConkey, "What is called regulation is in fact anti-regulation, because it interferes with the actual processes of regulation built into the market." (McConkey 2011)

Regulatory failures in the USA referenced by McConkey include the preparations and response to Hurricane Katrina, which were judged by the media to be woefully inadequate. Another example is the increase in coal-generated pollution that actually resulted from regulations on scrubber technology for cleaning effluents. In the US, states with strict licensing of electricians have up to 10 times more electrocutions than the national average (because licensed electricians charge more, which increases dangerous DIY electrical work). Internationally, the banning in the USA and Europe of the insecticide DDT due to environmental damage may have caused unnecessary deaths from malaria. In 2008, the WHO reported 243 million cases of malaria, including 863,000 deaths, mainly in Africa. DDT would have prevented some deaths, but its use is controversial.

How Humans Outgrew the Dominance Hierarchy

A key tool of the state is imposed hierarchy. Anthropologists believe that six million years ago, our early pre-human ancestors, like chimpanzees, were still controlled by a dominance hierarchy. The alpha animals – usually the biggest and most forceful – had a relatively fixed rank, which they vigorously defended by employing coercion to obtain priority in access to food and sex. Alpha animals had more offspring, which meant the group benefited from their genes.

Many thinkers mistakenly consider that humans naturally form a dominance hierarchy, or pecking order, like those of other social mammals, such as dogs, chimpanzees, and chickens. This mistake has political ramifications, for if humans still established a fixed dominance hierarchy in modern societies, it would inevitably produce a "pyramid of power" with the leaders of the state at the apex, composed of the alpha individuals who dominated those of lower rank.

However, the evidence shows that human social organization altered fundamentally during evolution. Certainly, humans still exhibit hierarchical behavior, but it has been radically modified due to the evolution of human intelligence and collaboration.

When large-brained humans developed intelligent thought, its benefits were much greater than mere physical strength. Modern humans do not dominate the planet because of their strength, but because of their thinking power. So, natural selection acted on the human behaviors generated by intelligence and caused an increase in the power and size of the human brain.

However, the degree of hierarchy in a society affects the expression of intelligent behavior by the general population. People subject to hierarchy are simply not free to use their intelligence to optimize their "fitness."

For example, in military operations people are forced by a state to fight and the probability of their survival is not closely related to their own intelligence or other traits. Similarly, employees working in a hierarchical company are frequently frustrated at the constraints imposed on their working methods, which prevent them applying their full intelligence to the variation and selection of methodologies necessary for the efficient achievement of corporate goals.

In both military service and employment it is common to hear individuals complain of the "stupidity" of their seniors in the hierarchy. The real problem, however, is not human stupidity but the imposition of hierarchy by the state and the corporation. The state is directly responsible for the military hierarchy, and indirectly responsible for corporate hierarchy, which it controls through a complex web of laws that define employment, corporate structure, limited liability, and related aspects such as intellectual "property" rights.

Similarly, during the Industrial Revolutions that transformed Europe, the Americas, and Japan, and are now transforming China, India, and Africa, each country tends to support "its" industrialists in international markets by passing laws biased towards the aggregation of power by corporations. The most relevant laws are those that regulate the duration, remuneration and working conditions of employees, and those that reduce the geographical mobility of workers and provide them with cheap mass housing. The parasitic purpose of such regulation is to "commoditize" unskilled and semi-skilled workers in order to keep their wages competitive. Such workers become more like robots than humans, and can use their intellect very little in earning their living. The state and the partially state-controlled media conveniently blame the conditions of the less educated workers on "capitalism."

In order to understand who controls the economy of a modern state, we need to differentiate the free market – which could only exist if men and women were entirely free of any controlling state – from "state" capitalism, which comprises hybrid corporations with limited liability and other corporate law that releases businesspeople from the absolute personal accountability that is essential to the health of free markets. Free markets are simply the natural exchange relationships between people that exist in a society with no state control, in which the law is based on the strict prohibition of all harms, plus absolute personal accountability.

In the small, interdependent human bands of the evolutionary era, most tasks were carried out collaboratively, and therefore intelligent behavior would have sharply conflicted with hierarchical behavior that lingered on from human ancestry. If alpha humans had routinely ignored the intelligent contributions of those of lower status, the fitness benefits of intelligence would have been lost.

For example, supposing a particular male was mated with an especially intelligent female. If the two collaborated well, her intelligence would have contributed to better decision-making about the great number of large and small issues that arose in the life of the couple and the nurturing of their children. Good collaborative decision-making would have increased the survival prospects of themselves and their children, so that more of their genes would have been passed on. But if the male were a bully, or incompetent at cooperation – irrespective of his intelligence – the partnership would not have worked so well and the woman's intelligence would have been be frustrated, partly eliminating the benefit of that advantage to their fitness.

Similarly, in a group of hunters, intelligence would have enabled them to hunt more efficiently and obtain more protein, thus increasing their reproductive potential – but only if they collaborated well as a group, by sharing information and coordinating their ambush tactics. Any member who would not share information relevant to locating prey, or was unable to participate in group consensus, or to become a team player, would have seriously undermined the group's success. The group would have applied sanctions to poor cooperators, reducing their fitness and the number of offspring they were likely to bear.

The same pressures of natural selection must have acted on men and women who collaborated in plant food collection and preparation, childcare and other tasks. Individuals unable to collaborate well would have lost status and therefore fitness, and thus passed on their non-collaborative genes less frequently. Over thousands of years, such selection reduced the occurrence of many human genes that had formerly evolved for aggressive success in the dominance hierarchy.

For humans, hierarchy can be regarded as the "failure of collaboration." We now know beyond any doubt that human intelligence and collaboration increased radically in comparison to those of chimpanzees. It follows that the genetic basis of the dominance hierarchy has been progressively eliminated by natural selection.

Another piece of evidence that social rank became less important during the Paleolithic period is the alteration in the appearance of modern humans, who have become lighter in build, with small canine teeth, and a total loss of the erectile hair used by other primates for threat displays. Some subgroups evolved light skin that exhibits reddening (blushing) and light eyes in which iris dilation can be observed, both of which reveal emotional states and are useful in collaborative communications. All this suggests that human society evolved to exhibit less aggression and threat displays, at least within the group, and that also means less fixed hierarchy.

The original dominance hierarchy, as exhibited 1.7 million years ago by pre-humans, extended a social rank to each member of a band, and enabled that person to utilize coercion to take advantage of all those members lower in rank. In any modern human society, behavior associated with the dominance hierarchy would be regarded as theft, assault, or rape, and the individuals concerned would be labeled as "criminals."

What behavior do we see when we look around at our fellow humans today? In most social situations, humans are mutually courteous, offering hospitality and equal respect to others. When we look at groups of modern people at work or leisure we generally see relations resembling meritocracy, rather than the chimpanzees' dominance hierarchy.

Of course, equal status and contractual behavior are limited to mentally competent adults. People who are mentally incompetent, due to disease, infancy, or impairment due to alcohol or some other narcotic drug will, for their own benefit, be denied some autonomy by persons temporarily acting as their guardians.

Some people may consider that the family is a hierarchical structure, especially if they have lived in a patriarchy, a matriarchy, or a community where women or children are subject to reduced autonomy due to religious prescriptions. In my view, this is a relatively modern and pathological form of the family. In human bands of the Paleolithic period, the biological family was fairly loosely organized within a close community, and autonomy and relatively equal status were emphasized.

I believe that the dominance hierarchy was modified by evolution to create an entirely new form of rank or status, which I will now discuss.

From Dominance Hierarchy to Contractual Hierarchy

Although the dominance hierarchy has disappeared, hierarchy it-self has not. The dominance hierarchy was replaced by what may be called "contractual hierarchy," which is compatible with our modern idea of meritocracy. The social control that evolved in humans is so comprehensive and universal that every modern society today has for-mal laws to control delinquent behavior and ensure that people usually relate to each other by contract rather than coercion.

Below, I list some examples of contractual hierarchy in use today. Note that these examples all comprise the use of hierarchy or status to fulfill a real social need for leadership. In a group of chimpanzees or dogs, alpha individuals can use physical power to dominate other indi-viduals and take their resources, such as food and sex. But contractual hierarchy enables any person with a useful skill to adopt a temporary leadership role with the consent of the community.

Let us consider the kinds of social rank we commonly see in mod-ern societies.

Informal contractual hierarchy: In modern social life, a group such as a private club that decides to organize a particular activity may recruit the specialized services of a member (for example, a cook or a navigator or a handyman) and then defer to that person, providing him or her with temporary rank that enables the task to be completed more easily. Another context under which people are assigned a temporary rank is when a friend or relative acts as "guardian" to an individual who is temporarily incapacitated by a brain disease or consumption of a mind-altering substance such as alcohol.

Formal contractual hierarchy: Also in a social group that pursues, for example, a hobby or leisure activity, the officers of a committee, such as a treasurer or secretary, may have formal responsibility for the oper-ation of the association. Other members will defer to those individuals and acknowledge their contribution to the group. Of course, the power of such officers is limited in scope and duration.

The guardianship of children and disabled adults also constitutes a formal hierarchical role that has a useful social purpose. It is needed be-cause some human groups do not have the mental capacity to make all of their own decisions. Parents and stepparents are the guardians of chil-dren, and professionally qualified individuals may be guardians to the mentally incompetent. Friends often need to become the informal guardians of those temporarily under the influence of mind-altering substances, including alcohol. Individuals managed by a guardian should retain their human rights and thus be legally protected from accidental or intentional harm.

Contractual disciplined hierarchy: In a police force, or armed forces, each member has a rank and those in senior ranks can exercise considerable powers over those of inferior rank. In the armed forces, officers may order those of lower rank to expose themselves to extreme risk, or to kill "enemies." Even though millions of deaths result from military activities, this is clearly not a dominance hierarchy, because the military officers are not permitted to attack, rape, or steal from those of lower rank.

The orders that may legally be given to people in a disciplined service are usually laid down in regulations that are available for inspection. Joining a disciplined service requires members to sign a contract, and therefore it is a contractual form of service. Furthermore, it is entirely restricted to the context and duration of the service concerned – outside the service, the individuals revert to being "civilians," under the terms of their contract, and the dominance behavior ceases.

The hierarchy of state coercion: Governments and their civil servants comprise unnatural hierarchies that are created to control mass populations. In democracies, civil servants who are unnecessarily "bureaucratic" or inefficient may be subject to strong criticism. But in socialist states, the state bureaucracy may act as a pernicious oppressor, stifling spontaneity, creativity, and free speech, and crushing the very sources of human self-actualization.

Social classes based on meritocracy and wealth: In a society controlled by the rule of law, people can obtain power by creating wealth in the form of goods and services. In a completely free society, people would compete on a level playing field and differentials between the richest and poorest members of society would be modest.

Wealth differentials would be modest, because, in a free market, people are permitted to compete for *every* opportunity, and the power of such competition would tend to minimize differences in wages, prices, profits, interest rates, and other economic variables. If some businesses earned large windfall profits, competitors would rush in to share the bounty, and prices and profits would be forced down to normal levels. If some workers were underpaid, investors would rush in to take advantage of their low wages, which would actually drive the wages up towards the average level for that class of work.

Most important of all, a free market society would be completely reorganized. Employment might be mostly replaced by other forms of market participation, because it tends to "commoditize" workers and prevents them obtaining their true worth in competitive markets, as businesses do. Many abuses based on state coercion, such as intellectual "property" and limited liability, would disappear in their coercive form, placing humans on an equal footing. This huge process of equalization would take place globally, as well as within each community. In fact, without the huge power of state coercion, humans would be as relatively equal as they were in natural hunter-gatherer societies.

At present, due to skewed laws created by coercive governments, some individuals achieve astronomical wealth and status, in contrast to the underclass, many of whom have negative equity. The abnormally high differentials that we often see today can only exist where the market forces are interrupted by external coercion. Such coercion is caused by the actions of governments acting to intervene against market forces. All governments pass a large number of laws that constrain human action and therefore suppress market forces. In this way, the government is the source of extreme hierarchies based on wealth.

If the state did not intervene in the free market, and market forces were allowed to minimize wealth differentials, it would become manifest to all that the state is an unnecessary parasite. Thus the state, irrespective of the political system in use, must cultivate abnormal, exaggerated hierarchy in order to justify its centralized power to intervene.

Contractual servitude (employment): Employment is a kind of servitude in which the individual takes up a position in a hierarchical organization. Recruitment, however, is contractual, and the labor demands made on an employee are usually constrained by a contract of employment. Thus, the dominant-submissive behavior pattern is limited by both contract and context.

Contractual slavery (indentured labor): Indentured servants are people who are contractually bound to work for an employer for a specified duration. Contracts for indentured labor usually extend for a period of years, and the work to be done may be vaguely specified, so the system invites many abuses. Modern indentured servitude includes, for example, illegal immigrants paying their passage by long work-hours in harsh conditions, often at subsistence pay rates to support themselves.

The United Nations has ruled that indentured servitude should be illegal in member nations.

As in the case of full slavery, it can be argued that a contract for indentured servitude is subject to great uncertainty and cannot be fully comprehended by the contracting parties, especially the servant, and therefore it cannot be the subject of a voluntary agreement. If a proper contract for indentured labor cannot be made in principle, then such contracts are void, and this is now the case in most countries.

Indentured labor is surely close to the dominance hierarchy, but the fact that it is rare and generally illegal illustrates the point that the pure dominance hierarchy is no longer a normal part of human behavior.

Coercive slavery: Most people imagine that slavery is a thing of the past, but researchers at "Free the Slaves" (www.freetheslaves.net), formed to eradicate slavery, claim that there are about 27 million slaves in the world, many times more than there were at the peak of the African slave trade in the 19th century. Today's slaves are less likely to work in agriculture, or wear metal manacles, but slavery still means the complete control of one person by another.

"Violence is used to maintain that control; and economic exploitation," said Kevin Bales, one of the founders of *Free the Slaves*. "When we're in the field and we want to decide whether a specific case is slavery we often ask the question: 'Can this person walk away, even if it's into a worse personal situation?' If they can't, then it is likely that they are slaves."

Some people argue that military conscription, in which a state forces men and women, and sometimes children, on pain of death, to become a part of the armed forces, should be classified as slavery. Slavery is common during warfare. In WWII, Germany enslaved about 12 million people in concentration camps, a high proportion of whom died or were killed. In the same conflict, Japan enslaved an unknown number of "comfort women" as unpaid prostitutes for its military personnel.

Much of modern slavery occurs when people from the developing world seek help in moving to industrialized nations to seek a better quality of life and are taken advantage of by those offering to smuggle them across borders. About 6-8% of the people considered to be slaves are trafficked for sexual exploitation.

The acceptance of slave workers in many places, such as the Middle East, is related to the fact that slavery only became illegal in some countries in the 1960s. The origins of slavery, like so many other corrupt aspects of human society, were in the agricultural age that gave rise to the state as a form of social organization. As stated previously, prior to agriculture, human productivity was not high enough to provide an incentive for slave labor.

State coercion: Governments inherit their power over societies from the original conquerors that created their state, and they maintain a monopoly of military force to support their control of the general population. At first, this might seem like a return of the dominance hierarchy, but it is not, because the persons that secure political power usually have to submit themselves to a legitimizing process, such as an election by the public, or an elite group. Governments exercise power through the law, and thereby gain the appearance of legitimacy.

Even the most ruthless dictators implement their dominance mostly through legislation, so that they can claim that their power is a legitimate expression of group will. In nearly all states there are clear limits to power laid down in constitutions, and politicians are occasionally punished for criminal acts.

Criminal hierarchies: Organized crime, including street gangs, has its own hierarchy, and power is exercised according to a specific code, which includes sanctions against defaulters. Although criminals may be ruthless, the existence of agreements between criminal organizations demarcating the nature and geographical limits of their illegal operations differentiate their social system from the dominance hierarchy. The system of agreements and punishments exercised by criminals has come into existence because criminals in dispute with one another have no recourse to the law, due to the illegal nature of their activities.

If the state did not limit human rights (for example, to sell certain drugs, or to market prostitution), then most such activities would be within the scope of civilian law. Alcohol kills and injures far more people than all illicit drugs added together. As well as criminalizing the activity of drinking alcohol, when the USA imposed prohibition in the 1930s, the experiment gave rise to a huge crime wave born out of the demand for the newly illegal product and this criminalization of a hitherto legal activity may even have resulted in increased alcohol consumption.

In spite of this disaster, prohibition was then placed on a range of drugs, including opiates, such as morphine, and stimulants, such as meth-amphetamines. This action has arguably had even worse consequences in terms of a huge increase in criminal activity, and a terrifying eruption of murders in the USA, and in the drug production countries, along with the failure of the prohibition to reduce drug consumption.

The main beneficiary of drug prohibition is the state, which can justify more coercive intervention in civil society. Individual politicians in many countries, and at many levels can be corrupted by the billionaire drug barons and lesser criminals that were created by anti-drug laws. The general public gains nothing from the prohibition of drugs. The effect of forcing the whole drug supply chain underground makes it much harder to know who is taking drugs and to provide treatment for them, or to protect children from the gangs created by the state.

The State Imposes Enforced Hierarchy

The disappearance of the dominance hierarchy in humans and its replacement by contractual hierarchy is a remarkable example of the power of both biotic and cultural evolution. The great advantage of human intelligence could not be used effectively if we were burdened by the "criminal" dominance hierarchy of the chimpanzee. When contractual hierarchy evolved in stone-age societies, it made the roles of human leaders compatible with social justice and the efficient use of intelligence by all members of society.

10,000 years ago, the catastrophic emergence of the coercive, parasitical state did not destroy contractual hierarchy, but it did distort it. The use of military power by small, conquering elites enabled them to achieve unnatural coercive control over large populations.

The existence of a single coercive leader as a parasite would not necessarily be catastrophic in itself. The problem is that, in order to control a population of millions, government has to construct a huge hierarchy of social classes in order to bring its control to bear on the whole population (just as the generals of an army can only control the mass of soldiers through the agency of a large hierarchy of officers). This hierarchy of millions, supported as parasites and backed by military power, is a tool for social control.

In the modern state, the equal rank of humans in their natural habitat has been replaced by a hierarchy that stretches from the leaders, who have "sovereign" (that is, absolute, or life or death) power over all others, down to the lowest members of society, who, in most societies during the last 10,000 years, have been slaves used for hard labor, with no property rights, even to their own bodies.

This huge graduated system of social rank is still necessary today for the exercise of power by the tiny elite at the top. To maintain the loyalty of those near the top, such as the industrialists and landowners, plus the middle classes, including the legal, medical, and accountancy professionals and other leading citizens, the elite must necessarily reward them with large benefits taken from the majority. The professions are given some degree of monopoly power over recruitment and their markets for specialized services. Professional monopolies damage the free market, driving up prices, and restricting innovation, but the state benefits by acquiring the loyalty of such groups.

All social groups that have the potential of leadership or political independence, such as trade unions, NGOs, and the environmental movement, are courted by the state to some degree, helping to build the artificial hierarchy necessary for parasitic, centralized control. For those affiliated with the state, this means freedom, high income, and status. For the population in general, it means materialism based on state-controlled capitalism, a distorted caricature of the free market, and leaves the lower classes in desperate poverty and appalling living conditions.

Thus the most damaging consequences of modern government are not primarily due to the coercion or the parasitism of the tiny elite at the center. Rather, they are due to the unnatural, exaggerated hierarchy maintained by the government in order to stay in power and control the host population. The existence of an enormous social hierarchy absolutely destroys the social organization natural to the human species, and without that social organization, humans are much less able to adapt themselves or their technologies to the environmental conditions of planet Earth.

Humans are competitive, but their natural social organization, which evolved over millions of years, prohibited the initiation of force in pre-agricultural societies, thus channeling their competitive drive towards socially beneficial activities such as creation and exchange, as well as harmless leisure activities based on "play." But when technology placed military power in the hands of a tiny minority, the normal social organization with its prohibition of force was abolished and the political "leaders" acquired the power to do great harm.

State Ideologies are Fraudulent

The social hierarchies used by coercive governments to control mass populations should be rejected by the public as unnatural and damaging, but few members of the public realize that they are the victims of a pathological society, because nearly every individual has been indoctrinated as a young child by ideologies that seek to justify criminal governmental behavior.

Furthermore, humans have strong group loyalty, because group membership was essential for survival in the evolutionary era. The purpose of a state ideology is to persuade a population that the group can only survive if it supports the values expressed by its leaders. Note that all political ideologies must necessarily be false, because the state system is an imposed parasite. Below are some examples of ideologies employed by states.

Political scientists argue about the pros and cons of different ideologies, such as social democracy, communism, religious fundamentalism, and socialism. But, from a biological perspective, these are all variants of the same sovereign state in which a parasitic elite has virtually all the power to legislate and to tax and to commit the society to warfare.

All modern governments had their origins in military victory of their group over other groups, and then the continuance of a monopoly of power. Every state government is a separate social group, attempting to hold power over all other groups within its society. Although all governments spend part of their resources to address the needs of the population in general, inevitably their priority must be to retain and exploit power in the interests of their own ruling group.

A small elite group can control a mass population in only one way: through a hierarchy in which the value system supports the legitimacy of the ruling elite. The hierarchy must be substantial enough to exercise control and the state must seek allies in every part of the population, including the army, the police force, the law, the professional classes, the educational system, and the mass media.

Below, we present extremely simplified, generic descriptions of the main ideologies utilized by nation states to justify their parasitic power over their host communities. The main aim is to show that the coercive, parasitical state is biologically unnatural and harmful to humans, irrespective of the ideology used to disguise it.

State Ideologies are designed to Obtain Obedience

The only rational political "ideology" for a society comprises the rules that evolved with the original hunter-gatherer band, which was the only society for which humans were genetically adapted by evolution. All the economic and political theories created in modern times are simply futile attempts to justify the illegitimate power of the military conqueror – the state.

Supremacist ideology

Supremacist ideologies gain the support of a society by claims that its members are superior to other groups and are naturally in conflict with other ethnic groups, nations, or social classes. Supremacists include the fascist governments of Italy, Germany and Japan in the World War II. European empires of the 15th to 20th century were partly motivated by misconceptions of white European superiority.

Communism

Communist ideologies gain the support of the working classes in a supposedly inevitable historical struggle between social classes. Communist ideology requires the state to own the means of production, and permits more state power over the lives of individuals than any other social system. Instead of supporting the human nature that actually evolved, communists believed they could create a "new man" who would work altruistically for the state. All communist states have failed, and most have failed catastrophically.

Religious fundamentalism

Religion is closely related to the collective identity and morality of humans, and a majority of the human population find it useful in providing a philosophy of life and assisting in the raising of children and other basic aspects of the human lifecycle. Religion also plays a key role in "tribal identity." Most governments find it useful to claim that their policies are supported by a popular religion, because no-one can challenge the legitimacy of a supernatural god who is by definition outside of human understanding. Religious fundamentalist ideologies frequently sacrifice human rights in favor of the centralized power of the state and its religious institutions.

Personality cult

Charismatic leaders play a part in all political systems by creating trust in state power and helping to legitimize its parasitic control of the population. In dictatorships, conflicts are often sought with other states, and the aggressive posture of a charismatic leader seems to encourage the loyalty of the population, even if human rights are withheld.

Socialism

Socialism comprises a variety of ideologies that range from communism, in which the state owns the means of production and controls most aspects of life, to communitarian philosophies that may be compatible with commercial markets, but which use taxation and government intervention freely in the interests of economic egalitarianism. Socialist reformers may have rational goals, such as the reduction of wealth differentials between rich and poor, and world peace, but they mistakenly pursue these goals through centralized dictatorship, rather than by accepting the naturally balanced society that would result from human freedom.

Social Democracy – sovereignty of the people

Democracy implies that citizens can remove a government that they dislike, which is a step in the right direction, away from absolute monarchy or religious fundamentalism, in which the general population is "owned" by the state. In practice, however, the sovereignty (absolute power) taken from monarchs is adopted by the democratic majority, which can then confiscate the human rights of the minority as surely as any dictator.

Although democracies tend to be less extreme than purely fascist or communist states, they incorporate aspects of enforced equality (through nationalism and welfarism) and of enforced inequality (through hierarchy based on regulation of professional monopolies, restriction of trade, licensing, etc.). Thus democracies can be said to incorporate a proportion of what can be called "communo-fascism," e.g. a mixture of enforced hierarchy and enforced equality. For this reason, democracy has lost much of its credibility worldwide.

Nationalism

Nationalism is the most universal state ideology, because sovereign states exist in mutual insecurity and must prepare their subjects for offensive or defensive warfare. If humans are successful in creating an adaptive global civilization, warfare will become impossible through the legal constraints on political leaders, and economic competition will be attenuated by the global network of collaboration that is certain to cross ethnic and regional boundaries.

Nationalism is a deadly evil, but it can be easily eliminated by the abolition of sovereign power. When humans abolish sovereign power is abolished, all humans will live under the same law. Given that states fail to achieve what humans need, why have we not created supra-national institutions?

Why are People Deceived by Ideologies?

All the ideologies used by coercive states are patently based on false information and some appear ridiculous. So why are they so effective in creating slave-like passivity in populations of tens of millions of people?

The main reason is that humans, despite their high intelligence and powerful preference for freedom, have evolved a strong biological desire to serve their social group. During the late stage of human evolution, when groups were often forced to kill each other for resources, the individual could not survive without the support of an aggressive group. But the group could not survive without the support of its members, so natural selection may have favored loyalty, especially in times of aggressive conflict with other groups.

Loyalty to one's family and friends in a small band of people is good survival behavior and rational. Modern societies with millions of people result from the success of the human species, yet they provide a habitat that is abnormal from the genetic viewpoint. When such a society is controlled by a parasitic state, loyalty to it ceases to be a virtue, since the existence of competition, rather than collaboration, between nation states is entirely damaging to the human species and to the individuals within it, other than the controlling elites.

Only free people can Create a Complete Civilization

If we consider the history of state power, one conclusion is irrefutable: if civilization is "living by contract" it cannot emerge from any society in which sovereign power is exercised. If the only civilized power is that based on contract, it follows that the only legitimate form of human government is the "bottom-up" management of society that evolved in nature. This raises the issue of how to apply the natural form of human social organization to the mass populations of industrialized societies.

All societies generate conflict but, in an adaptive society, modeled on the natural social structure that evolved with humans, most conflict is resolved harmlessly, because every individual has a stake in the maintenance of reciprocal goodwill between group members. Similarly, welfare is implemented without a second thought, because individuals know that equitable behavior is the expected norm, and that others will reciprocate with equity when the need arises.

This kind of moral reciprocity cannot exist in a society larger than about 150 persons, according to British anthropologist Robin Dunbar, who found a correlation between primate brain size and the average size of their social groups. For humans, the size of the neocortex dictates that 150 is the maximum size of a group in which individuals can relate to every person and also understand the relationships between them. (Dunbar 1992).

In contrast, a democratic government deals with welfare by first stealing resources from the general population through taxation, which is always unfairly gathered, due to the inherent difficulty of defining "income" equitably and the numerous means of avoidance dreamed up by accountants. Secondly, when the government provides welfare to claimants, including poor people, large corporations with special needs, and industries that are deemed worthy of subsidies, the distribution is related to lobbying power, and not morality. Therefore, taxation is an amoral system, biologically unsuited to redistribution of resources in a human community.

In fact, coercive resource redistribution of any kind is immoral in principle, and will be unnecessary in a truly civilized society, in which open markets reduce differentials and minimize the need for welfare, and moral behavior strongly supports appropriate welfare.

Chapter 7

Replacing the State by Free Communities

*T*he sovereign power of all current governments arose from the military conquest of the subject people. How do political scientists justify the power of any state to control its population or its territory? They don't. As political historian, Istvan Hont writes: "We still do not (and perhaps cannot) possess a theory that can provide an ultimate justification of national boundaries." (Hont 2010)

Governments originally took over by force, and then insisted on maintaining a monopoly of force. The ownership of states changes in the same manner as criminal territories change in gangland. As Hont notes: "Europe in 1500 included some five hundred more-or-less independent units; the Europe of 1900 approximately twenty-five." The state is simply a historical legacy from which people have found it difficult to escape.

If the human species wishes to be fully civilized, it must replace sovereignty with legitimate, consensual self-government. That means rediscovering the natural social organization that evolved with humans, but was corrupted by the harmful side-effects of technology 10,000 years ago.

This will be our species' "second attempt" at civilization. In order to avoid the conflict over resources that triggered the invention of warfare, the human species must ensure that sovereign power is utterly prohibited and that global markets are absolutely free.

If humans wish to break free from the deadly stranglehold of the state, they need to create a new system of global, natural law that will support the non-aggression principle, as I explained in Chapter 2. Only this will eliminate the damage done by the state. But what kind of human community will replace existing societies? Of course, once humans are free of the shackles of the state, the human species will blossom and expand, both culturally and economically.

Future society is unpredictable, but we can be sure that humans will choose to re-create small communities based on high-trust relationships, like the bands in which early humans lived. Now, with the hindsight of the damage done to humans by the sovereign state, we must support the biological needs of our species for morality, autonomy and equitable justice on a species-wide basis.

Conflict between Small Communities in Mass Society

If the pre-agricultural band, comprising several extended families, is the normal human society, then the same entity will reappear automatically in mass societies when the distorting force of the parasite state is removed. The challenging issue is how thousands, or millions, of such small social units can be aggregated to represent the governmental needs of large-scale, regional societies.

I propose that the civilized relationships between human bands will result from their interaction with one another, mediated by the prevailing law, just as the harmonious relationships between individuals are reinforced by laws. We already have experience of how humans respond to laws. At one extreme, nation states have different laws and no effective international law; this system cannot resolve conflicts, and conflicts grow into warfare, with millions of deaths. At the other extreme, small religious communities with well-studied, but consensual, rules can keep crime levels close to zero.

Large numbers of small communities that comply with identical natural law will be able to form peer-to-peer networks that will be trusted by their members and therefore can provide financial and social services. If millions of bands are aggregated by means of Internet communications, and are capable of acting in unison under the direct control of their members, then they can express their social and financial power on a regional or even global level, without the necessity for coercion.

Autonomous communities will require absolute freedom from sovereign power. This means that full, voluntary governance is only possible on a global scale for the whole human species. Any country attempting to implement voluntary governance without global coordination would face possible coercion from the existing states, which act out of amoral self-interest.

When the coercive, parasitical states is finally abandoned, humans will still want to associate themselves not only in small communities, but in larger associations of regional, tribal, religious, or any other affiliation that they see as advantageous. But there will be one enormous difference. All large-scale organizations will be voluntary and virtual. "Virtual" means that, unlike the sovereign states, the communities that choose to join together for any cultural or economic project will not necessarily occupy a contiguous area of land. Instead, populations with different affiliations will be mixed in every region. This will not generate conflict because there will be no sovereign power over which to fight.

Ownership of Our Own Bodies

Most of us would agree that men and women should own their own bodies – yet we do not, in any current society, because the sovereign power of the state enables it to set aside that ownership whenever it is beneficial to the ruling group. For example, the laws against abortion in many countries constitute the state's use of force to overthrow a woman's natural right to ownership of her body.

The most extreme view that contravenes self-ownership is the belief that a woman who has been raped and has a day-old fertilized egg in her womb, must be forced to allow it to develop and give birth to the child of the rapist. A fertilized embryo is simply a group of cells that has no conscious brain, no morality, and no human shape – it has the potential to create a human being, just as one egg and one sperm before fertilization have that potential, but neither constitutes a human being. If some people think that a woman's rights to own and manager her own body can be taken away by force for the sake of a few unfeeling cells of a fertilized embryo that were built by that same woman's body, then they are rejecting the contract of civilization – the non-aggression principle – in favor of the principle of "might is right," a principle that can and regularly does quickly lead to unutterable horror.

At the opposite extreme, a woman who wishes to abort a pregnancy after several months, when the fetus may be viable, is contemplating a drastic decision. But the right to make this decision is the woman's and hers alone, quite irrespective of whether other people may agree or disagree with her decision. For example, it may be that the birth of a baby would put the mother's life is at risk, or that the baby would be severely handicapped – such contingencies would engender sympathy with her decision. However, if the fetus were healthy, and she terminated it because she felt that it would be a burden to her in her planned career as a stripper, public sympathy might wane. But, either way, the opinions of others is immaterial, because under the contract of civilization – the implicit contract that is the only one that saves us from the unutterable horror of the jungle – the woman's body is hers and hers alone, to control provided that she does not harm another human, and a human is, by definition, someone who has been born.

Some people claim that a fetus inside a woman's body has rights that supersede those of its mother. But the only concept of rights recognized in all societies is the implicit consensus against the initiation of force described above. Rights are simply the extension, by a social contract, of the desire of humans to defend themselves against the initiation of force. No rights can overcome the natural right of ownership that men and women have over their own bodies.

A fertilized embryo cannot defend itself, nor demand to be defended. Although a woman and her relatives may place extreme value on the survival of her fetus, the "right" of its survival as part of her body belongs to the mother and there is no logical meaning in claiming that the fetus itself has rights. This is quite irrespective of the "viability" of the fetus. Even if the fetus is due to be born on the very next day, it is not yet a "child" because human life commences at birth.

I must make it clear that I am not advocating termination of pregnancy – but I am advocating the absolute right of (competent, adult) persons to make decisions about their own bodies. I believe that respect for human rights is essential for the health and happiness of individuals and their communities. For example, it is very natural for mothers and fathers to protect the fetuses that are their future offspring, even at great cost to themselves, because they highly value their future children. The love of parents for children is an extremely strong safeguard for most fetuses. The rights that a just society grants to a mother over her body offer a much stronger guarantee for most fetuses than the hypothetical "rights" that are attributed to the fetus, which is helpless.

What about the rights of the father over the fetus? Stable parents tend to develop a deep mutual sense of loyalty and duty, especially with regard to the success of a project to produce children. It is natural for prospective mothers and fathers to collaborate deeply over attempts to produce a child, and perhaps even more over the traumatic decision to terminate a pregnancy. There are sometimes extremely compelling medical reasons to terminate a pregnancy, for example, to avoid the birth of a child with extreme handicap or lethal disease. Yet, the potential mother is not the property of the prospective father, but a human being; she must have the final word over what happens to her own body, including the contents of her womb.

The same, would, of course, apply to the father. Supposing that a couple has eight children and both partners agree strongly to seek the best contraception. Their mutual discussion might identify the best solution as being that the father should seek a vasectomy. Yet, the final decision is his alone: he is not his mate's property, but a human being who owns his own body.

Where the powerful protection of the fetus by the parents of the future child is missing, then concern for the fetus is misplaced. It is parallel to the anger of vegetarians in the killing of animals for meat. Vegetarians have every right to value animals highly and to refrain from eating meat. But nature contains no restraints of any kind against the daily slaughter of millions of animals by their predators. Humans are also predators that have slaughtered animals to eat for millions of years. Uniquely, humans have evolved morality, and laws, that enable them to usually refrain from harming one another. These laws are only agreements, and if one side breaks that agreement, the other side will reciprocate, which may result in uncontrolled slaughter.

Animals, of course, cannot make a contract with humans to refrain from violence, and so humans continue to kill and eat them. Many vegetarians are opposed to this practice, but if they act upon their feelings by using force against other humans, they are breaking the contract of civilization and are likely to experience retaliation, either from their victims, or from the law that should act on behalf of victims. While it is good that some people can empathize with animals and attempt to protect them, any attempt to force others to value animals as the equivalent of humans is irrational and likely to involve criminal behavior.

In summary, however much individuals wish to change the behavior of others to comply with their own preferences, if they initiate force to implement their preferences, they must be classified as criminals.

Conscription for Warfare

Civilized behavior is based upon the implicit social contract to refrain from using force against others unless they use force first. This contract means that we should "own our own bodies." But when parasitic governments wish to use people as proxies to fight their wars against other states, they soon abandon the pretense of civilization and employ conscription to enslave people and force them to train as soldiers to kill innocent strangers upon command. Enslaved humans killed hundreds of millions of people during the 20th century, about three times more than all the wars in history before that time. Modern "total" warfare kills more civilians than soldiers, and future wars using nuclear weapons have the potential to increase civilian casualties to the hundreds of millions. Yet, because the state has the power to conquer its subjects, the population has accepted that the state "owns" them.

All these abuses by the state represent the negation of the natural social order, in which the genetically influenced choice of free human individuals drives the process of evolution that protects the thriving of any natural human society. In the more natural societies of the evolutionary era, people owned their own bodies, and only if this continues to be true is real civilization possible.

Rather than argue endlessly about these individual rights, it is simpler for those who believe in human freedom to express their belief that men and women should "own" their own bodies. Ownership by an individual of an item of property, including the human body, should mean that the owner can do *anything* to that property that does not contravene the rights of others.

But the corollary is also true; nobody has the right to force a free man or woman who has not harmed anyone, to do something they do not want to do. So conscription into an army is impossible in a free society.

People Easily Lose Sight of the Value of Freedom

Of course, many people do not believe in personal freedom. They believe that they, and others with similar views, especially if they are a majority of society, have the right to stop others doing things of which they disapprove, such as practicing homosexuality, or doing certain kinds of work without joining the relevant trade union, or choosing to reject the dominant religion, or sunbathing naked, or smoking cigarettes in private, or not wearing a seat belt. When challenged, such collectivist bullies may claim that minority behavior is inconvenience for others, and that self-destructive activities may increase hospital bills paid out of taxation.

However, people are not born merely to please others, and if some people feel that other members of society are objectionable, they can find ways to avoid their company. As for hospital costs, in a free society, we are not obliged to be charitable. It is entirely up to our individual

moral conscience whether we choose to help people who injure themselves by reckless or depraved behavior. We cannot use the "charity" of
the state, which steals our resources as taxation to run socialized medicine, as an excuse to steal away other people's right to live their lives as
they wish.

The simple fact is that people act most responsibly when they are
made responsible for their own lives. Collective, socialist solutions
simply remove that responsibility and increase the role of the parasitic
state. There is no justification for the use of force except self-defense.
People who believe that the "majority" has a right to take away the rights
of the individual person who is not harming others are as evil as rapists
or thieves. Communism, fascism and democracy are all ideologies that
employ sovereign power won by military conquest to abuse and loot the
innocent public. The right to do anything that is harmless to others
evolved in nature, and is the only basis for civilization. When we use
collective power to reduce individual freedom, then we build our societies on a foundation of injustice.

The ultimate aim of supporting human rights is to greatly improve
the quality of life for most people, and I hope that my readers will mostly
agree with me in this. However, it does not follow that we can consider
individual cases and decide whether to support human rights or to overrule the individuals involved because we think we know better. Some
people do have the hubris to think they know better – especially communists, fascists and other supporters of totalitarian creeds. But often,
unimaginable horror has followed in the wake of those who have sacrificed individual rights because they thought that they knew better.

Property rights

The ownership of fixed property such as buildings and land is often
controversial. Land is a finite resource, and billions of people would like
the opportunity to compete for control of it. The global distribution of
housing and land is particularly inequitable, with some individuals owning thousands of acres and building great mansions and factories, while
millions of the poor live in shanty towns, squatting on land they do not
own.

The state is the culprit, because it has blocked the free markets that
would have led to more equitable distribution. The super-rich and the
politicians that sell favors to the elite benefit from the inequitable distribution of resources. The majority are told that determination and hard

work will enable them to acquire property, but this is only partly true. For millions of people in poor countries, simply obtaining food and clean drinking water is out of reach. Therefore, it is virtually impossible for a large part of the world's population to acquire property; even a house in which to live.

The solution to this inequity does not lie in taxing (stealing from) the rich to support the poor as a caste of slaves living near to subsistence. The solution lies in creating fair and fully competitive markets for everything, so that human reward accurately reflects individual industry and ability. A just society requires the total abolition of the hugely distorting pressure of state coercion on markets. An absolutely fair and open market in land must exist everywhere, by removing the state restrictions that have created inequality.

The traditional ownership of large land areas by aristocrats, who acquired the land and the people on it from the state, generally contravened the earlier ownership of the same land by its native inhabitants. The inequitable distribution of land and housing in modern times reflects the artificial power of corporations based on state law, the state's creation of a social hierarchy by differential rewards for social classes, and the state's embrace of the capitalist/employee division, which means that a minority of people are players in markets, while others are simply commodities bought and sold as units of labor. Even more extreme, of course, are the grotesque distortions in land ownership that result from state policies of colonialism, imperialism, and racism.

Property is the great, criminal conspiracy at the heart of human "un-civilization." If we are to create a real human civilization – an adaptive society – then a primary task is the passing of uniform global laws to protect property rights, including the first creation of property ownership from the wilderness, and the transmission of title to land and buildings for every person on the planet. Absolute equality of access to land markets, absolute transparency of process, and absolute abolition of state power over the economy are the keys to an equitable solution.

Creating Systematic Global Property Rights

Existing property rights in land have often resulted from the principle of "might is right." In the 19th century, Europeans displaced native populations in the Americas, Africa, Australia, and elsewhere, through both the spread of European diseases, against which the indigenous populations had no immunity, and armed conflict, including genocide.

In the case of new property in finite resources such as land, there has to be a system to determine how people can become owners. Philosophers have tended to romanticize the creation of property by claiming that individuals naturally "earn" the right to ownership. For example, UK philosopher John Locke (Locke 2007) proposed that ownership was created when an individual "mixed his labor" with something removed out of the state of nature, such as land or the plant or animal life on it.

Under global law, the key to justice in the creation of new property is not a perfect system of creating new rights, as much as perfect equality of access. Provided that people feel that they have the same opportunity as all others to acquire new property, the exact method of creating new property from wilderness areas may be unimportant.

Immigration Control in the Free Market

For most people, the scrapping of nation state immigration controls would be another beneficial step forward in personal freedom, similar to the hugely beneficial freedom of movement obtained when the aristocratic feudal system ended in China, Europe, and Japan. Feudalism locked people into villages and towns, so that they became virtually the property of local hereditary lords; modern progress in civilization was impossible until that system was abolished. Today, the coercive, parasitical nation state acts like feudal aristocrats, blocking international freedom of movement, curtailing technology transfer and the freedom of trade, and creating artificial poverty.

Some people will object that, if property rights replaced the sovereign state, large numbers of people might emigrate from poor countries to rich countries, causing damage to culture and the environment at their destination. Currently, rich countries control such immigration by means of passports and visas in the supposed interests of their citizens.

There is often intense disagreement about such policies, because employers in rich countries, and the relatives of poor immigrants, want to permit immigration, while trade unions afraid of job competition, and people who feel threatened by sudden changes to the cultural environment and the demand for local services, do not want to allow the immigrants access. What would happen in a fully civilized society where the arbitrary force of sovereign government had been abolished?

Perhaps the first thing to say is that the large-scale emigration from poor countries to rich ones is a temporary problem caused by the barriers to equalization of wealth in the world put up by sovereign states. If sovereign power is abolished, free markets (absolute freedom of movement for money, technology, people, and goods) will tend to drive the reduction of wealth differential throughout the world. When wealth is much more equitably owned, large migrations of people will cease, because the incentive of better living standards will disappear, while the disincentive of alien culture and language will remain.

But some unwelcome migration may still occur and it is understandable for communities to desire protection against the disruption caused by the sudden large-scale immigration of foreigners.

In a mass society free of state power, natural-sized human communities can collaborate voluntarily in the same way that autonomous individuals can choose to collaborate voluntarily. The resources of millions of individuals can be aggregated without coercion, and used democratically for any social or commercial purpose.

Such projects may include the use of financial resources by communities to insulate local culture from alien immigration. Regional groups that acquire sufficient ownership rights over their houses, streets and other infrastructure can, by peaceful means, prevent the sudden influx of large numbers of immigrants.

In principle, this could constitute irrational racial discrimination. However, peaceful discrimination against other groups is self-limiting, because of its commercial cost. Groups that discriminate racially have a lot to lose in a free society, which explains the rapid reduction of overt racism in current societies, influenced by the globalization of trade and the necessity to maintain normal relations with trading partners from other racial subgroups. Nevertheless, the ability of autonomous communities to protect their cultures from unwelcome and extreme cultural change is desired, is needed, and is compatible with civilization.

The solution for small, wealthy communities that fear immigration is to contract with like-minded people and collectively purchase the rights to residential areas and urban facilities for the exclusive use of their own group. This solution might be useful for groups that prefer not to integrate with the mass population, such as religious minorities, people who wish to live in a particular language environment or culture, and those with alternative lifestyles, such as nudists. Of course, such private communities could not exclude outside groups from using the transport links and other public facilities necessary to travel between their own preferred communities.

When individuals are no longer slaves to the nation state, they will also have legal equality to all other adults in the species, under global human law. But until now, industrialization has introduced great inequality between humans. Large corporations can dominate individuals, imposing one-sided contracts. Sometimes, corporations cause great harm through reckless industrial operations, knowing that the state will not hold them accountable for their actions.

Federation of Community Economic Power

Allowing people to naturally determine their own social organization will result in a re-emergence, in one form or another, of the normal band model of less than 100 people. Within each small human community, a cluster of adults will interact with one another on a voluntary, peer-to-peer basis. Similarly, in a mass society, it is likely that clusters of such small communities will utilize Internet technology to enable their members to aggregated their individual resources whenever desired. This will mean that huge investment capital will be available from millions of individuals who will be entirely autonomous, and yet benefit from their membership of a strongly affiliated group. Such groups can invest in anything, but local infrastructure and businesses will be particularly appropriate. Over time, local groups can have a large ownership stake in their regions. The members of a community will be able to opt-in or opt-out of any specific investment project. Investments supervised by community expertise will be trustworthy, because financial experts working for a community will be answerable to all the individual members.

The same kind of aggregation of voting power will enable groups to be confederated at a regional and even global level, enabling decisions made about global law, for example, to be controlled by the global population without any political mediation. Incidentally, when this happens, it will eliminate most of the wealth differentials that give rise to the need for welfare.

More important, the family structure of the band will provide the social context in which people needing help will receive it as they did in nature for millions of years. For needy individuals outside of any specific family, it will be extremely easy and inexpensive for the band to agree on voluntary charitable subscriptions to provide necessary welfare, education, and medical treatment.

Humans are compassionate, and a free society will also be considered "just" by a great majority of its members. Therefore, the willingness to be charitable, already manifest in state-dominated societies, will be a backstop to human suffering. Note, too, that welfare embezzlement will be reduced to almost zero in a face-to-face society in which those in charge are the adults of the local community.

When whole communities fall on hard times, perhaps through a natural disaster, the confederated structure of society will also provide ample assistance, on the same principle

Extending Property Ownership

Extending property ownership can help poor people who rent housing, or who live in shanty towns, to own their own property, to be connected to utilities and services, and thereby gain access to participate in the economy and overcome their poverty.

But merely extending property ownership has one drawback. For example, supposing coral reefs become private property – some owners might take the short view and cut the coral up to sell to gift shops. Likewise, country parks might be sold off as real estate and become urban sprawl, and city parks could be replaced by more profitable skyscrapers. How do we manage conservation in societies with no coercive state?

The first thing to understand about a society free of coercive government, is that it has the same total resources and these will grow more rapidly in free market conditions. We all know that communism led to inefficient industries and poverty that in turn resulted in the destruction of many natural resources. In principle, all current states are coercive and operate on the same principle as communism, except that their power to control society is temporarily reduced.

Free markets work so well because they enable people to get what they want, which means that if people want conservation, they can get it. The purchasing power of a free society will be expressed through the voluntary confederation of many small communities. Within each community, every individual will decide in what she or he wishes to invest. A community, or confederated communities, can retain fund managers as a service to members.

So it will be very easy for millions of people to invest, using management companies owned by their confederated communities, in which they can place a very high degree of trust. In short, such mechanisms will enable conservation projects to be funded, provided that they have popular support. Conservation in isolation cannot constitute an economically self-financing activity. Conservation projects will usually become self-financing only when their existence raises the quality of life, and therefore the revenue earned by a much larger development. I discuss this below under "Public Goods."

Land is a finite resource and in order to have an effective market in land, land reform may be necessary at some locations to remedy very inequitable means of allocation resulting from wars or colonization. For example, where colonization has concentrated the land into the hands of a few owners, leaving local populations landless, then a remedy may be needed.

This is a sensitive issue, for legitimate property rights that have been earned should be treated as sacrosanct, in order to optimize security and justice in the market. In the past, land reform by sovereign governments has often been arbitrary and unjust.

Therefore, equitable land reform can only be carried out according to internationally agreed rules formulated by a body with no regional bias. Whereas those people who are subjected to land reform by current governments may sometimes feel that they are victims of an inequitable political agenda, this grievance would surely decrease if land reform was a global remedy, the purpose of which was purely to secure equitable and fair markets.

Free Market Elimination of Compulsory Purchase

When major new infrastructure such as railways or airports is built in today's economies the developers usually need to buy large areas of land from existing owners. Some owners may refuse to sell, or hold out for unreasonably high prices, so to overcome this problem, governments step in and force them to sell, under a compulsory purchase law which is known in the USA as "eminent domain."

One argument against eminent domain is that it was intended that the government be given powers of compulsory purchase only for major infrastructure that was in the public interest. However, it is arguable as to what is in the public interest. More recently, the US Supreme Court has allowed compulsory purchase for ordinary commercial development, which amounts to arbitrary government.

In an adaptive society, there can be no coercive government to intervene arbitrarily in the economy on the side of firms or consortia that plan to build infrastructure such as railways or airports – even if it is socially desirable that they should be built. Therefore, another mechanism will be needed, free of arbitrary state power. Such a solution will have to be global, to conform to the basic requirement that all coercion must ultimately rest on the non-aggression principle and should be universal and bear equally on all humans. To illustrate the kind of solution that would be appropriate, I proffer the concept of "collective domain."

I propose Collective Domain as a free market solution to facilitate purchase of land for large scale developments, including necessary infrastructure, such as railways, roads, and airports. This solution is based on the assumption that any land and buildings may at some time be subject to attempts at purchase offers by developers of major infrastructure projects.

To operate this system, the title deeds to all freehold or leased property must be written in a way that recognizes the possible need for collective relinquishment of affected properties in the face of projects of higher economic value. The creation of collective domain requires that all real estate contracts should incorporate requirements for a *collective decision* by all affected owners to sell or not in the event of an outside offer to buy land for major redevelopment.

Thus, if an infrastructure development company wants to build on occupied land, the company owners must approach all affected property owners, and make them an offer, which would typically be the estimated market value plus a significant uplift to represent the value placed by the existing property owners on such things as the inconvenience of moving or their sentimental attachment to the property. The price demanded could be, for example, 20% more than the market value, a figure that might represents the "real" cost to the existing owners of relinquishing their property.

Under such a system, property owners who refuse to sell purely for tactical reasons (called "holdouts"), and who might otherwise be in a position to extort excessively high prices for their land, will have no opportunity to do so. Also, the government will not be able to force a sale unfairly at market value or take bribes from the buyers, both of which cheat the property owners. If any property owner feels that another site for the proposed development or another route for the road or railway would be better, he or she may try to gain the support of the collective owners to table that proposition.

If any owner has a property of exceptional value due, for example, the presence of an archeological or heritage site, this can be expressed in the market valuation of the property. To minimize conflict over such issues, we need both laws and codes of practice that recommend how people collaborate to be created at a global level, as part of the principle of human civilization that all people are equal under the law.

Collective domain would ensure that developers of large projects such as railways, canals or airports would have to pay the real market cost for the land they purchased. People threatened by new development would not have to protest against arbitrary state power; instead, they would simply have to make a commercial decision and accept the results of a ballot among the group of people subject to the same offer as themselves.

Such a system recognizes that construction of new infrastructure is absolutely essential, but that it can only be justified if its value to society enables it to pay the real market value of the homes and businesses that it displaces. This requirement is best met when the owners of the purchased properties have democratically accepted their collective relinquishment. This solution rests on the non-aggression principle.

Public Goods are Collective Property

Economists claim that certain things, such as military defense, are "public goods" that must be supplied by the state, because they cannot be supplied by the commercial market. The reason given is that defense and other public goods are "non-excludable," which means that all members of society will benefit from them, and therefore should be forced by the state to pay their share of the cost.

In a free society with no coercive state, the majority could agree to contribute funds to buy weapons for national defense. However, if a minority of people refused to pay their share, they would be "free riders", subsidized by those who did pay.

Some people opposed to state coercion argue that defense could be supplied by market mechanisms and their efforts, often bolstered by the mathematics of game theory, show great ingenuity that may well be useful in managing the market mechanisms of future free societies. Nevertheless, no clear alternative has been found to fund defense without coercive taxation. Lawyer and economist David D. Friedman, discusses many approaches to free market defense, but without notable success, in his book *The Machinery of Freedom*. (Friedman 2009)

If it did not prove practicable to create free market defense, he says, "I would still regard the government as a criminal organization, but one which was, by a freak of fate, temporarily useful. It would be like a gang of bandits who, while occasionally robbing the villages in their territory, served to keep off other and more rapacious gangs. I do not approve of any government, but I will tolerate one so long as the only other choice is another, worse government."

In my view, both the proponents and enemies of state coercion miss the point when they argue about the practicalities of free market defense. What such people are ignoring is that warfare itself is, in the modern age, solely a product of state coercion. When we remove from governments worldwide their arbitrary privilege of coercion, and force political leaders to be equal to ordinary citizens under the law, war will, literally, vanish. Any subsequent initiation of force will no longer be warfare – it will simply be crime. And if leaders are equal under the law and subject to the glare of publicity, then violent crime will become extremely difficult for them to accomplish.

The real solution to the problem of funding "the public good" of defense is to implement global laws that remove coercive government and the need for warfare. I explain how to implement such laws in Chapter 8.

Bridges are "Non-Rivalrous"

Another reason why economists say that public goods should be supplied by the state is that they are "non-rivalrous," which means that, if they were provided by the state and paid for out of taxation, the social cost would be the same but more people would be able to use them thus increasing their productivity.

Use of a bridge by one person, for example, does not prevent additional users, but if a private bridge builder charges a toll for crossing the bridge, the usage is limited, and may be regarded as inefficient compared to a toll-free government bridge that will be used by a larger number of people.

However, this argument assumes that if more people use something, efficiency has necessarily increased. This is not the case. In a perfect free market economy, every individual would pay for what they used and for nothing else. This would bring about the most effective investment of social resources that could be conceived. If the state uses force to make some people subsidize the use of a bridge by other people, there is no overall increase in efficiency.

All investment has an opportunity cost, which is the value that would be generated if the investment were used for something else. If the state forces taxpayers to subsidize some of those who use the bridge, the opportunity cost of the investment is unknown. Also, if tolls are not charged, the bridge is more likely to be congested and those businesses that obtain most value from using the bridge, and that would otherwise be prepared to pay high tolls, can be blocked by users who gain much less, generating inefficiency.

This argument applies to everything in the economy. Consumers obtain the optimum combination of goods and services at the best price when they are obliged to pay for what they need, but are protected from being charged for what they do not need.

After defense and the law, there are many other things that are described as public goods, because their acquisition requires collective action in the market place, and collective action in the market is always more difficult than private buying or selling. However, all such collective actions will be resolved easily in free market conditions. I will discuss some of these below.

Bee Pollination and Other Beneficial Externalities

Sometimes, bees used for honey production are kept in hives close to farmers' fields, so that the bees pollinate the farmers' crops while collecting nectar, with mutual benefit to both businesses. However, if there are plenty of alternative sources of nectar nearby, farmers may have to pay the beekeepers to locate hives on their land. Or, if sources of nectar are scarce, beekeepers may have to pay the farmers to permit the hives to be sited on the farmland.

However, if a large number of farmers and bee-keepers would have to be included in negotiations, then high transaction costs may ensue, and prevent the negotiation of advantageous arrangements. Therefore, the state may legislate to force cooperation between the beekeepers and the farmers to obtain this "public good." (Coase 1960)

The error in this state intervention is that, if the value of cooperation is already high enough to cover the additional social cost of legislation, then it may also cover the cost of an alternative free market solution. In the free, self-governing societies of the future, all individuals will be members of local communities that will need to be confederated, ultimately, up to the level of the global population, in order to deal with major economic projects. Undoubtedly, the rules for inter-community cooperation will be standardized, as voluntary, industrial "Codes of Practice" that will provide models that can easily be emulated, without the necessity for complex negotiations, or state compulsion. When free market transactions are standardized and computerized, transaction costs virtually disappear.

Non-Revenue Earning Assets such as Parks

There are some cases in which facilities needed in civilized life seem to be public goods, because their value to society cannot easily be collected from those who enjoy them. At first sight, the creation of parks in cities seems to fit the requirements for a public good. All the people who live in, or visit, a city will value a park and there is little doubt that a city with an above-average area of green spaces will be preferred to other cities.

This means that parks contribute to the success of cities, helping them attract new residents, shops, commercial companies looking to locate offices, and visitors, including tourists who bring money from outside. But a park is a capital investment that provides a return on its investment, which is spread unevenly over all residents and visitors to a city over decades, or even hundreds of years. This may mean that it is *impossible* to calculate the benefits received by particular individuals, or to charge them fairly for those benefits.

If a fee is charged for use of the park, it would have to be extremely high to provide an adequate return on the high asset value of the city center land used. And even if a low charge was levied, it would exclude access to the park by low-income people who have the greatest need for the amenity, and this would reduce the value of the park to the city. It may be that some parks could be created from charitable trusts set up for the purpose by wealthy benefactors, but charity would be unlikely to satisfy the overall need for parks.

The key to solving the public good problem of parks is to realize that, in future, the market system will necessarily embrace all aspects of the infrastructure of civilization, including the construction of new cities. In a competitive, globalized world, cities will compete with one another for all incoming investment, including commercial corporations, retailers, high-income residents, and the hospitality trade, including conferences, exhibitions, and tourism.

The intensification of inter-city competition will mean that those responsible for developing any parts of both existing and new cities will have to work on a commercial basis. That means taking account of the all relevant prices and costs as signals of the desires and needs of all the people in the region. This contrasts with the development of past cities, which often resulted from the whims of aristocrats, kings or dictators.

In the 20th century, many cities saw a perplexing collision between the incessant social engineering of the coercive state, especially the communist, socialist and democrats who thought that they knew what people wanted – and the forces of "the market" – which actually represents the financial choices made by millions of men and women who actually lived in the cities. Bureaucrats cleared away the slum housing of the poor and built standardized, high-rise blocks that looked neat on paper, but turned into desolate, gang-infested war zones. Architects dreamed up ideal estates made of concrete in which every human need was met – but nobody wanted to live in them. City planners dictated to the commercial interests that developed railways, ports, houses, offices and roads – but the result was always bureaucracy, high costs and poor service.

In contrast to planned cities, there was increasing evidence that cities that were not planned were actually more harmonious and attractive. For example, in the UK, during the 19th century, Manchester grew from little more than a village to become a giant industrial metropolis over a few decades of the industrial revolution without any planning. Frederic Engels, the disciple of communist intellectual Karl Marx, was astounded and bemused how spontaneous order could arise without "scientific" communist planning. The answer, of course, is that the market expresses the needs of ordinary people, providing synergies and solutions that optimize resources for all.

Like Manchester, hundreds of places in the USA started as gold rush towns, watering holes for cattle, railway stops or provisioning centers for farmers and cowboys, and grew organically to become great cities, without much planning.

In future, when cities are seen as commercial entities that must be optimized to provide a good return to *all* their business investors, then market surveys will reveal what people want, and that information will be used by individuals and companies to design each aspect of new cities in order to best satisfy the needs of all residents, businesses and visitors affected by the city, rich and poor alike. The creation of attractive parks will then become, not a loss-making obligation, but the creation of an important amenity that will help to make cities attractive – and, therefore, profitable – to everyone who experiences them.

By monetizing parks as amenities that improve the city's overall return on investment, the "public good" problem disappears. In a world of competing cities, city development will be commercial, but must take full account of the long-term return on investment in every kind of amenity that makes cities attractive. This is often likely to include a re-integration of social levels in mixed neighborhoods with pedestrian areas, parks, and other amenities that fit thriving, heterogeneous, natural human communities.

Who develops cities in a free society? The answer must be free individuals, free companies and free communities, that take account of price signals that represent the wishes of the millions of people who use the city in various ways. Some new cities may be built on land freshly assigned from wilderness or other undeveloped areas. This may require the participation of the regional community, expressed through confederal organization of self-governing human groups. In other cases, cities may be purely commercial ventures, probably adhering to voluntary global codes of practice that update the human requirements that cities meet. Either way, organic development must replace top-down social engineering.

Wilderness also Adds Value to the Quality of Life

In any region, the proportion of "wilderness" in which nature can predominate is also a basic concern to humans, since the destruction of all wildernesses would probably mean the destruction of the human species. If science establishes that humans cannot survive on Earth without a proportion of wilderness areas in which nature can predominate, then retention of wilderness regions should become part of "the natural human law" (see Chapter 8) that protect humans from harming one another. Such standards for conservation of wilderness areas and for public access to them will be expressed firstly as globally agreed laws that are ultimately based on the non-aggression principle, and second, as advisory codes of practice for distribution of wilderness within regions. The proximity of accessible wilderness will likely be a factor in the commercial success of a city and its region.

The state has taken over much of the education and medical services in the last two hundred years, and the price has been constantly inflating costs and low productivity, compared with other parts of the economy. It is time to re-examine the purpose of these services and then return them to the free market in order that the most advanced technology can be utilized in service delivery.

If we want to know how the poor will afford hospitals and education, we merely have to look at the USA today, where 70% of people below the poverty line have electricity, toilets, water, refrigerators, TV, mobile phones, cars, and air conditioning. In a future adaptive civilization with a level free market, the poorest people will be rich by today's standards. In addition, charity will be likely to blossom in a society in which communities and individuals are autonomous and the law is devoted to social justice.

Both medical services and schools represent obsolete delivery chains that have hardly changed since the 19th century, with little or no profit incentive, highly unionized staff, and generally very low utilization of equipment. It is easy to imagine fundamental change in the goals of medicine and education as well as the way that services are delivered.

It is extraordinary that medicine has remained a largely remedial service, when 80% of disease is related to lifestyle. The greatest social effort should surely be to eliminate the causes of disease. Doctors and hospitals provide remedial services, but in future, global databases should be able to link patient records with lifestyles and identify the causes of all non-genetic disease conditions. Examination and treatment delivery could also be automated to gain the huge cost advantages that have revolutionized manufacturing and other industries.

Compulsory Schooling Should be Abolished

Public schools were originally designed to train children in disciplines suitable for factory work and military service, and they have never been re-thought to address the needs of children in the modern age. The very idea of having up to two decades of education at the beginning of life, before children start to work, should be rejected. A more reasonable model would be for children to gain real work experience at the earliest possible age to help them build their individual identities, in parallel with education-on-demand available for their whole lives on the free market. Such a practice will not only help children identify and nurture their natural talents from a young age in their lifelong quest for "self-actualization, but also switch the focus of teaching from the mass-production processing of human "drones" towards the tutoring of students that have a deep love of their activities and are highly motivated to learn.

Let's Put Real *Morality* Behind Welfare

In a mass society, the provision of welfare "entitlements" is one of the key justifications for the heavy taxation wielded by coercive, parasitical governments. But why is so much welfare necessary?

There are two causes, both avoidable. First, enormous wealth differentials have been created by government's intervention in free markets. An adaptive society would abolish laws such as limited liability and current intellectual property rights that have created billionaires versus people with negative equity. I explain this problem and its remedy in Chapters 9 and 10.

Second, the centralization of society that resulted from state power has almost eliminated the extended family as the basis for human adaptation to the habitat. Only the "nuclear" family remains, and a high proportion of these seem to be dysfunctional, especially in the USA and Europe, creating a huge mass of people who have no one to help or be helped by, because they have become disaffiliated.

During evolution, when humans lived in small itinerant bands, mutual welfare was a part of survival behavior, since every individual depended on the integrity of the band, and the band could only be maintained with the support of its members. Furthermore, the band comprised one or more extended families, so most members shared family relationships. As a result, all humans have inherited genetically based behavior that supports mutual welfare in normal social conditions.

The effect of the state on human social organization is to destroy the integration of extended families and replace it by the reciprocal duties and privileges of each individual towards the state. Welfare is needed to support people who are incapable of supporting themselves, due to old age, or physical or mental disability. In addition, in an economy divided into employers and employees, unemployed workers and their families tend to need the support of society. The state steps in to fulfill this role by taking resources by force from the majority and redistributing them to those in most need.

This process is hugely inefficient, requiring millions of state employees to undertake a process that is ultimately against nature. People who legitimately earn money do not like to have it taken away from them, so that the very complex process of determining how much tax each person should pay is obstructed by the constant need to monitor the population and attempt to minimize tax evasion.

When the tax has been collected, the state has to determine who is deserving of receiving its bounty as welfare payments. In a partly free society, it is very easy for elements of the population to work for cash while posing as unemployed or unfit for work. Welfare fraud becomes a normal way of life, destroying citizens' trust in government or society.

Of course, politicians are high in the ranks of beneficiaries, but the subtle and close relations they have with trade and industry makes such corruption largely undetectable.

A greater loss caused by current government may be the loss of morality. In a natural society, people support welfare because they care about others, and those who are helped have a sense of gratitude and obligation that encourages them to minimize the burden they present to society. However, in a state controlled system, there is no sense of gratitude, merely one of entitlement, accompanied by the desire to maximize the claims that are made. Those who are heavily taxed to pay for the system may feel resentment, especially if they are familiar with the depth of the fraud accompanying the system.

A particular problem accompanies welfare that is paid out of taxation, which is the trend today. Brink Lindsey (Lindsey 2002) describes how collective social insurance was initiated by the 19th century statesman, Bismarck, who created the German Empire and was its first chancellor. The purpose of such welfare was to generate dependency on the state. "Whoever has a pension for his old age," said Bismark, "is far more content and far easier to handle than one who has no such prospect."

Lindsey explains that governments could compel workers to provide for their own retirement, but that would not inspire the proper feelings of dependency and subservience. Instead, governments prefer a pay-as-you-go system funded out of taxation. "The pay-as-you-go system flies flagrantly in the face of market logic," says Lindsey. "Indeed, when such ventures are attempted in the private sector, they go by the name of pyramid or Ponzi schemes and constitute criminal fraud."

In a pyramid scheme, the money is never put to productive use, because all the benefits received by participants are derived from the recruitment of new participants. In due course, the number of new participants dries up and the scheme collapses. The same thing happens to state pensions or other welfare paid from taxation. As the proportion of old people in the population rises, pensions, medical insurance and other welfare schemes collapse.

In contrast, the free societies of the future will be based on small, autonomous, and collaborative groups that are confederated to manage mass society, and can hire welfare management specialists directly. Welfare schemes will therefore serve the community holistically, because no parasitic state will exist to provide a conflict of interest. In other words, humans will work *with* nature, rather than against it, as people did for millions of years before the state took over.

Who Protects Society against General Threats?

Another general principle is that the members of a society are the only people who enjoy its benefits and value it and they must be jointly responsible for costs incurred to maintain the society. The same principle must apply to the species, once humans have united in its management.

Consider a major and general threat to human civilization – say a major asteroid strike. Asteroid strikes against the Earth serious enough to kill off a large proportion of organic life have happened many times before, but at long intervals of time. So although such a strike is not probable in any particular year, it would not be a surprising event either. If scientists were able to predict a likely future strike, they would try to formulate methods of attempting to deflect it, which would probably be extremely expensive. The question is: who would pay for the project?

Justice demands that the beneficiaries pay – that is, the whole human species – and most of us would give the tiny amount chargeable to each individual without demur. If anarchists, for example, refused to pay their share of the protection against the asteroid strike, on the basis of demanding total independence from other humans, they would be demanding to live outside the social contract of civilization itself. But it is the social contract of civilization and nothing else that is the basis of the law against the initiation of force. Once a person insists on being "outside the law", he or she becomes an outlaw, and the life of such an individual can no longer be protected by any laws based on a the social contract of civilization. In practice, such a choice is not viable: one reason is that these outlaws could be targeted by criminals, and as such, they would receive no protection or assistance from the police and the judiciary services.

People want to support their community

It is therefore clear that even in the free societies of the future, an individual who refuses to pay for measures necessary for the survival of the human species will be sabotaging the society on which the individual absolutely depends. Humans are a social species, and historically, they have generally supported their own society in times of need. In fact, humans have consistently been ready to fight and die for their country, even though nation states are arbitrary creations, and the governments that start wars are coercive parasites! I therefore conclude that the potential need to counter threats to the existence of humans on earth will be met by support from the whole human population.

Chapter 8

Global Natural Law for Absolute Human Equality

*T*o overcome the misuse of coercion by nation states, humans need to unite in a voluntary plebiscite to agree the simple global laws necessary to support the genetically inherited morality that we now know as the "non-aggression principle." Implementing the non-aggression principle can prevent all people, including political leaders, from initiating force for any purpose.

Many people may consider this project too ambitious, but anthropological evidence indicates that men and women have already lived by consensus in small egalitarian bands for much of the two million year evolutionary era, and they have learned how to prevent the emergence of coercive leaders who would have destroyed the group's moral culture.

Modern humans have inherited the habit of living mostly according to the non-aggression principle and we can all observe daily evidence of this. The exceptions to this rule, such as warfare and state control of the economy, are instigated by the imposed, parasitic culture of the state that we discussed in Chapter 2.

Scientific Law is Much Simpler than State Law

In order to appreciate the viability of introducing global law, it is important to realize that scientific global law is a much simpler concept than traditional state law.

The fact that modern law is *not* science-based is an anomaly. In industrialized countries, most of the professions, such as accountancy, architecture, the many disciplines of engineering, and medicine have been based on science since the 19th century. The reason is that practitioners of these disciplines need scientific methodology to fulfill their role in the modern world, which is based on numerous technologies.

The law was not made into a science and one reason is that this did not suit the state. Traditional law is convoluted, fragmented, and difficult to understand. Since the law is outside the comprehension of lay people, the government and the malleable legal profession can create laws that suit their own purposes, rather than the primary need of the general public for equitable dispute resolution and the sanctioning of criminals. The law has become enormously complex, incorporating regulations and restrictions on practically every conceivable aspect of life. This not only makes the law incomprehensible to the public, it also makes it too costly for use by most of the population.

Paradoxically, if the scientific community is commissioned to draw up a framework of global laws that will support civilized behavior for the whole human species, the actual laws necessary can be very simple. In 1850, Frédéric Bastiat, a great French writer, economist, and statesman, recognized the way that the law was being abused by the modern state. His monograph entitled *The Law* is a masterly discourse on the real function of law and how, when government uses the law to manipulate society according to its own arbitrary preconceptions, the result is a progression towards socialism and communism, with all the ills those societies bring.

Bastiat defines law as "The collective organization of the individual right to lawful defense." Each person has natural rights to defend his person, his liberty, and his property, which he calls "Three basic requirements for life."

"If every person has the right to defend, even by force, his person, his liberty, and his property, then it follows that a group of men has the right to organize and support a common force to protect these rights constantly."

Bastiat points out that this law cannot legitimately be used for any other purpose. "Since an individual cannot lawfully use force against the person, liberty, or property of another individual, then the law, which acts as a common force – for the same reason – cannot lawfully be used to destroy the person, liberty, or property of individuals or groups." (Bastiat 2007)

Natural Law is Based on Human Biology

If we consider what formal, explicit laws are necessary in any society to achieve the same result as was achieved by evolution in the pre-agricultural band, it appears that as few as four fundamental laws can be identified as indispensable; these together can be described as "natural human law."

First, group members must refrain from harming each other's persons or property. This is the "non-aggression principle," that is the basis of civilized behavior and which is still a central tenet of most moral and legal systems today.

Second, in order to protect persons and their property from force, the global human species must have the means of assigning property rights in a consistent manner. This must include the creation of rights in completely new property in wilderness areas or, in future, on other planets, and the assignment of these rights to claimants.

Third, the members of all human groups must collaborate in implementing the above laws, by defending fellow group members and their property against the initiation of violence by persons inside or outside the group. Without such collaboration, the first two laws would be contravened with impunity. In modern conditions, "collaboration" usually means accepting an appropriate share of the extremely low cost of implementing the laws.

Fourth, there is one more condition for the survival of any civilized community. If any community is to survive in the long term, its members must accept equal responsibility for the survival of the community in the face of any internal or external threat. In modern conditions, this law means that all humans who accept the contract of civilization must accept their share of the cost of defense of the species against extreme (but very rare) threats, such as climate change (if it is proven), or a potential asteroid collision with Earth. Since the human species can probably not survive indefinitely without becoming completely civilized, I believe that this condition, too, should be treated as a law.

Since the value provided by any voluntary association is shared equally among its members, any costs of maintaining the association must also be shared. Commonsense tells us that, if the members of any human group do not support its existence, then it will disappear. This must therefore apply to a voluntary civilization.

In practice, without civilization, very terrible things happen to humans (consider what happens under coercive, parasitic government, which is only part civilized), so it is reasonable to ask every human to agree to this condition, and to expect universal compliance.

It should be noted that the agreement of individuals to accept the cost of implementing the contract of civilized life is not a tax. It is simply the logical consequence of deciding to live in a civilized community. Prehistoric people who chose to live in a particular community would have also accepted their personal responsibility for the "social contract" implied by this decision, although the "cost" to them would have been the behavioral modification necessary for adults to collaborate in directly defending one another from aggression.

We can now list the essential laws of a fully civilized human species:

1. Contractual agreement among the members not to initiate force against others or their property.
2. Equitable laws for assigning property rights.
3. Contractual agreement to accept the individual's share of the cost of implementing laws 1 & 2.
4. Contractual agreement to share the cost of the defense of civilization against any external attack (Such as an asteroid colliding with Earth or climate change that may threaten to destroy the human race).

The above four laws are not arbitrary: they simply express the conditions necessary for the maintenance of civilization among any human group. Nobody "discovered" these laws; they evolved as implicit social constraints in prehistoric societies, simply because they express survival or "fitness" behavior. These laws create a social contract that has the powerful effect of forcing people to "live by contract," which is the formula for civilized behavior. Furthermore, after two million years of evolution, it is likely that all humans are to some degree genetically adapted to comply with these survival laws, even though individual cultures have distorted human relations.

Scientifically Mediated Coherent Tort Law

If we replace national law with the simple laws necessary to implement the non-aggression principle, we can live by compliance with this law, without any arbitrary coercion from government. But while the application of such natural law must have been very simple in pre-industrial human bands, its application in a large society based on numerous technologies is much more complex.

What if a million motorists each produce some air pollution that in aggregate is responsible for the death of 10 innocent people? Does society shrug off the deaths as the price of modern transport? If a steel foundry worth billions of dollars pollutes a town and makes some people ill, has the law been broken?

In modern societies, most pollution and destruction of nature is accepted as the price of economic productivity. This is because governments attach a high value to economic production, but a much lower value to the life or well-being of small numbers of people among a population of millions.

In contrast, an adaptive society must be self-governing and is based on a social contract – an agreement between all its members. If people choose to voluntarily agree upon the law that will constrain their own actions, as well as those of others, they must insist that the constraints on all individuals are identical. This means that genuine social contracts create a level playing field in which people are free to pursue any activity, provided that it is harmless. If an activity harms other persons, or their property, it must cease or be subject to legal redress.

In order to apply natural law in modern societies that use complex technologies, we must use scientific expertise to accurately measure the consequences of commercial and private activities that utilize technology. Such measurements will reveal whether specific technological practices will result in significant harm to others, and whether that harm is within the limits that society has decided to tolerate. I call this extension of basic legal principles "coherent" law, and discuss it below.

Many things harm people or their property, but in very small doses, the same things are usually harmless. For example, trace amounts of toxins such as cyanide or mercury in food may be harmless, while significant amounts may make people ill, or kill them. Small sounds may be unnoticed, but at high volume they may cause immediate injury. Air pollution is undetectable at very low levels, but at certain levels, it becomes a nuisance, and at higher levels, threatens people's health.

"Coherent" law requires that databases of scientific knowledge are maintained, so that society can make informed judgments about threshold values at which things that are nuisances become harmful and must be prohibited. In an adaptive society, it is necessary to prevent by law the operation of motor vehicles, power stations, or factories when their joint operation is at a level that can be expected to cause the injury or death of innocent people.

It is surely reasonable that the law should prohibit equally the initiation of all kinds of force. For example, existing laws prohibit the use against other persons of guns, knives, heavy objects or other physical weapons, including poisons and toxic gases. It is clear that industrial plants should be held legally responsible for any harm they cause to local populations. A classic example of this was the Bhopal disaster of December, 1984 in Bhopal, the capital of Madhya Pradesh, India. A pesticide plant operated by Union Carbide India Ltd emitted a lethal poison, methyl isocyanate, into the atmosphere. Many of the people affected by the disaster were too poor to be documented, but estimates range from the immediate official death toll of 2,259 to figures from outside observers that are ten times higher.

The purpose of coherent law is both to enable rational planning of the location and design of such plants to take place and also to assign responsibility for harms that do occur. Even if the law prohibits harm, and scientists accurately evaluate the level of technical side-effects that are likely to harm people, some people will still be injured or killed when events occur that could not reasonably have been anticipated. Such events are simply accidents that cannot be prevented by any reasonable means.

What will coherent law mean in practice? It will simply mean that productive industries and vehicle owners will have to clean up their act sooner, rather than later, in accordance with the rights of people not to be injured by reckless production of poisonous fumes or other harmful technologies.

Coherent Law needs an Apolitical, Scientific Foundation

The principle of natural law is solely concerned with a global agreement to prohibit the initiation of force, and to protect the human species if it is threatened by natural disaster. Since all people need to be protected from the initiation of force, these goals are apolitical and should be non-controversial.

The actual creation of natural law must also be absolutely apolitical and non-controversial. In order to achieve that, it will be necessary to create a global foundation to create a simple form of law that can be adopted everywhere. To ensure that laws are framed without regard to the political interests of any human group, the foundation must be staffed by a large, multicultural group of people, including scientists, sworn to serving the human species rather than any subgroup. Members of this group must be frequently replaced by fresh recruits to minimize the opportunity for corruption. The foundation's working procedures must be absolutely public and transparent, and available to the whole

Civilization

9. Global natural law
8. National state law
7. Feudal law
6. City state law
5. Village law
4. Chiefdom law
3. Tribal law
2. Hunter-gatherer law
1. Dominance hierarchy

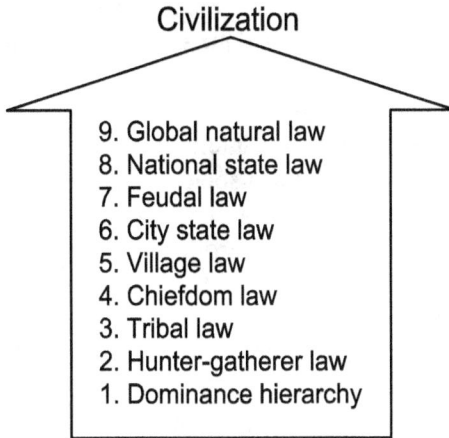

Fig. 7. Evolution of the Law. All human societies have depended on laws. As societies grew in size, the law evolved to suit the ruling group. The final step to a technology-based civilization requires the creation of "global natural law."

human population 24 hours a day on the Internet, and other media.

Why the Law Must Be Global

Individual nations cannot abolish coercive government, because the 200 states that exist today are interlocked at many levels. If coercion were overthrown in one state, other states would close ranks to re-establish the rule of force. Therefore, complete civilization can only be achieved by the consensual adoption of a system of global law.

The introduction of globally uniform and biologically natural human law will create an adaptive civilization that will benefit all humans, because it is an absolutely apolitical project. That is, natural law does not benefit any one group at the expense of another group.

Natural law has only a single function: to protect the general population from the initiation of force, whether the force arises from common criminals or from governments. Natural law is the universal protector of equal freedom under the law for all humans.

In an adaptive society, the law must be globally controlled by an elected body comprising numerous and diverse people from every major human group, to serve the species as a whole. The goal must be to create global meritocracy through absolute equality under the law. Such equality will naturally include the leaders of all human groups, so that the process of civilized conduct – "living by contract" – becomes universal, and all coercion is criminalized.

It is easy to believe that universal global law will soon sweep away national laws when we consider the progressive integration of smaller legal jurisdictions into larger ones in the past. Historically, we appear to be progressing through at least nine levels of legal jurisdiction, as shown in Fig. 7.

This sequence outlines the evolution of human law. Surprisingly, only hunter-gatherer law fully supported human intelligence and was an appropriate match for the natural form of human society. Humans were forced into ever larger societies by the constant insecurity arising from the threat of warfare. All larger societies were controlled by exploitative military parasites, and the laws made in these societies were biased towards the purpose of exploitation.

The challenge for modern humans is to reintroduce the laws that guide human behavior into the civilized relationship that resulted from the evolution of the human brain, together with the moral system and collaborative behavior that complemented it.

Cultures can be Diverse and Free under Global Law

The adaptive society requires that a unified global system of natural human law should replace all coercive national law, in order to bring about a situation in which all actions not prohibited by the law are permitted. This law bears equally on all members of the community, including its leaders, who can have no more rights than other people.

At the same time all arbitrary forms of government must be abolished and replaced by the self-government of individuals and of local communities. Thousands of small self-governing communities can be federated in order to tackle regional projects. Similarly, global collaboration can be achieved by the federal arrangement of millions of small communities. The social influence and commercial resources resulting from pooled communities may be very great, but the legal rights of such entities can never differ from the separate rights of the individuals who constitute them. This is what "civilization" means: individual rights and responsibilities.

The goal is not to achieve world government, but to create a uniform world standard for civilization, comprising numerous diverse societies. Each society will manage its own economic and cultural activities on a completely autonomous basis while accepting the unified law, on the basis that it reflects the unchanging biological needs of our species.

In such a global adaptive civilization, all individuals will be subject to identical human rights, while participating in a specific society that may diverge greatly from its neighbors culturally and economically.

As travel becomes easier, and many societies become multicultural, so that people originating from different cultures often live side-by-side, people are increasingly realizing that when completely different legal rights are supported in different jurisdictions, they cannot possibility all represent "justice."

Current Differences in Law Make Justice a Sham

In every country, the so-called justice dispensed is likely to be partially fraudulent, because it is not aligned with the common preference for equity that is the biological inheritance of all men and women. The only absolute justice is absolute equity.

For example, under Moslem Shariah law, women who commit adultery may be stoned to death. In contrast, in the United States, adultery is not a crime, and if a woman – or a man – is abandoned by their spouse, the government takes money by force from taxpayers and may support the person as a "single parent family." Both of these legal approaches cannot be just, and I believe that neither is, since both entail the initiation of force against innocent individuals.

Even the nuclear family has degenerated due to the welfare policies of the state. Many children grow up in households with a single parent, due to divorce and also women having children out of wedlock. In 2007, 28% of American children grew up in single parent households. (US Census Bureau 2009) Although children can survive with single parents, especially if they are supported by a village-like community, children without two parents in industrial societies are more likely to suffer developmental problems.

Another example is the different treatment of homosexuality. Male homosexuality is still illegal in about 80 countries, punishable by prison sentences up to life, and sometimes whipping and incarceration in psychiatric institutions. The death penalty is applicable, but rarely implemented, in seven countries. (Cviklová 2012) On the other hand, same-sex marriage is currently legal in 16 countries. (CFR 2013)

UN Human Rights Declaration benefits States, not People

As we have discussed, scientific law would be extremely simple in principle, but would require extensive scientific support in order to effectively control all the harmful side-effects of technology.

An example of how ineffective and impractical nation states are in thinking about international law can be found in the UN's Declaration of Human Rights. The United Nations, an inter-governmental body, adopted the Universal Declaration of Human Rights in 1948 as a statement of rights and freedoms intended to help secure universal and effective recognition and observance for such rights. The trouble is, being an inter-government project, it is incompetent.

The biggest criticism of the Universal Declaration of Human Rights is that it is merely a collection of commonly desired wants dreamed up by bureaucrats to garner support for the UN. Some "rights" on the list could only be delivered by ignoring the real rights of other people. And any finite list of rights could never be comprehensive, and would always leave loopholes for governments to oppress people because the real, inherited right of every human is to be free, which is a state of infinite possibilities. A genuine statement of human rights must permit all things, other than those things that harm others.

A huge omission from the UN charter is the vital right to use force in self-defense against an aggressor. This is an interesting omission, because the only rational justification of *any* law is that it represents the collaboration of individuals to jointly support their individual, natural right to self-defense against attack by criminals.

Article 3 of the UN Charter states that: "Everyone has the right to life, liberty and security of person." That surely cannot apply to murderers who are often executed, or even criminals who are imprisoned. Article 5 prohibits degrading treatment or punishment, but the imprisonment of lawbreakers is a degrading punishment that is carried out by every society.

Article 19 gives us all the right to freedom of opinion and expression, and the right to "seek, receive and impart information and ideas through any media and regardless of frontiers." But article 12 states that no one shall be subjected to "…attacks upon his honor or reputation." How can we criticize criminals in public office, or retailers of harmful junk food or alcohol without damaging reputations? In practice, such a "right" is more likely to punish the innocent critic than to protect his or her freedom of speech.

Article 16 states that men and women are entitled to equal rights as to marriage, and at its dissolution. That seems to imply equal shares of marital wealth, yet pre-nuptial agreements (part of our rights in a free society) expressly avoid equal treatment. In the absence of prenuptial agreements, law courts determine the allocation of marital property, but equal sharing has never been the guiding principle.

Article 16 says that the family … is entitled to protection by society and the State. But the family is surely a biological entity that does not need such protection? If the state legislates on marriage, it is surely restricting the choices that people would freely make. And if married people are protected in some way, such as tax concessions, then non-married individuals are being correspondingly discriminated against, and thus robbed of their "inalienable" rights.

Homosexuals now demand the right to marry, but if marriage is primarily a private contract between two people to share assets, to stay together for life, etc., they have always had this right, even if public disclosure of such marriage would often have invited discrimination. Some homosexuals may wish to marry under state auspices in order to receive welfare payments or tax deductions on mortgage interest, and some may wish to raise children. In a just society, each issue should be settled by the only relevant criterion: does the practice involve the initiation of force against others? Is the practice harmful in any way, to children as well as adults?

It is worth pointing out that tax advantages merely for being married are clearly unjust – mating is a part of human biology and it does not require legal encouragement. However, if a community voluntarily agreed to support the cost of raising children, then logically, homosexual parents, or step-parents would have identical rights to those of married couples. There is, however, some evidence that adopted children with same-sex parents can suffer gender confusion, especially boys with two female parents. (Mohler 2004)

Article 17 says that no one shall be arbitrarily deprived of his or her property. Taxation, which now exceeds 50% of income in some democracies, is surely theft by government that makes nonsense of this article? Since all government activities could be performed more efficiently by the free market, most taxation for government purposes must be "arbitrary."

Article 22 claims for everyone the right to social security. How can that be a right, since it involves taking by force the resources of some to pay others, rendering them unequal under the law?

Article 23 is even more mischievous, promising everyone the "right to work, free choice of employment, to just and favorable conditions of work and to protection against unemployment." But in a free society, employment is a contract between free individuals, one of whom agrees to carry out work and the other to pay remuneration. If everyone has a "right to work," who is going to be enslaved to provide the work? This article clearly reflects the influence of the Soviet Union and Marxism immediately after the Second World War.

Article 24 absurdly promises everyone "holidays with pay," hardly practical for the self-employed, unemployed, or, for that matter, full-time parents.

Article 25 claims for everyone the right to a standard of living adequate for health and well-being and a list of other benefits only available to a minority in rich countries.

To summarize my view, the trouble with the United Nations is that it *does represent the power of nations*, which are arbitrary divisions of the human species, created by military conquest and existing in mutual insecurity that prevents them from being at all "united." Nations are held together by political elites that practice coercion, false ideology and artificial hierarchy as tools of control.

I do concede that the UN was created in the aftershock of the horrors of WWI and WWII and I have no doubt that many people of honorable intention thought that a global talking shop for governments was the road to peace. History shows it was not.

The trouble with political solutions is that politics is not a science, and discourse based on its ill-defined terminology and "realpolitik" assumptions, tends to be close to valueless. Compare that with, say, the discipline of aircraft engineering. When we board a jetliner, we accept the airline's promise to take us safety across the world, and the airline usually keeps its promise. The airline's ability to do that rests not only upon the training and care of the pilot and crew, but upon the patient men and women who used hard science to design and maintain the airplane. In contrast, the promises of politicians have a level of credibility similar to those of professional confidence tricksters.

In all, the Declaration of Human Rights is amateurish public relations for big government, politically motivated, irrational, and worthless. The very fact that the United Nations, subscribed to by most governments, can produce such a flawed document on a subject as crucial as human rights, is a terrible warning about the current quality of human government.

Formalizing the Citizens' Contract

Civilized relationships are based on a mutual agreement not to initiate force, which we usually take for granted. But this agreement is so vital to human civilization that it may be desirable to make it a formal contract, to be agreed when any young person reaches the age of maturity. The act of voluntarily joining civilization upon reaching adulthood could be a powerful stimulus for individuals to value and respect civilized life.

Such a "right of passage" will reinforce the public awareness that people must be given exactly the same legal rights in every country of the world, without regard to race, religion, or nationality. This will be a powerful counter to the ideological state indoctrination that emphasizes aggressive tribal identity and prepares people for conflict and warfare.

Imagine if every member of every society, upon reaching adulthood, solemnly swears to uphold the contract that underlies global civilization, to live without the use of force and without tolerating privilege of any kind. Such a ceremony will become an enormously significant honor and a valuable opportunity for self-appraisal at the time of embarking upon the great adventure of adult life.

Who Will Pay for Law in Free Societies?

The law against the initiation of force is natural to humans and has always existed. As long as there have been humans, every society has required that each member of society should support his or her share of the burden of implementing that law. This cost is very small, because natural law is such a small part of the massive web of laws that has developed in all modern societies. But the rule of law is an unavoidable cost of civilization, and every society must pay that cost.

Of course, while the law itself must be scientifically defined and globally agreed, the courts, police services, and lawyers will operate commercially like everything else in a free society.

The implementation of law can be a free market activity, but it must be subject to stringent public standards. It seems likely that anyone in a free society will be able to arrest a criminal, provided civilized procedures are followed. Further, the implementation of justice in law courts will not be subject to a lawyers' cartel, nor a coercive state. Private enterprise courts will deliver cheap, efficient, high-quality justice, entirely based upon globally agreed biologically natural human law.

The highest courts will be global in scope and staffed by individuals who are rendered "incorruptible" by their short tenure, by scrutiny by scientific specialists on behalf of the public, and by constant monitoring by the global public, using video streaming of all such activities through the Internet, which will eventually be accessible to all people throughout the world.

Present Laws that will Disappear in Free Societies

One area where the law has expanded rapidly and harmfully in recent times is that of industrial regulation. Although industrial and commercial processes do need a system of control, this should emerge from voluntary standardization and codes of good practice, since the only legitimate controls in a free market are the controls that make industry more efficient, and therefore will be supported by all parties that accept free trade.

Today people are so habituated to the vast amount of state regulation that they have come to believe that it is necessary. If the government makes traffic rules for speed limits, red and green lights and driving on one side of the road, perhaps they should regulate other things as well? Rothbard (Rothbard 2006) says: "The fallacy here is not that traffic should be regulated; of course such rules are necessary. But the crucial point is that such rules will always be laid down by whoever owns and therefore administers the roads. Government has been laying down traffic rules because it is the government that has always owned and therefore run the streets and roads; in a libertarian society of private ownership the *private* owners would lay down the rules for the use of their roads."

Rothbard also points out that, in the 19th century, commercial US railroads interconnected for mutual benefit, allowed cars on each other's tracks, and adopted a standard rail gauge. The railroads also pushed to reduce the 54 time zones then prevalent down to the four used today. In other words, private industries are perfectly capable of regulating their affairs for efficiency and safety by voluntary agreement, so state coercion is not required.

A historical era when good regulation would have been of crucial value occurred during the first Industrial Revolution, when workers were exposed to dangerous machinery, chemicals and pollution. Industrialists in international markets for coal, steel and manufactured goods were forced into intense competition, and they responded by exploiting workers ruthlessly, often in inhuman working conditions. Governments did not wish to sabotage the competitive ability of their "own" industrialists, so they ignored workers' rights as long as possible. States pretended to "help" workers by building the cheapest possible housing and infrastructure and by passed laws preventing the free movement or "combination" (market organization) of workers, to lock them into a subordinate role. How very different things would have been if the economic control of society had not been in the hands of the state, and if the whole population had been represented in the marketplace by organizations that could deal as equals with large companies and whole industries.

Abolishing Victimless Crimes

A part of existing modern law comprises those regulations that are intended to protect ordinary citizens by taking away their human rights. For example, laws making the use of safety equipment compulsory will not be possible in a free society. This does not mean that unsafe behavior will be encouraged: on the contrary, a natural adaptive society will have higher moral standards and in most cases, managers responsible for working environments will insist on safety measures using contractual pressures, so that no social compulsion is necessary.

Laws against sexual orientation or prostitution would not be possible in a free society. At present, there are laws prohibiting illicit drugs, which kill about 250,000 people a year, but no similar laws against alcohol, which kills 2.25 m people, or tobacco, which kills a staggering 5.1 m. people. (WHO 2009) In a free society, there would be no such laws, but legalization would force out of business the international criminals that supply drugs, and an adaptive society would be much more active in combating the hazards of such drugs and of leading the way towards a healthy lifestyle.

Some existing laws are intended to discourage behaviors which are self-destructive, and which would be discouraged by most rational people in a free society. Nevertheless, laws against "victimless crimes" appear to be both irrational and extremely counter-productive. Although many such types of behavior should be the subject of powerful social discouragement, they should not be the subject of law, since coercive interference in the natural rights of another human being is unnatural according to the universal practices of humans in pre-industrial societies. Also, of course, it is impossible to justify the control of one adult person by another if the person so controlled has done no harm to others.

If we accept that the rulers of society have rights over individuals even when they are only harming themselves, then we are accepting that the individual does not own his or her body. Who owns our bodies, if not ourselves? If the rulers of society own our bodies, then we are not equal under the law.

Why Anarchism is Not Viable

There are some political groups who imagine that humans can live in a civilized manner without any centralized laws. Anarchists wish to dispense with the state, which is a rational position according to our biological knowledge, but some would also dispense with the law, which they see as a repressive tool of the state.

It is true that many modern laws are repressive tools of the state; such laws will not be adopted by those people who build a complete human civilization. However, civilization is a social contract to behave without coercion, and those who break a contract must be sanctioned, which is why human communities have always had, and must always have, laws and sanctions supporting the non-aggression principle.

There is no such thing as an *absolutely* "anarchic" society, because human families, especially those with children, depend heavily on mutual support and cannot exist for long in the "jungle" outside of civilization. This was true one million years ago, and it is just as true today, even though the environmental threats that necessitate humans living as a "social animals" have changed greatly.

Libertarians Should Support Strong Government and Law

Another political philosophy that tends to ignore the biological foundation of law is libertarianism. Libertarians include writers who advocate the privatization of law, with market competition between different moral and legal systems. However, although the implementation of the law should certainly be privatized, the substance of the law, as stated above, comprises biologically founded constraints that are revealed through scientific investigation, and can no more be mediated by market competition than can the laws of mechanics or electricity.

It is true that, in the small, face-to-face hunter-gatherer bands of the evolutionary era, the simple "laws of human association" were a part of every child's socialization, and genetically programmed into the moral conscience of every individual, so they needed no discussion. However, the instinctive peer-to-peer behavioral control system of hunter-gatherers cannot protect people from criminal behavior in a mass society in which people frequently interact with strangers and miscreants who can quickly travel hundreds of miles from the scene of their crime.

To create a contiguous civilization based on the law of human association, the "islands" of non-aggression created by human instincts in every small community must be linked by uniform global law that is implemented everywhere on the planet (and in the future, perhaps, on other planets). Without the rule of law, meaning the non-aggression principle, the majority of people would quickly be enslaved by aggressive armed groups, who would in time become coercive governments. And of that, we should be very afraid!

Chapter 9

Replacing State-controlled Capitalism by Free Markets

*I*n the 19ᵗʰ and 20ᵗʰ centuries, market-based "capitalist" societies
manifestly created more wealth and freedom than societies in which
the state used socialism, fascism, or religious fundamentalism to
justify its economic control. As a result, nearly all governments have
accepted the operation of markets in their economies, even if they have
compromised them with coercive intervention.

Despite this success, few people are enthusiastic about capitalism,
which has apparently created extremely wide wealth differentials between rich and poor. Other widely expressed criticisms include the view
that capitalist corporations pollute and destroy nature, support a materialist, consumerist philosophy, and cannot be held accountable for their
actions.

The criticism is almost entirely misplaced, because all so-called
"capitalist" societies are actually subject to incessant state intervention
and regulation, which has created hybrid economies that are nearer to
socialism than to free markets. In fact, the most successful "capitalist"
economy is currently governed by the Communist Party of China!

However, "capitalism" is often defined as a hypothetically perfect
economic system in which people whose person and property are protected by law are *completely free* to produce goods and services and retain the surplus value (i.e. profit) created as a result of successful competition in serving customers. The result of such a system would be that
those who were most efficient at serving customers would accumulate
wealth, which would enable them to create more enterprises that served
society well.

Such a system is as morally perfect as can be conceived, since it

Economic Freedom & GDP per Capita, 2011

GDP PER CAPITA, US$ 2011

$40,000.00	
$35,000.00	
$30,000.00	
$25,000.00	
$20,000.00	
$15,000.00	
$10,000.00	
$5,000.00	
$0.00	

$4,382.00 $8,523.00 $17,869.00 $36,466.00

Least Free   Third   Second   Most Free

ECONOMIC FREEDOM QUARTILE

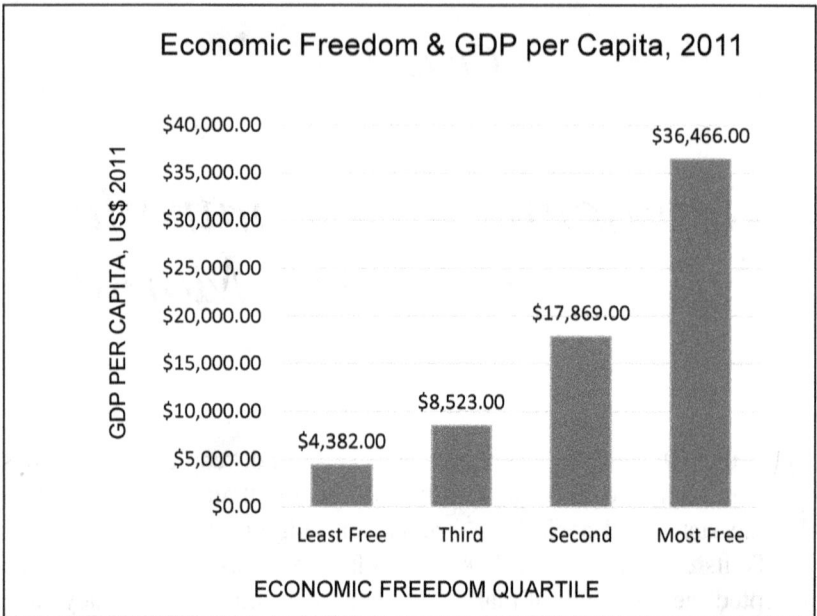

Fig. 8. Income as a function of economic freedom. The income per capita of societies is directly related to the degree of economic freedom as measured by 42 variables. Source: Fraser Institute, Economic Freedom of the World: 2013.

rewards productive ability and hard work with more profits and punishes laziness and inefficiency with losses. People must have food, clothing, dwellings, and many other things, and a system that rewards the individuals who supply them most efficiently is obviously very desirable.

In future societies that are free of state dictation, it is likely that great emphasis will be placed upon enabling children to explore their aptitudes and preferences, so that they are motivated to serve others in the most effective way, and to seek education that will assist them in their chosen role. If all children could seek "self-actualization" in this way, the existing exaggerated wealth differentials between rich and poor would be greatly narrowed. Another powerful force that can reduce differences in wealth is free market competition – if society permits this force to operate, as I shall discuss below.

But capitalism is only an equitable system if all individuals have equal access to the marketplace and can freely take part in the competition to serve customers and earn revenue. Unfortunately, the sovereign state system of government has a monopoly of force, which it uses to

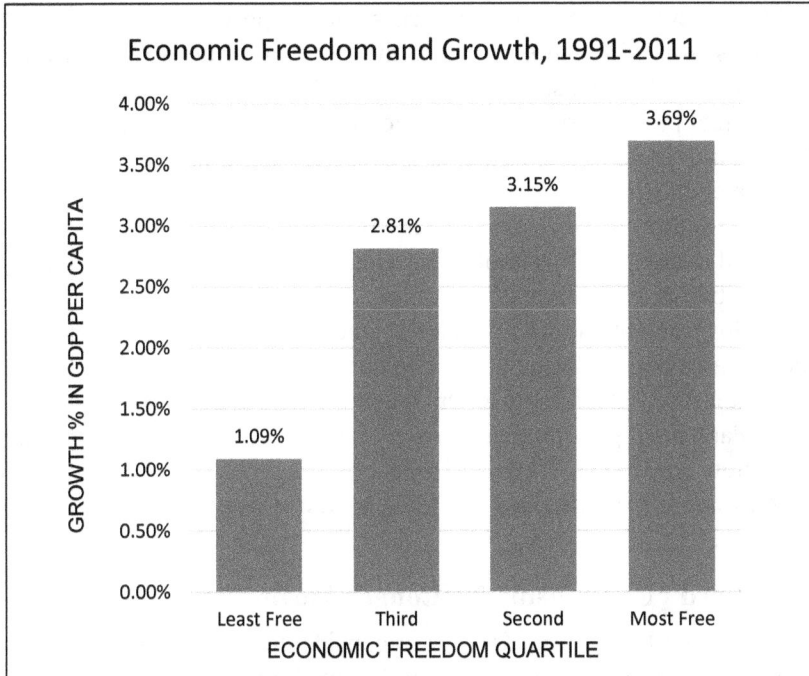

Fig. 9. Growth as a function of economic freedom. The growth of economies is directly related to the degree of economic freedom as measured by 42 variables. Source: Fraser Institute, Economic Freedom of the World: 2013.

create a social hierarchy. Large corporations, industrialists and many public bodies are given privileges that block the general public from market access and force them into "employment" which is a structurally inferior position in the economy.

Free Markets Reduce Wealth Differentials

Individuals vary considerably in their capacity to participate in the production or sale of goods and services, and so some wealth differentials are a consequence of ability. But in absolutely free markets, unusually high or low salaries, high or low profits, high or low interest rates, or other economic variables, attract competition that moderates all extremes and prevents excessive wealth differentials.

Under the state control of capitalism, this reduction of wealth differentials by competition has been neutralized because the parasitical state *needs* a social hierarchy to maintain control of the economy. The ruthless hand of the state intervenes and imposes a hierarchy that stretches from billionaires down to the starving millions of the world. The tools used by the state include monopolies such as limited liability, intellectual property rights, and employment law, state barriers to trade, foreign aid, including armaments provided to repressive governments, and the endless regulation of markets.

Therefore, a reduction in excessive wealth differentials could be obtained at any time by simply removing the state-imposed monopolies and the barriers to market competition.

Governments attack the natural free market *because* it expresses the morally perfect framework of relations evolved in nature, and *because* it is a self-stabilizing system that does not need any coercive guidance. Parasitical governments *have* to corrupt the free market, in order to operate societies as "human livestock farms" that can be controlled by artificial hierarchies and exploited by those using force against the majority.

The Word "Capitalism" No Longer Means Freedom

In the 19th century, Karl Marx considered "capitalists" to be the enemy of working people because of the appalling conditions in UK factories after the Industrial Revolution. What is not widely understood is that the tough conditions were the results of state legislation, not free markets. The British government expropriated the land of the peasants in the Middle Ages by the Enclosures Acts, and passed its ownership to the aristocracy. Previously independent small farmers were forced *by the state* to choose between exploitation by the new landowners, or to work in the factory system. In either case, workers faced a state-sponsored monopoly that would prevent them negotiating a fair living.

The British state also passed the Laws of Settlement, to stop workers from traveling outside the parish (local district) of their birth without permission, which prevented them traveling to jobs. In many countries, today's migrant workers are similarly excluded from work opportunities by national passports and work visas. In the UK and elsewhere, "Combination Laws" prevented workers from combining in trade unions to negotiate wages.

So the horrors often attributed to capitalism were entirely a product of state intervention in favor of big business. If "laissez-faire" (totally free markets) had really existed, men and women would have been free to choose their jobs or independent business activities and negotiate the best conditions and payment that could be gained, just as large-scale industrialists do. Wealth differentials would have been minimized by freedom.

Why was the state so ruthless? The obvious reason is simply that politicians are ambitious and acquisitive, like the rest of us but, unlike the rest of us, they can wield the sovereign power of the state like gods, to dispose of the general population exactly as they think fit. The profit in politics is "rent-seeking", which includes earning goodwill from providing state favors to the wealthy and powerful – goodwill that can one day be turned into money.

A second reason why the state is so ruthless is that patriotism provides the pretext for making laws that serve the needs of large-scale industrialists. In the 19th century, the early factories, mines, and steel mills served international markets with commodities like coal, cotton, and steel. International competition based on predatory pricing could bring the less competitive producers to their knees within a few months. Industrialists begged their governments to help them compete against foreigners by suppressing the wages of domestic workers. The state was happy to oblige.

It would probably surprise most people to know that, in the 18th century, the word "capitalist" described a beneficiary of state intervention, as libertarian writer Sheldon Richman notes. (Richman 2010) "Most notably, Thomas Hodgskin (1787–1868), a free-market liberal and Herbert Spencer's mentor, preceded Marx in this usage," says Richman. "By 'capitalist' he meant one who controlled capital and exploited labor as a result of State privilege in violation of the free market."

Karl Marx rightly condemned 19th century capitalism as exploitative, but failed to see that the poor conditions of workers were due to the state legislation that excluded them from the marketplace and delivered them as near-slaves into the hands of big industrialists. The state was legislating to create the same class structure in every new industrial country, and so the wages that industrialists could afford to pay were often limited by international competition.

The word "capitalism" is still widely misused to refer to the economic system in most industrialized states, as being laissez-faire, or absolute free markets. In reality, all democracies have a large degree of socialist control. The state in the USA, for example, takes half the nation's income in taxes, borrows astronomically from the nation's future wealth, controls the currency and generates long-term inflation, controls interest rates, runs a welfare state, operates compulsory schooling, and is moving into compulsory healthcare. Whatever economic problems face modern economies, the state is certainly responsible for them, whether or not we call the economic system "capitalism."

But today, the state has regulated business to such an extreme degree that enterprising businesspeople with their idealism and moral purpose have been largely replaced by limited liability corporations manned by professional managers, who are focused on profitability and nothing else. The word "capital-ism" has become a state ideology, associated with the professional managers of corporations obsessed only with return on shareholder capital. The accusations of greed and materialism made against capitalism are true, but the state made all the regulations that produced that result.

It may be time to stop using the word "capitalism" as an ideal, because we need to educate young people to seek self-actualization and fulfillment of a moral purpose when they become entrepreneurs, as is

Fig.10. Economic systems, from controlled to free.

Communism	State-controlled Capitalism	Free Markets
An economic and social system in which the coercive state controls the means of production, regulating the rest of the population with regard to almost all aspects of their lives.	The most common economic system, in which the state controls and regulates enterprises, which therefore cannot be held fully accountable to their customers or the law.	The most free economic system in which men and women risk their own capital, under the rule of law, and are fully accountable to their customers and all others. Such firms comply with the non-aggression principle.

only possible in a very free economy. State-regulated business and state-managed trade are the enemies of free markets and healthy societies. A more realistic spectrum of economic systems is that shown in Fig. 10.

Abolishing Limited Liability

Shareholders of limited liability corporations own all the profits they earn by trading successfully, but their liability for losses due to unsuccessful trading is limited to the corporate assets they invested as equity. This means that the debts of a bankrupt company are transferred to its creditors, primarily its employees and suppliers. This can lead to abuse, for the directors of a company know well in advance that it is likely to fail and so they tend to "milk" the assets prior to bankruptcy, secure in the knowledge that others will be forced by the state to bear the loss.

Natural justice demands that all members of society are fully responsible for the good or evil effect of their actions on other people. A society that does not reward the good and punish the wrongdoer cannot remain a moral society.

The fundamental problem with limited liability is that it separates responsibility for actions that are sometimes harmful from the actual individuals that made the bad decisions with the hope of profiting from them. In other words, limited liability removes morality from commercial companies, and replaces it with collective responsibility, so that individual culprits cannot be identified or penalized.

The principle of "incorporation," is the same as the corporate nature of the state itself, which enables political leaders to start wars that kill millions of people, yet avoid accountability, because the "state" is supposed to represent the whole nation.

Traditionally, small companies were owned by a single entrepreneur, or a group of investors who could be forced to compensate for losses caused to others, or punished for criminal harms committed. But the state has used limited liability and other laws to create large corporations that have thousands, or millions of shareholders. The company is a legal "person" under the law, and if it is fined for losses caused by its management, the fine is paid by the innocent shareholders, including the powerless workers who are investors through their pension funds.

Personal Versus Collective Responsibility

Why does the state not wish to hold individual businesspeople accountable for their actions? In the 19th century businesses with a few rich investors were often involved in risky overseas ventures in which there was a real possibility that the investors would not only fail to make a profit and lose their investment, but they might face large claims from third parties. This possibility of large losses limited the growth of joint stock companies, and so governments legislated to create limited liability. This protected investors by forcing other people to cover part of their losses.

The state's creation of corporations as "legal persons" meant that the business was itself responsible for debts and even torts. Although individual directors and managers could be held responsible for criminal wrongdoing, the principal of "collective responsibility" of the board of directors often made it impossible to identify an individual who could be held accountable for reckless or criminal decisions. Governments liked large companies that could dominate overseas rivals, and that were also simpler to tax and manage than many small or medium-sized companies.

Before corporation laws, a single business owner could often be held responsible for everything that a business did. But in a corporation, it became much more difficult to attach blame to the actions of a large number of professional managers, hired to maximize profits, without any ownership privileges. As a result, companies could grow to an enormous size without the same concern about the legal consequences of mistakes.

But, while governments prefer giant-sized companies created by special laws, are they good for society? One supposed benefit of incorporation is the creation of a network of huge companies that can together employ millions of workers. But the corollary of that is that millions of people who *might* have started their own companies and actively participated in the economy, have now become employees, struggling in the rat race.

Today, industrialists have only to indicate their need for employees and the state will adjust the school and college intakes to train the right mix of workers to satisfy their needs. Such social engineering has many of the qualities of communism – instead of life being a spontaneous adventure, people become "cogs in a machine." The increase in the size of companies, each with thousands or millions of investors, is in some ways more like communism than the free market, and that generates criticism of materialist values, and consumerism, which entail a decline in human well-being.

Large Companies Increase Wealth Differentials

Gigantic companies do produce gigantic profits, and this generates a large number of millionaires and billionaires. The state may like this idea, because it produces a social hierarchy that aids in the centralized control of the economy. However, large wealth differentials cause both extreme wealth and extreme poverty. This is clearly an evil, which the state addresses with high taxation and welfare payments – but it would be far simpler and more just to allow free market conditions to prevail, because this would result in many smaller companies and no billionaires.

Another reason why we should regret the creation of so many huge companies and the massive parasitic investment industry that supports them is the corresponding loss of the inventiveness and job creation of small and medium-sized companies. Even the state realizes that it is business start-ups that tend to create new ideas and to increase employment. But today, startups mostly don't dream about becoming bigger – instead they just seek to be purchased by giant companies that are unable to create new ideas themselves. This parasitic pattern is a loss to both wealth production and to the quality of life.

The popular resentment against corporate power creates a major misunderstanding in society, in which many people align themselves against "capitalism," without realizing that the misbehavior of corporations is due to corporate law made by the state, not by free market conditions that no longer exist.

Limited Liability is Popular with Litigators and Lawyers

One major driver for limited liability is that the principle of collective responsibility in business partnerships, and the invention of corporations and limited liability companies as "legal persons" means that victims of torts can now sue for part of an entire company's wealth, instead of being limited to the wealth of the individual who caused the damage and who would be culpable under natural justice.

When people are harmed by malfunctioning vehicles or equipment belonging to a company, or through the recklessness or error of a human operator employed by the company, they expect to obtain compensation. In natural justice, they should only be awarded damages when criminal intent or recklessness is involved, not for accidents that occur randomly at any time. But sympathy for the victim swings courts in their favor, and the fact that money is available from the relatively large resources of a commercial corporation may swing the judgment towards compensating the victim without much regard to real liability.

Would Limited Liability Exist Without the State?

Many libertarians argue that limited liability should be repealed, but one of the greatest libertarian thinkers, Murray Rothbard argues that, if the state did not create limited liability by law, any company could achieve the same end by free contract. He writes: "On the purely free market, such men would simply announce to their creditors that their liability is limited to the capital specifically invested in the corporation, and that beyond this their personal funds are not liable for debts, as they would be under a partnership arrangement. It then rests with the sellers and lenders to this corporation to decide whether or not they will transact business with it. If they do, then they proceed at their own risk." (Rothbard 2011)

I consider that Rothbard was wrong to ignore the fact that a libertarian "free market" can only exist if voluntarily agreed laws specify the conditions under which property rights and contracts are legitimate. A lawful libertarian society cannot be like the "free" society of the jungle in which "might is right" and there is no higher court to invoke in case of dispute – the jungle is certainly not libertarian, nor just.

Rothbard quite rightly attaches great importance to freely-made contracts, which are the basis of civilization. But he is mistaken in assuming that all private contracts must be supported, and that there is no higher authority than the contracting parties. The law must have criteria to determine which contracts are valid and can be supported by courts. Criteria will certainly include such factors as:

1. Contracting parties must be adults, of sound mind, and not intoxicated.
2. The parties must have agreed voluntarily, not under duress.
3. A contract must specify precisely what things are to be exchanged.
4. Neither party must have misrepresented the things that are offered in exchange.

For example, among the contracts that are never accepted in courts today are agreements to pay the uncertain and badly documented debts arising from private gambling.

Now, consider Rothbard's free market vision, in which a group of entrepreneurs (collectively known as a "company") advised potential business partners that they would only pay their debts from the assets of their business, including their paid-up share equity, and that they would refuse to contribute any further assets for this purpose.

My first objection is that such a company would have to clearly inform *every single person* with whom they made a contract, that their liability was limited. Every employee, every supplier, and every customer who purchased a product from it would have to be unmistakably informed that the company did not intend to meet its liabilities if these exceeded its accrued assets.

Such a statement is rather like a man who asks a woman out for an evening stroll in the woods, saying: "I've got a tendency to commit violent rape when the inclination arises – are you OK with that?"

In other words, in a truly free market, everyone would always have choices, and it seems unlikely that anyone would choose to do business with a company that preceded its offerings with the extraordinary announcement that it intended to dishonor its debts under certain circumstances.

It is true that, without limited liability, businesses might tend to stay smaller. But a common view today is that giant corporations are both immoral and monopolistic. In contrast, numerous medium-sized companies would offer more variety and competition, provide more people with business opportunities, and operate more morally. Which society would you choose?

The general public detests large corporations for their immorality. A few large corporations employ millions of people, thus dividing society between capitalists and employees. Large corporations are part of the fundamental reason for today's huge wealth differentials. The UN's World Institute for Development Economics Research reported that, in 2000, the richest 1% of people owned 40% of all global assets. (UNU-WIDER 2006) A large proportion of people, even in rich countries have no assets, and six million children die of hunger each year. (FAO 2005)

Historically, limited liability can be seen as a continuation of the state's policy, during the Industrial Revolution, of favoring the new factory owners against craftsmen, small farmers and other potential employees. The overall effect has been that most of the population has been excluded from the marketplace, to become employees, or, legally, "servants." The creation of large, favored corporations without full liability has created immoral business, materialism, and consumerism.

Replacing Employment with Market Relationships

Once we have understood the power of the marketplace to reduce excessive differentials and deliver economic justice, we have an important reason to ensure that all markets really are free from the use of force by either criminals or states. But even if markets were suddenly free, most people would be poorly equipped to benefit from them.

Today, almost everyone lives and works in economies that are loosely called "capitalist", but most people don't consider themselves to be capitalists – they reserve this label for the owners of businesses, just as Karl Marx did in the 19th century. Ordinary employees – what Marx called the "proletariat" – are legally denoted as "servants" and exploited.

A kind of social apartheid has been created, which divides the whole population into employers and employees, and the distinction, which was at first arbitrary, has been deepened and consolidated by two hundred years of unceasing government legislation and intervention. An enormous web of laws now controls the way that people can or cannot contract with each other and relate to each other. People are subject to what can be called "state capitalism" or mercantilism, in which one part of society exploits the majority, under state auspices.

If we accept that (non-state controlled) capitalism is a good way to organize a modern society, then *everyone* should be a capitalist. If free exchange between all adults, which we call "markets," is the most efficient way for people to relate to one another, then *everyone* should have a personal presence in the market.

Employment is undesirable because the contract of employment does not quantify the work to be done. It simply places the employee at the disposal of the employer, in a dependent role that is certain to generate exploitation and alienation. "Alienation" is the sense of futility that arises when work is emotionally meaningless.

When mass employment was introduced in the 18th and 19th centuries, independent craftsmen fought tooth and nail against it. But enforced state schooling has manipulated generations of children with lies, so that modern employees are like listless chimpanzees in a bad zoo, ignorant that their misery is caused by enslavement.

Ultimately, state coercion must be abolished in order to recreate normal human social organization. In such societies, markets will simply express human interaction based on free contract. Every individual will have many economic relationships and therefore a place in the market. Although individuals may sometimes choose to be employees (for example, if they are learning a new skill), such roles will not be typical.

Economist David D. Friedman has expressed preference for a society where "almost everyone is self-employed" and "instead of corporations there are large groups of entrepreneurs related by trade, not authority. Each sells not his time, but what his time produces." (Friedman 2009)

Self-Employment is a First Step

New and flexible ways of selling "human services" will evolve, in which the workers are all entrepreneurs. For example, some workers will both own and work for a company that provides various human skills to organizations that need them, just as other companies provide raw materials or electric power. Workers in these "human skill resource service suppliers" will no longer depend upon a single employer, and therefore redundancy and unemployment will no longer be serious threats. Organizations will benefit by outsourcing their human resource needs to service companies, and obtaining reliable workers, with no strikes or other social conflicts.

Another advantage is that, in times of recession when companies have fewer orders on hand, instead of firing some workers, which causes considerable suffering, they will be able to simply reduce their purchases from the labor service companies. Of course, remuneration levels will be lowered in a recession, but no individuals will necessarily be "out of work" and the losses will be shared more equally. If everyone becomes a "market participant" unemployment will cease to exist.

The most likely future, when state control is abolished, is a completely free market situation in which the sharp separation between "business owners" and "employees" disappears. Instead, most individuals will have a flexible role in which they are owners of equity in some businesses, and suppliers of services to others. Individuals will no longer be isolated, but members of communities or companies that can negotiate directly with organizations requiring professional skills or labor.

Small Companies and the Conflict with Coase's Theorem

If employment disappears, there will be a lot more individuals and small enterprises in the market. Economist Ronald Coase wrote about "The Nature of the Firm", explaining why firms exist, and why entrepreneurs do not simply hire the services of all the individuals needed under contract. Coase said that this is because of the high costs of the transactions, including the research necessary to find the cost of a service, the search for efficient suppliers, and the negotiation of contracts. (Coase 1937)

But the paradigm for firms and their employees was developed during the chaos and the conflict of the Industrial Revolution. I do not think that "transaction costs" is the main reason why so many millions of people who had been craftsmen or small farmers were forced out of the market and into wage labor as servants. The current trend is away from employment, as more people work from home as freelances or set up small businesses. If, in future, all people are self-employed or own equity in service companies that provide specific labor skills, then the relationships between such workers and their clients will tend to be longer-standing than employment contracts, as happens in normal business relationships. So the cost of searching for skills will be lessened. In addition, self-employed people are subject to the discipline of initiating and maintaining multiple market relationships and may be more reliable than employees.

Furthermore, when workers are organized as service contractors to fulfill the labor needs of large companies, the absence of individual key workers due to illness or other causes will cause less of a problem because the labor service provider will be able to provide substitutes. Labor provided as a business service will also be free of strikes. This will enable large firms to plan their production on the basis of a more predictable labor service. This increase in the reliability of workers will be an advantage to free market enterprises.

Finally, automation is currently replacing unskilled workers, and that may increase entrepreneurship at the expense of employment.

But if wage labor is a disadvantage, why was it adopted? Karl Marx, the main originator of communism, portrayed the owners and workers of capitalism as social classes, the bourgeoisie, and the proletariat. Thus, he believed that technology inevitably changes the class structure of a society and produces injustice and class conflict.

In a free society, however, technology cannot by itself change social structure unless the new relationships created are welcomed by the general population. If the state had not assisted factory owners, free market conditions would have absorbed the shock of the new technology. Factory workers would have organized themselves into labor service companies, achieved the market presence to negotiate wages, and by reducing their dependence on a single employer, avoided the scourge of unemployment.

In the 21st century, we are slowly seeing an increase in entrepreneurship, and the rapid growth of outsourcing, which will tend to reduce the size of the largest corporations and increase the number of small enterprises. Eventually, we can predict that it will become normal for all people to offer their skills on the market, either as freelancers, professional consultants, or as equity participating members of human resource vendors. Suppliers of human resources will deal with their customers on equal terms and wage labor will be largely abolished, just as formal slavery has been abolished.

Freeing Consumers from Materialism

Humans are competitive, and in prehistoric hunter-gatherer societies, acknowledgement must have been provided to those who performed well in a socially useful activity, such as cooking, hunting, or collecting food. Due to industrialization, many people now work in factories or offices and do specialized jobs that cannot be understood or evaluated by others.

For many people, the only way to obtain acknowledgement for their contribution to society is by exhibiting their remuneration through the goods and services it buys, an activity termed "conspicuous consumption."

Conspicuous consumption is damaging to human culture when there is a strong need to protect the environment by conservation. Furthermore, the quality of human life is degraded when we cannot appreciate and acknowledge our neighbors, except by proof of their spending power.

Many economists and philosophers mistakenly assume that the roots of consumerism lie in technology and are therefore inescapable. But consumerism is simply a product of the distorted social organization generated by the state.

If state coercion can be neutralized by global laws implementing the non-aggression principle, then humans will automatically re-organize themselves into groups emulating the self-governing societies in which they evolved for millions of years. The priorities of such autonomous societies will be to protect the individual's opportunity to pursue self-actualization. The actions of parasitic groups will become illegal. Children everywhere will be raised to understand the adaptive lifestyle of a civilization in which everything is conducted by contract or by charity, without coercion.

Marketing and Procurement Should be Equal Partners

In a normal free market, buyer and seller should have equal rights. They both, after all, play an equal part in every purchasing transaction. Yet, in consumerist societies, nobody considers individual consumers to be the equal of large corporate retailers or manufacturers.

Powerful marketing organizations "target" consumers with "sales campaigns," based on "strategies" of psychological manipulation, as if they were enemy soldiers or hunted prey. Inevitably, people are misled by billions of dollars of persuasive advertising channeled through the Internet and other media.

Civilized behavior is based on contractual agreements, but in state controlled societies the complex and one-sided contracts written by lawyers for consumers to sign to obtain products and services are not meaningful. This is because they appear in small print, are too long to read, and can usually only be altered by the vendor.

In high-tech areas, such as computer software, the long, detailed contacts drawn up by lawyers to control consumers go mostly unread by the people who agree to the terms and conditions of use, so that no genuine contract is made. Lawyers claim that a contract is made, even if one party does not know (and could not easily know) its terms. Bad government has degraded the quality of the contract, which is the basis of civilization itself.

The proximate reason for the weakness of consumers in the face of mass marketing is that the buying power of the individual consumer is so small compared with the sales of corporations. However, the total market power of consumers is obviously as great as that of suppliers. Thanks to the powerful communications technology of the Internet, consumers are already starting to organize themselves nationally and globally to better serve their own interests.

When state coercion is abolished, consumers will organize themselves into regional federations with the same power as the largest vendors. Not only will such equality protect individual consumers from abuse, by providing the resources for legal representation, but also procurement will become a large and routine aspect of the consumer market. This means that groups of consumers will be able to design, develop, and specify their own products, even those in niche markets, by purchasing on a regional or global basis. This will create greater stability and mutual satisfaction, due to the equal power of buyers and sellers.

The Artificial Division Between Work and Leisure

The artificial division between work and leisure is another undesirable consequence of state power and the misuse of technology. Anthropologists estimate that the average hunter-gatherer spent three hours a day "working" on such things as dwellings, clothing, and obtaining and cooking food. And even the "work" of the hunter-gatherers still living today is never a dull routine, but rather like a useful game played between relatives and friends.

Yet modern man, supported by capital equipment that is supposed to have raised productivity hundreds of times, has to work from eight to ten hours a day, not including the extensive periods spent at home cooking, cleaning, and maintaining houses, gardens and motor vehicles.

The irony is that all modern humans could live normal lives in pursuit of self-actualization and supported by marvelous technology, simply by the removal of state coercion and the normalization of social organization on a global basis.

Reforming Unjust "Intellectual Property"

Intellectual property is a form of protectionism that attempts to give rich countries and large corporations the power to own technology and creative works and sell them for high prices, while depriving poor countries and small firms of the right to develop similar technology. IP rights also provide corporations with state monopoly power, while depriving new creators and ordinary citizens of the benefit of using creative works.

For hundreds of years, ruthless industrialised states attempted to control trade in order to increase the value of their exports, while buying goods as cheaply as possible from less industrialized nations. Virtually all economists now agree that protectionism is damaging to trade and to human development throughout the world. It is essential that humans reach the same conclusion about IP rights – state monopoly is an evil cancer and must be cut out.

How Monarchs Created Patents to Prevent Free Trade

Throughout history until the 18th or 19th century, people everywhere were free to create new writing, art, or mechanical inventions, incorporating ideas from existing works, without any hindrance. Copying was considered not only normal, but a widespread and crucial part of human activity. When people copy clever ideas this creates and spreads wealth and technology, reducing the gap between rich and the poor.

But parasites, especially governments, sought an unearned share of the wealth created by others. In England, in the 15th century for example, the monarch would employ state force to grant a monopoly in a particular good in exchange for a sum of money or a favour. The monopolies were usually granted by "letters patent," or letters from a sovereign or other head of state that granted to aristocrats or favored associates the right to hunt, fish, or to kill and eat certain animals. From the start, patents were a form of rent-seeking parasitism.

In 16th century England, patents were granted for monopoly manufacturing of soap, glass, knives, and sailcloth – things that had previously been made for hundreds of years by anyone with the necessary skill and resources. Patent monopolies did not start as a system to spread technology, but were an illegitimate system to prevent the spread of technology and to enrich the government and the aristocracy. The modern patent system has been amended to make it less outrageously unjust, but it is still a barrier erected by the haves to keep out the have-nots.

The Birth of Copyright in Censorship

Copyright, like patents, originated from the desire of parasitic governments to control society for their own advantage. In 16th century England, new printing technology was making possible the dissemination of radical ideas that might encourage people to question the power of the monarchy, the church, and parliament. Direct censorship of individual books was becoming impracticable, so the government began to award monopolies for book printing to prominent and loyal printers or stationers.

In 1557, the monarchy gave special powers to the Stationers' Company, the trade guild for printing. "The two most important powers... bestowed on the Company were a broad national monopoly and extensive search and enforcement powers," says legal historian Oren Bracha. "The charter provided that no one in the realm should exercise the art of printing directly or through an agent unless he was a freeman of the Stationers' Company or a royal patentee. As for enforcement, the Master and Warden of the Company were authorized to search the houses and business premises of all printers and book sellers in the kingdom; to seize any material printed contrary to any statute, act, or proclamation; and to imprison offenders." (Bracha 2005)

Of course, IP rights have changed over the years. But if IP rights were created as an immoral expression of state power, is it really likely that their role has become benevolent?

How Patents Slowed the Industrial Revolution by 30 years

Patents cause enormous damage to society. In the 18th century, they held up industrial progress for decades. Well after the steam engine was invented in 1712, James Watt and his partner, Matthew Boulton patented their design. Another inventor, Jonathan Hornblower, produced a superior engine, but Boulton and Watt sued him. Hornblower stopped production and ended up in jail, while Watt became rich.

Watt and Boulton made several hundred steam engines, but their patent monopoly prevented other types from being produced, resulting in only 1,000 steam engines being produced in the UK by 1800. However, when Watt's patent expired, inventors were free to sell designs for many applications, including steam boats and textile mills. The total horsepower of the UK's steam engines grew 21 times by 1815. Some historians have concluded that the Industrial Revolution was delayed by about 30 years due to that one patent, and many inventors were unable to realize their creations. Yet the ludicrous claim is still made that patents increase innovation!

In the early 1900s, the Wright Brothers held several patents on the airplane. Other aircraft manufacturers tried to build planes using the Wrights' inventions but were frustrated by the demand for very high patent royalties. Inventor Glenn Curtiss held patents on aeronautic technology, such as ailerons, tail surfaces, and a new engine, yet the Wrights wouldn't license their patents to Curtiss, who had to fight them in court for years.

The Wrights were ahead of their competitors in aerodynamic control, but behind in engine design, moveable control surfaces, and other vital features. If they had teamed up with competitors such as Curtiss, instead of wasting their energy fighting for patent royalties, they might have soared ahead.

A few years later, patents caused the American aircraft industry to fall behind that of Europe. Therefore, in order to be competitive against the German air force in World War I, patent barriers to aircraft design had to be quickly removed. Once the patent monopolies had been eliminated by pooling patents, a golden age of American aviation followed. The patent pool stayed in effect until 1975; companies who wanted to preserve a competitive advantage did so by using trade secrets.

Once again, patents were shown to hinder innovation. What is more, patents are generally too expensive and difficult to defend for individual inventors or small companies to use at all.

In 1895, patent attorney George Selden obtained a patent for the automobile and, although he had never built a car, he used the patent to extract royalties from car makers for years. He defeated Henry Ford in court and placed advertisements in the press warning Ford buyers that they "might well be buying a ticket to jail." During the case, Selden built a car but it was not a practicable design. A year before the patent was to expire, it was declared invalid except for cars with a specific type of engine, which was never used.

Researchers Back Abolition of Intellectual Property Rights

Boldrin and Levine (Boldrin 2008) provide a thorough review of intellectual property law and come out flatly against it.

These authors observed the tendency of IP rights to grow more powerful and concluded that patents should be abolished rather than re-formed. "Certainly the basic threat to prosperity and liberty can be resolved through sensible reform," say Boldrin and Levine. "But intellectual property is a cancer. The goal must be not merely to make the cancer more benign, but ultimately to get rid of it entirely. So, while we are skeptical of the idea of immediately and permanently eliminating intellectual monopoly – the long-term goal should be no less than a complete elimination. A phased reduction in the length of terms of both patents and copyrights would be the right place to start. By gradually reducing terms, it becomes possible to make the necessary adjustments – for example to FDA regulations, publishing techniques and practices, software development and distribution methods – while at the same time making a commitment to eventual elimination."

Over-charging is the Cause of Copyright Piracy

Corporations that lobby the state for a monopoly over digital music, literature, or software accuse ordinary people of "stealing" their property. But ordinary people have moral consciences, which tell them that the cost of their copying to the owner is zero, and therefore they are not stealing.

The conflict arises because copyright owners often demand astronomically high prices for digital copies that cost almost nothing to produce, which is profiteering from a state monopoly. Supposing that, in a few years, owners of digital material reduce their prices to a few cents per copy, and Internet micro-payments are made easy. Millions of customers will then happily buy music, literature, and other software without a second thought and this will provide enough income to recompense the authors and a modest supply chain. The customers will then be paying for the convenience of Internet distribution, just as they pay retailers for distribution.

The great mystery is why copyright owners – and governments – need to be hit over the head before they recognize the immorality and futility of holding the public to ransom with state monopoly IP laws.

Designers' Profits do not Need Protection

When companies spend money on designing products, they hope that good design will make their product more successful in its market. But only a tiny minority of designs become popular and make exceptional profits, and no-one can predict which designs will succeed. Therefore, the only designs that are copied are those that have proven to be successful, meaning that, by the time they are copied, the manufacturers have made a profit and recouped their investment. So even exact copying of successful designs cannot prevent their designers earning a profit.

But the manufacturer's profits will be reduced in the long term if other producers notice its success and copy the product, taking away some of its market share. Owners of successful designs would therefore like to have a monopoly so that they can continue to earn money from their designs for years. However, society does not have any particular obligation to maintain the profits of good designers indefinitely. Most people are only paid once for their work: why should inventors and designers be paid many times for the same work?

Trademarks are designed by producers to assist in recognition of particular brands, and therefore the use of trade marks by other producers falsifies product description and must be illegal in any rational jurisdiction.

Although all moral people should be against IP Rights based on state monopolies, the public should support creative people such as inventors, designers and software authors in the face of certain kinds of unethical behavior, such as the appropriating their inventions when they are offered for sale. The most effective support is by boycotting the financial interests responsible for the abuse, as described below.

Automated Boycotts of Unethical Commercial Behavior

In a free society, it will be extremely easy to organize boycotts by customers that will have a huge and immediate effect on commercial companies behaving in an unethical manner. For example, today, some kinds of social control, such as the control of extreme indecency in the media, or invasion of privacy by media representatives, cannot be attained without oppressive legislation that destroys the freedom that is necessary for a healthy human culture. However, in a free market world, it will be very easy for consumers' dissatisfaction with vendors' products or services to be expressed by coordinated boycotts.

When a decentralized society is constituted from millions of tiny autonomous communities, Internet technology may be used to provide customers with the means of disciplining the suppliers of services by withdrawing their patronization for a short period. When a particular service industry displeases consumers, the most active individuals will initiate a boycott using a software application developed for the purpose. All other consumers will be invited to join the boycott and will simply have to respond to the invitation with one or two mouse clicks to join or not, and to specify the period of boycott they consider appropriate. This means that the company providing the service will be financially punished for displeasing its customers and is likely to apologise and take remedial action as rapidly as possible.

In practice, of course, the exercise of such consumer power will rarely be necessary, because the providers of services will soon learn that unethical behaviour will never go unpunished. Note that the control of suppliers by consumers is precisely what markets are intended to do, and also that this behavioural control mimics the control over each other and over their leaders that free men and women evolved during human evolution.

To many people used to the "dog-eat-dog" world of nation state ruthlessness, the idea of such a boycott may sound idealistic. However, morality is built into every human being for a purpose. If we choose to reclaim our evolutionary heritage and live once more in a moral society, technology can help to adapt society to make that possible.

Chapter 10

Opening Markets to Every Person on Earth

*M*arkets are frequently described by politicians as if they were machines that should be subject to some kind of state regulation to protect the public. Yet markets that are free of state control comprise *nothing* except the public itself. "Markets" are simply our name for the relationships between ordinary men and women choosing how to exchange goods, services, or money that is already their legitimate property; in most cases, because they have earned it by their own endeavors.

Therefore the slightest interference with any market must be considered as either the theft of legitimate property, or an attack on the right of people to exchange what belongs to them. Such interference is a crime, whether it is conducted by common criminals or by a government that acts on a criminal basis. The state's curtailment of market freedom is an attack on civilization itself. Civilization can best be described as "living by contract." Contracts are promises, and morality requires that all people are free to make promises and obligated to keep them. Therefore, absolute market freedom is a condition of civilization. Until all markets are completely free, humans cannot be completely civilized.

The Myth of Market Failure

Proponents of state intervention typically believe that market freedom has been tried and has failed to deliver equity to the whole of society. Such critics are correct in finding great injustice in society, but if they examine markets in a disciplined way, they will find that great injustice has been caused, not by the market system but by the intervention of the coercive state.

In reality, the free market *cannot* actually harm anyone. A free market is merely free individuals who choose to trade, exchanging one thing for another because they see mutual advantage in it. If they both value what they gain from the exchange more highly than what they relinquish, then the total value of social resources – which rests on individual subjective preferences – has been expanded by their action, so that society benefits.

If we look back at earlier societies that exhibited injustice, we can usually see that the state was the culprit, not the free market. For example, the feudal societies of China, Japan, and Europe were mediated by the armed aristocrats, or warlords, who controlled each principality or fiefdom. Considering Europe, even those who believe in state power must admit that the suffering of the serfs and peasants in the Middle Ages was caused, not by the free market (which could not exist in such a hierarchical society) but by the coercive government. The state controlled an unnatural social pyramid through armed force, and often justified it as the will of a supernatural god.

Since the fall of the medieval feudal systems, governments have developed many more subtle ways to control the general population. Nevertheless, the continuing power of states to control markets, resources, and industries throughout the world still creates societies in which nearly all human exchanges are restricted and regulated by external coercion, the sole purpose of which is rent-seeking: that is, gaining resources without creating social value.

The intense competition between national governments chokes off the trade that would otherwise tend to equalize the wealth of different peoples. For example, most Americans, Europeans, and Japanese are relatively rich, yet one quarter of the world's population is virtually starving. In a free global market, the poor would utilize their low wage rates and desire to work hard as a means of providing competitive goods and services to wealthy countries, and would rapidly catch up economically. This extremely desirable outcome is slowed down by the managed trade policies of both rich and poor nations. Differentials of wealth are undesirable, yet rich nation states continue to work towards maintaining them.

Emergence, not Top-down Control, Creates Wealth

Market activities depend on the law of contract and the laws that prohibit the initiation of force, and which therefore channel human endeavor into collaboration, rather than criminality. But no coercive intervention is required to regulate the whole market, thanks to the "invisible hand" of the market, as described by Adam Smith.

Smith first explains the invisible hand in *The Theory of Moral Sentiments* (Smith 2000), in which he describes a selfish landlord who is led by an invisible hand to distribute his harvest to those who work for him. The landlord makes "nearly the same distribution of the necessaries of life, which would have been made, had the earth been divided into equal portions among all its inhabitants." Thus the selfish landlord advances the interests of society. In the same book, Smith describes the desire of men to be respected by the members of the community in which they live, and "their desire to feel that they are honorable beings." Thus the emergent stability of markets is also related to morality.

Today, scientists in the biological disciplines study many "complex systems" in nature and understand that their stability is due to "spontaneous order" based on evolution operating on the genes of organic life. For example, life within beehives, anthills, and termite mounds is complex and well-organized, but it maintains its stability without the intervention of outside intelligence. Human society is even more stable and coherently controlled as a complex system. Markets (i.e. human exchange) are simply one aspect of human biology that can achieve spontaneous order for a whole economy, and that must be protected from parasitical disruption by criminals or criminal governments.

Unfortunately, modern governments do not hesitate to intervene in the production of goods, their distribution, or trade, justifying such intervention by claiming that the market (that is, ordinary people) cannot do the job. Every time a government intervenes in absolute freedom, it benefits one group by cheating another group, and reduces the efficiency of the whole market.

Free Global Markets Equalize the Wealth of Countries

If we can free global markets from political intervention, exaggerated wealth differences between societies will disappear quickly. If differentials of any kind arise in free market conditions, they are pounced upon by competitors, causing differentials to shrink or disappear. We can observe from history how poor countries become rich when the political obstacles are removed.

For example, during WWII, the USA and Japan were enemies that could not trade. Not only were Japanese people much less wealthy than

Americans, but the quality of many goods, especially manufactured consumer goods, was much lower in Japan. After the war, the USA wanted Japan as an ally in the Cold War against the Soviet Union, and therefore it allowed technology transfer. The Japanese learned Statistical Quality Control from US specialists. The greatest specialist in quality control, Dr Edwards Deming, made such an enormous contribution to Japanese industry that the highest management prize in Japan was named after him – it is called the Deming Prize. The Japanese applied Deming's quality techniques with more vigor than other countries and became the world leaders in quality manufacture.

In contrast, the USA was the only country with an intact manufacturing sector after WWII. They had become complacent and placed less emphasis on quality, with the result that they fell behind other countries and had to catch up later.

The respective trade policies of the US and China meant that their people were not allowed to trade during the Cold War and until both nations made changes in those policies in the 1980s. US workers earned at least ten times more than the Chinese for the same work. When China joined the WTO and trade increased, many companies simply shifted manufacture from the US to China, creating jobs and wealth in China, and narrowing differentials. There is still no international free market, of course, but because the market is partially free, the Chinese economy is expected to overtake the US economy within a few years.

This same story has occurred repeatedly worldwide. When a quarter of the world's population was controlled by the British Empire, colonial policies restricted advanced manufacturing to the mother country, while the colonies provided commodities and less skilled labor. But after decolonization, market freedom expanded and former colonies, such as Singapore, Australia, New Zealand, and Canada prospered, and in many cases, overtook the UK in per capita wealth.

Competition Always Reduces Differentials

Classical economic knowledge, which has been confirmed by over two hundred years' of evidence, indicates that economic differentials, including those between the wealth of individuals, are reduced by the action of free market forces. Differentials are continually reduced in free markets when cash, people, and technology are permitted to migrate to where the demand is highest.

The principle is simple. If the wages of workers in one industry are higher than another for the same kind of work, then many poorly paid workers will try to raise their wages by moving to the highly paid area. The industry that pays poorly will have to raise wages to retain workers, and the one paying high wages may be able to lower rates a little.

The same thing will happen with profits. An industry that earns unusually high profits will attract more investment, increasing production until the products made exceed demand, and their price falls. When the prices of the products fall, the high profits will also fall. The same mechanism controls and stabilizes interest rates, dividends on shares, the rent for land and property, and indeed all the other variables in the economy.

One of the great, fundamental problems of modern life, the coexistence of huge wealth and immense poverty, can be almost entirely eliminated by allowing humans to act free of state intervention. Moreover, we know that acting freely is what humans did for two million years before the invention of the state, and that the only biologically normal type of social organization is one in which all adults are autonomous and act freely.

State Intervention Increases Wealth Differentials

And, of course, when states restrict the free market, differentials automatically increase. In countries with totalitarian governments, the ruling elite tend to be very rich and the general population very poor. This was true under hardline communism in Russia, China and other places.

Some people may choose to believe that differences in wealth are due to the inherent characteristics of populations. This racist prejudice was credible in the 19th century, but modern experience has quashed it. China was poor for three hundred years due to the repressive power of emperors and later, the state-dominated Communist system. But as soon as more liberal policies were introduced by Deng Xiaoping in the 1980s, economic growth resumed, and China is heading to become the world economic leader after a few short decades. India is now hot on China's heels, getting richer for precisely the same reason – the abandonment of state restrictions that prevented the majority from taking part in markets.

Some differences of wealth result from human variation, such as how hard people focus on serving the needs of others, how many hours they spend working, their physical and mental health, and their natural aptitudes, including their ability to analyze difficult problems and make good decisions. Such differentials are modest in degree, because individuals with one competitive advantage often have weaker abilities in their other talents.

It seems that modest differences in wealth are welcome and necessary. When individuals are industrious and study hard to improve their understanding of customers, or their ability to serve them better we tend to applaud them. Most of us are very happy to see that people who exhibit talent, industry or charity are rewarded by a higher standard of living, because we know that, without such people, we could not live good lives ourselves.

However, the exaggerated and extreme wealth differentials between billionaires and the starving poor are a different matter altogether. These huge differentials are purely the consequences of our distorted social organization – in particular, the actions of socialist, caste-ridden governments of some third-world countries and the arrogant, racially supremacist and nationalist governments of some industrialized countries.

Ludwig von Mises, the leading exponent of the Austrian School of economics supported this view as early as 1949: "All varieties of interference with the market phenomena not only fail to achieve the ends aimed at by their authors and supporters, but bring about a state of affairs which – from the point of view of their authors' and advocates' valuations – is less desirable than the previous state of affairs which they were designed to alter. If one wants to correct their manifest unsuitability and preposterousness by supplementing the first acts of intervention with more and more of such acts, one must go farther and farther until the market economy has been entirely destroyed and socialism has been substituted for it." (Mises 1949)

It is abundantly clear how true von Mises view turned out to be, when country after country scrapped their policies of nationalization and gross intervention in the decades after World War II. Finally, in 1989, the Soviet Union fell, demonstrating incontrovertibly the futility (and the horror) of state control.

Nevertheless, governments continue to pull the wool over the eyes of the public by practicing as much intervention as they dare, while making sure to leave enough of the market for the parasite state to be supported.

Today, we hear a lot about globalization, and the freedom of movement of money and partial freedom of trade, which have tended to equalize the price of goods and the cost of capital. But the really astounding exception to human economic freedom is the government control of human labor movement.

Global freedom of labor would disarm the sovereign state

Before WWI in 1914, there were only about 50 sovereign states, and people could travel to any country to invest or to work, without the slightest formality, and irrespective of their wealth or poverty, using gold coins that were universally accepted. If this human right to travel had been retained, wealth differentials between countries would now be very low indeed. But the number of states increased to over 200 and borders were quickly manned by armed guards, who demand to see passports.

The huge wealth differentials caused by the closing of borders and the damaging effects of sovereignty have been well examined by economist Lant Pritchett: "First, for most poor countries, "globalization" is a much less primary concern than sovereignty, and even the most aggressively liberalizing countries have yet to overcome the disintegration consequences of sovereignty. Second, the range of "equity" issues usually discussed in this context are all dwarfed, *by order of magnitude*, by the wage gaps across equally productive workers created by the enforcement of US (and other rich countries') borders." (Pritchett 2010)

Complete freedom of human movement without passports should be a long-term goal of those seeking lower wealth differentials, or the reduction of illegitimate state power over the individual.

States Prevent Social and Economic Adjustment

Coercive governments, as we have seen, continually distort the naturally meritocratic social order, and they have another enormously negative effect upon their societies. They pass legislation and make regulations that control almost every aspect of the population's economic, social, and sexual lives. Whatever the ostensible merits of individual laws and whether they are well-intended or not, the sum effect of constant legislation is the same: to prevent free contract between members of society. Without free contract, society becomes "rigid", which prevents the quicksilver, subtle, and unpredictable processes that would restore adaptive conditions in the face of technological change in a free society.

A useful metaphor for the overall effect of coercive government is the pouring of glue into a mechanical watch. We know that a watch can only function if the friction between its numerous moving parts is low. If any kind of viscous liquid is poured into the watch, or if any process increases the friction between the parts, the watch will immediately cease to keep good time. That is what all governments do to the economy, *irrespective of their intentions*; every single law is one more restriction, one more barrier, one less free choice to be made by the general public. This burdening of all adaptive effort by bureaucratic regulation eventually prevents the rapid adjustments to new conditions that enable a real free market to be both fair and productive.

Competition: Is it Freedom or Hell?

Most people have a love-hate relationship with competition. Socialists and many academics associate competition with laissez-faire capitalism and large, ruthless corporations. Consumers may identify competition with the "rat-race" and with advertising that persuades people to buy things they don't always need. Yet when people have to buy their groceries at high prices from the only shop in their district, they know that the only remedy is competition from one or more additional shops, to quickly bring prices down.

On the other hand, free market advocates talk about competition like a religion, but when business owners smell competition, they often lobby the government to ask for protectionist trade barriers or licensing requirements to keep low-cost suppliers out.

The simple truth is that the freedom that makes competition possible is vital to human life, but excessive competition is stressful, so we nearly all try to sidestep it by any legitimate, or often illegitimate, means.

How Excessive Competition Arises from State Restrictions

Governments make thousands of laws and regulations, each of which nibbles away at the available human choices like a mouse eating a block of cheese. The total effect of thousands of laws and regulations is to force the whole population into the remaining narrow bands of legal activities. All individuals are forced into artificially exaggerated competition for education, jobs, and business contracts and this artificially increases their stress levels.

Most people think that state controls on trade reduce competition. However, although such trade barriers stop the competition that would bring prices down, in another way, they increase competition. Home producers that wanted to buy the cheap foreign products as part of their business operations can no longer do so, so they will have to struggle harder to survive. The importers and distributors of foreign products will have less business and employ fewer people. The home producers that replace the foreign imports will, without the spur of foreign competition, continue to be inefficient, and fail to break into export markets.

Resisting cheap imports is only one of a huge variety of things the state does to strangle free trade, in both international trade and the home economy. When the state reduces the range of choices for people in hundreds of ways, the general population eventually ends up competing for fewer and fewer legitimate businesses and jobs. Every time another trade is regulated by license, or a profession is given a monopoly, or another industry is regulated, more people are forced to share fewer legal paths to earn their living, and this means more competition and stress.

The rat-race is really a product of the state, and the solution is to open up all market opportunities so that everyone can be enterprising and seek unique ways to make a living in which they can best serve the rest of society while avoiding the most intense competition with hundreds of similar competitors.

All the stress produced by "consumerism," including incessant advertising, unemployment, rat-race commuting, and corporate hierarchies, result directly or indirectly from state intervention in the market. If individuals and local communities were self-governing, consumers would be empowered by the combination of their confederated communities, which would provide them with an economic power base greater that the largest corporations. If buyers and sellers were thus equal in the marketplace, buyers would not tolerate the materialist, "Consumer Society," because they do not like it. Sellers, including the largest corporations, would have to negotiate with organized customers as equals.

Nature gave humans equality and the armed state took it away. But when human freedom is fully restored, ordinary individuals will be able to buy or sell goods, services or labor on an equal footing with the largest commercial companies. Furthermore, both buyers and sellers will be happier if they are equal under the law.

Free Markets Create Minimal Competition

I repeat, the most intense competition actually results from state *restrictions* to economic activities that remove choices and force people into competing for a narrow range of options. In contrast to our intuition, *minimal* competitive stress – and, in fact, minimal competition – arises when there are no restrictions and therefore the widest range of choices.

In free market conditions, differentials in wages, interest rates, profits, and overall wealth are minimized by *potential* competition, but the freedom to avoid competition by differentiating individual performance reduces the actual occurrence of wasteful competition and the stress it causes.

Thus, the dream of many academics and other thinkers to live in a world free of exaggerated commercialism would be realized by absolute free market conditions that would dissipate market energy over the widest range of choices, mediated by the smallest price and income differentiation. It is indeed an irony that the ideal world that socialists dream about is achievable through *laissez-faire* human freedom, not by state control.

Removing All Barriers to Trade

Free trade means that all persons have the right to buy or sell anything to which they have property rights. Free trade has been shown to be the most powerful system for wealth generation. Free trade also enables poor people to reduce wealth differentials and is therefore a tool for social justice. Why, then do governments restrict trade? The reason is that governments can only maintain their parasitic, centralized control of society by policies that increase wealth differentials. Ultimately, social justice is the same as social freedom; if governments supported low wealth differentials they would have to abdicate their control of society and lose the dishonestly acquired benefits that go with it.

The most sophisticated category of trade barriers are the so-called technical barriers, which constitute the artificial creation of conflicting national standards in order to prevent the emergence of global markets that might be dominated by foreign manufacturers. Governments often maintain idiosyncratic national standards to protect domestic manufacturers. Examples include electrical plugs and sockets, plumbing pipes and fittings, safety standards for motor vehicles, and food safety regulations. In the future world of global free trade, customers' organizations will select which standards to adopt, thus optimizing both competition among standards to improve technical quality and price competition to improve manufacturing efficiency. A free global market would allow goods and services to be produced as cheaply as possible, to the benefit of the whole human species.

Powerful countries often impose sanctions against their citizens trading with rival countries which they consider unfriendly or out of line with civilized practices. The motivation is to inhibit the economic and military development of the targeted countries, but the most certain effects are, first, to harm the ordinary citizens of the targeted countries, second to inhibit mutual holiday and business travel that tends to facilitate cultural harmony, third, to further alienate targeted governments politically, and fourth, to increase the chance of warfare.

The Chinese Experience

For example, the Chinese economy has been the largest in the world for 17 of the last 20 centuries and the Chinese people had the highest standard of living in the world until the 17th century. Yet, due to the policies of emperors and the isolation of Chinese society and resistance to industrialization and western ideas, China fell behind, starting from the 18th century.

When China failed to initiate an industrial revolution it was weakened by foreign predation and fell into deep poverty. By the 20th century, communism was introduced as a corrective for social inequality.

But communism requires a state monopoly of economic activity and therefore, to prevent individuals from initiating economic activity, the state had to set up a vast hierarchy based on individuals who accepted the communist ideology. When such a hierarchy was used to impose massive centralized power, wealth differentials grew between the powerful and the less powerful.

Communism prevented the creation of economic value by individuals and destroyed the price signals that guide investment in free economies. The all-powerful state made mistakes, just as all individuals do, but the state's mistakes were huge and caused economic catastrophe, resulting in tens of millions of deaths.

In the 1980s, the Chinese economy was opened up by Deng Xiaoping and the country began to trade again. The western world still imposed many technology restrictions and quotas against China, but with entry to the WTO (World Trade Organization), these fell away. Once it was partly free of foreign and national state restrictions, the Chinese economy began to grow rapidly and it is now the world's second largest.

Labor Costs in Industrialized and Developing Countries

The wages of factory workers in industrialized countries are often ten times higher than those in developing countries. Consequently, a large volume of manufacturing has moved from rich countries such as the USA, Western Europe, and Japan to developing countries such as China, Vietnam, Indonesia, and Thailand. This is one more example of the powerful moral effect of the market system in reducing differentials of wealth.

Workers in rich countries are "feather-bedded," when compared to those in developing countries, by state border controls and many trade restrictions that block equal market access to less wealthy farmers and manufacturers. When state barriers to trade are lowered and multinational companies invest in developing countries, poor workers may exult in their new opportunity to live more normal lives. Yet trade unions and socialist groups in rich countries, in their bid to continue their own "feather-bed" differentials based on state force, never fail to complain that wealthy corporations are "exploiting" foreign workers.

If anyone doubts the advantages to the poor of freer markets and globalization of the economy, trying explaining those doubts to the wealthy workers in Japan, who lived in a feudal economy until the export drive began in the mid-19th century, or to workers in Singapore, which was a poor and squalid British colony until its markets were opened after decolonization, and who are now among the wealthiest citizens in the world.

The free movement of labor between countries is as important as the movement of financial investment, technology, and trade. In the past, people could easily migrate to work in almost any country, but the system of passport control spread rapidly at the start of the 20th century and locked workers into their own countries.

The experience of the USA shows the benefits of an open immigration policy, because that country's great wealth was created largely out of the immigration of entrepreneurs and workers from other parts of the world, but today, opposition to immigration has become a major political issue. Today, restrictive immigration policies are narrowing the pool of imported talent and the USA is becoming less competitive.

The economist Milton Friedman argued that, up until 1914, free immigration to the USA enabled many people to find work that made America rich. If the same policy were permitted today however, millions of migrants would arrive to take advantage of the generous welfare payments, and this would make the country poor. Friedman pointed out that Mexicans that cross the border illegally to find work in the USA are still helping the country increase its wealth, because they cannot qualify for welfare of any kind. Friedman concluded that such situations, "show how bad laws make socially advantageous acts illegal and therefore, lead to an undermining of morality in general." (Friedman 1978)

Remove Market Privilege for a Moral Society

The legal concept of "equity" based on the inherited human preference for justice, was honed by evolution for millions of years, during which justice could often mean the difference between life and death. Today, we can occasionally see fierce controversies in sport, because of concern over perceived injustice, yet the broad sweep of play takes place under a strict set of rules almost faultlessly implemented by the referees and other officials.

Yet in our commercial relationships, the concept of fairness generally has no place. Companies have limited liability, and a hugely complex web of rules dictates the parameters in which companies can be set up and business conducted. International trade that ought to be a voluntary activity between free individuals is circumscribed by inter-government deals, WTO rules, tariffs, quotas, sanctions, and technical trade barriers. Nearly all such rules exist because rich countries wish to prevent the equalization that will result from free trade with the have-nots. Such restrictive policies work against justice as well as general prosperity.

Without Privilege, Differentials Shrink

Human civilization is degenerate and the entwined economic and military relations between governments are at the heart of the degeneracy. When humans reform global markets, abolish the power of states to rig them, and deliver a "level playing field" and the legal equality that has been delayed for centuries, all privileges will be eliminated and all monopolies terminated. The end of privilege will also see the end of exaggerated differentials. Free markets will relentlessly reduce differentials – of income, wealth, interest rates, and profits. An end to exaggerated differentials will mean an end to the exaggerated class system based on such differentials, and in particular, the end of poverty and hunger.

The ideal form of human society is absolute freedom under laws that prohibit direct harm to persons or their property. When we return to that ideal, which originated in nature, we will have the first fair society for 10,000 years.

Professional monopolies constitute one more form of restriction upon economic freedom. In a free market, all workers would choose what services they would offer to customers, and their success would depend upon the degree to which they could identify customer needs and meet them.

Opening Markets by Abolishing Monopolies

However, in order to maintain the hierarchy necessary for centralized control, the state does not permit this natural relationship for certain trades, such as legal services, accountancy, military services, engineers, doctors, and priests. Practitioners must be licensed by a state agency, or for priests, an organized religion. In fact, the number of skilled trades subject to mandatory licensing has exploded in recent decades.

Professionalism is generally desired by workers, because a professional monopoly controls entry to the profession, which lowers unemployment and raises the status and remuneration of the members. Society in general may lose, because customers have to pay higher fees to a monopoly profession, and may also be unable to obtain precisely the service they want, because service has been partly standardized to benefit the collective membership of the profession and the state.

Professionals create the belief that they have specialized knowledge and skills that cannot be judged or assessed by the public — they know what is best for their clients. Professor Stephen Davies (Davies 1983) makes the point: "Above all this relationship is paternalistic. The professional is in a position of authority over the clients and makes choices on their behalf from this superior viewpoint. This, we are told, is for the good of the clients who are incapable of deciding what sort of medical care they want, what kind of education their children should have, what type of houses they should live in, etc. They are seen in fact as incompetent. It is the professional who decides what their needs are and how they should be met."

The public has no control over the monopolies provided to professionals by the state. It is assumed that professionalism is related to standards of excellence, but there is not much evidence for that. Misconduct by professionals is tried and punished by their own controlling bodies, and the worst punishment is expulsion, which may eliminate income from that occupation. Some professions, such as teaching, have a national pay scale in which remuneration depends upon length of service rather than performance.

The number of occupations that are controlled by the state and can be considered as professions is growing fast, especially in the USA, where the virtues of free markets, on which early US success was entirely based, are apparently forgotten. The license to practice often depends upon examinations controlled by a monopolistic professional body.

Professional monopolies, like any monopolies, are bad for society, because they take away the free choice of the customer, putting too much of the power into the hands of the producers and of the state. As more occupations are regulated by the state, the damage to the economy and to social justice increases.

Professional monopolies began in the 17th and 18th centuries, when the modern states came into being. The state gave privileges to key occupations as part of the class system, in order to buy their loyalty, and maintain the parasitic state system in power. As UK playwright George Bernard Shaw wrote: "All professions are conspiracies against the laity."

In 1983, Stephen Davies wrote: "The present (UK) government has, rightly, been determined and severe in its attack upon the monopoly powers of trades unions. Professions are middle class trade unions, equally coercive, more influential and powerful, and perhaps even more damaging. If the government takes its own rhetoric seriously, it should seize the nettle and take action against them now."

Put more simply, professions are monopolistic privileges provided by state force and they should be exposed to the same open, competitive environment in which most people have to earn their living.

Market-based Professional Certification

Nevertheless, the public does require an effective means of ascertaining the competence of people who offer their services, especially for vital roles such as medicine. At present, the fact that someone has passed professional examinations does not clearly indicate their experience or competence, and details of their track-record are not available, due to patient confidentiality among other things.

When state power is abolished, federated communities will represent all the customers of professional services. Therefore, it will be quite easy to persuade professionals to act in accordance with their customers' needs. So, if potential patients would like to receive the appraisal rating of all a doctor's previous patients – anonymously, of course, to maintain patient confidentiality – then this may be made available. Information such as this will not only give patients a far better way of choosing service professionals, but it will provide the market feedback necessary to maintain the standards of professional service.

Replacing State Fiat Currency by the Gold Standard

The control of currencies by armed nation states is clearly a destabilizing force in the world because of the ability of states to print money, which dilutes the currency and swindles the general population out of the value of their savings. The associated ability to manipulate interest rates of issuing banks distorts the allocation of investment in the economy.

In the 19th century, major currencies like the British pound and the US dollar were not generally subject to inflation, due to the gold standard. Consequently, as manufacturers constantly increased their productivity, the prices for most goods fell. International trade was facilitated, because the currency could be relied on to provide constant value, and there was no need to constantly hedge against fluctuations.

Many free market economists believe that currencies should be freed from state control, so that people can select the media of exchange that is most stable and efficient to use. If trading is freed from state control, it is quite likely that most people will prefer to use currencies that can be redeemed against precious metals or commodities, rather than the fiat currencies that depend upon having faith in the body that issues them.

The control of banking by governments also severely limits the huge advantages that would otherwise be obtained by free market banking. Real free market banking would have a phenomenal effect in funding small businesses and returning mass populations from state dependence to market participation.

NGO Microfinance Pulls the Poor back into Markets

Microfinance is one of the most powerful tools in the fight against global poverty. Starting in the 1970s, small independent microfinance institutions (MFIs) began lending tiny amounts to poor people. The MFIs may be credit unions, NGOs, and sometimes conventional banks. Most microfinance is in Asia, with a substantial amount in Africa and the Middle East, and much smaller movements in Latin America and the Caribbean.

The microfinance movement was started by Muhammad Yunus,

an economics professor in Bangladesh, who lent US$27 to 42 women in 1976, after the banks refused to help them. Yunus's philosophy is to help the poor to help themselves: "Give a man a fish and you feed him for a day, but only by teaching him how to fish do you feed him for life."

The Grameen Bank, which Yunus founded, has already loaned over US$13 billion to poor people with no collateral, and has achieved a recovery rate of over 97 percent. The Grameen Bank model has since been emulated by thousands of MFIs around the world.

Traditional banks will not provide microfinance, because the poor have no property to provide security against default, and because the transaction cost of a tiny loan is greater than the profit. MFIs cover the transaction cost by charging an interest rate from 30% to 70%, which is higher than a normal bank, but much less than a money-lender. And instead of asking for collateral, MFIs obtain security by dealing with groups of borrowers, so that peer pressure reduces defaults.

Micro-loans are made to typically hardworking micro-entrepreneurs to fund small businesses such as weaving baskets, raising chickens, or buying wholesale products to sell in a market. Such businesses can lift people from near-starvation to a viable family life. Most of the micro-loans are made to women, because 70 percent of the world's poor are women, who have higher unemployment rates than men. (World Bank 2011)

MFIs represent the opposite of state power – free market capitalism for the poor. The success of microloans indicates the real nature of poverty, which starts with exclusion from markets, including banking, caused by state power. The answer to poverty is not taxation and welfare, which breeds dependency, passivity and helplessness, but rather the opening up of the market to everyone on the planet. Once we remove the sovereign power of governments, the growth of micro-businesses will become the rule, not the exception.

Yunus claims that there are two mutually exclusive motivations for capitalism: "Maximization of profit" and "Doing good to people and the world." (Yunus, 2006)

However, a primary reason why capitalist corporations are dedicated to maximization of profits is that of limited liability and other corporate legislation, which is the handiwork of the ruthless, parasitical state.

In contrast, businesses started by individual entrepreneurs or families that live in normal human communities are rarely concerned with the maximization of profit, because they are founded on the inspiring visions that arise in the minds of entrepreneurial men and women. It is human nature to dream – but it is not human nature to act like an accounting machine.

Chapter 11

Promoting an Adaptive Global Civilization

*T*he task of freeing civilization from the coercive, parasitic state and creating an adaptive habitat for the global population will require the collaboration of hundreds of millions of people.

Enormous benefits to the wellbeing of all humans will be realized by gradually abolishing the conqueror's monopoly of power that has been inherited by the parasitic state and making global laws against the initiation of force and in compliance with the "non-aggression principle." This one action will prevent warfare and prohibit the use of technologies whose routine side effects injure or kill humans. The adaptive society will harmonize technology use with both the well-being of the human species and the integrity of the earth's ecology.

Maladaptive features of current societies, such as warfare, exaggerated wealth differentials, pollution, state controlled capitalism, consumerism, and materialism will disappear. The general global public, whose work creates the resources on which civilization is built, will at last be enabled to demand – and obtain – the adaptive living conditions necessary for intelligent, moral humans to thrive.

The recovery of the normal social organization that evolved with our ancestors, and the end of 10,000 years of slavery to the armed state, promises to constitute "the greatest adventure in human history."

Educating the Global Public

The great project to create adaptive civilization will require the most extensive educational program in history, in order to transmit the first scientifically based concepts of a rational civilization to all cultures and in all languages. Below, we discuss the social groups and issues that need to be addressed.

In order to obtain global acceptance of a return to a natural civilized social structure, it is essential that the global population be taught as much as possible about the history of their species, including the harmful side-effects of technology and its most damaging manifestation, the emergence of the coercive, parasitic state.

Many writers lament the fact that the general public is so passive in its response to political issues, and even to issues of self-preservation, such as saving money for their retirement or maintaining a healthy diet and lifestyle. The reason for this passivity is that the parasitic state has stolen the normal role of ordinary men and women in the governance of their own communities – the role of discussing the threats and issues that face their society and deciding what to do about them. The centralized state has even replaced family welfare and most of the education of the young.

Many people will be skeptical that the global public can take a more active part in the management of their lives. Under state control, people are remarkably passive, even stoic, in the face of many aspects of the quality of life that are in decline. It is easy to believe that the political or religious differences between groups will continue to block collaborative initiatives, such as the trend towards the creation of adaptive civilization.

An optimistic view of how the general public can defeat the parasitic control of the state is expressed by US voluntaryist and anti-war activist, Adam Kokesh, who believes that technology is equipping people to see through government deceptions. He points out that each generation has more advanced communications technologies to monitor the injustice resulting from the state's use of force. "Today's kids had smartphones in high school, with the incredible power of the Internet," says Kokesh. "We have the truth button in our pockets, one-click away. You can lie to us but not for long. The bullshit detectors get better and better with every generation."

Given this power to monitor the state, Kokesh believes that people will soon achieve a society without state coercion. "I see freedom is simply a by-product of our ability to apply logic and reason and see that there is a better way than dealing with one another by force, fraud and coercion. The development of a free society is our destiny as a species and it is inevitable – they cannot stop us." (Kokesh 2012)

The main thrust towards controlling the illegitimate use of force by states must start with education and lead to public demands expressed in the international arena. As the global population becomes more conscious of its common heritage and needs, people everywhere will begin to demand more uniform and natural human rights. A concern for human rights will lead naturally to the demand for a standard form of global law and for a global debate on which human rights are natural and essential.

Enforced schooling has taken children away from the family for most of their youth, greatly weakening the family structure. Centralized welfare enables single women to support children financially, but it has made men dispensable, so that 28% of US children grow up in what are often "dysfunctional" single-parent families. In the natural prehistoric human bands, there could be no "dysfunctional families," because children grew up in a close network of relatives and were therefore not exclusively dependent upon anyone, even their own parents.

As scientific truths about human history become common knowledge, it is my belief that millions of men and women will be galvanized by the possibility of re-assuming their natural autonomy and taking back ownership of their lives from the parasitical state structure.

Cultural Exchange

Although political authorities can easily incite conflicts between national, racial, or religious groups, such conflicts can be defused by direct contact between populations. The quest for civilization will justify major efforts to expand the exchange of students, media representatives, and cultural specialists between cultures. Tourism already provides a framework for contact, but people campaigning for a new civilization will need to organize cultural exchanges to debate and resolve the issues facing a peaceful and harmonious global civilization.

A substantial and fast-growing proportion of the global population, especially the young, utilize real-time Internet communications many times each day. When state borders disappear, they will already be habituated to the global travel and global communications that enable humans to be mutually hospitable and to share their solutions for common problems that arise in modern civilization.

Scientists Slow to Recognize the Pathology of Civilization

As we discussed in Chapter 3, the human metabolism and the natural human lifecycle are subject to slow Darwinian evolution but they must be protected from distortion by the fast evolution of the habitat. Most people, including scientists, have tended to accept the erroneous idea that the human lifecycle and its supporting culture should conform to changes in technology. But the natural human lifecycle is part of the sacred "humanity" of our species, and just because people are flexible enough to tolerate the distorting effects of inappropriate technology does not mean that such technologies should be used. When technologies harm people, they become weapons, and their use should be universally prohibited by the public and its leaders.

As previously explained, technology and the part of human culture associated with that technology evolves rapidly by evolution of civilization, but the human species and the part of culture that maintains the natural human lifecycle, evolve very slowly, by biotic evolution. If scientists or other thinkers support the coercive alteration of the human lifecycle or social organization by the state, they are participating in the destruction of their own species. Distortion of the human metabolism (unnatural diet, polluted air and water, for example), or social organization, such as enforced hierarchy and socialist-style regulation, not only cause severe stress, lowering the quality of life for most people, but also disrupt the evolution of the habitat.

The scientific community has enormous potential for good if it can recognize the need for the human species to close ranks and adopt biologically natural law and morality. The scientific basis for closer global collaboration of the species is irrefutable but it is obstructed by the power of over 200 coercive governments that see science as the key to military and economic domination of other states. The human species has experimented with various political forms of centralized power for several hundred years; long enough to establish without doubt that neither peace nor social justice are obtainable by coercive governance. The case for an adaptive civilization that evolves by a process of emergence, driven by the adaptive preferences of billions of individuals and consensually managed communities, is irrefutable. Support for a biologically natural, and apolitical form of social organization should be part of the philosophic outlook of any scientifically educated person.

NGOs Should Unite in Global Social Reform

NGOs (Non-Government Organizations) are created to pursue specific goals, often related to the reform of society, and they therefore constitute potential support for the creation of adaptive civilization.

The term "NGOs" was coined by the United Nations to refer to non-profit groups that are independent of government, although some are funded by government, but have no government representatives as members. Political parties are not considered NGOs. Due to variations in the definition of NGOs, the number of such bodies is unknown, but there are said to be 3.3 million groups in India alone. Therefore the total membership of such bodies forms a significant percentage of the world population, and their membership surely includes some of the most active and intelligent humans on the planet.

At present, each NGO is concerned exclusively with one aspect of human life. Thus, in the hierarchical organization of the nation state, NGOs are in conflict with each other (e.g. gay rights advocates versus religious fundamentalists, family planning rights groups versus anti-abortionists, trade unionists versus free market adherents). NGOs also compete to pull state policy one way or another by lobbying.

If state power is gradually suppressed, and a more natural human society emerges, the competition between NGOs to win a share of the taxation taken by force will disappear. Instead, NGOs will tend to be united by their desire to alter human society, typically in the direction of what they perceive to be "human rights." They may then see that their best interest is in collaborating with other NGOs to adjust the necessary trade-off between the various goals of reform. Therefore, the education of NGOs about the need for adaptive global civilization is a very high priority.

Religious Groups and Scientists must Collaborate

The creation of a global human civilization that is well-adapted to its habitat depends upon achieving a consensus on the prohibition of the initiation of force throughout society. Religious communities are important in achieving such a consensus because they not only profess a desire for peace and harmony and a concern with moral values, but they constitute a clear majority of the global population.

In contrast, the community of scientists is small, but it has a great influence on government and the media. Science is also amplified by the large body of engineers and technicians that mostly embrace a scientific view of the world. Furthermore, the majority of humans now live in crowded cities that are based on the intensive use of technology, and this tends to promote a widespread demand for scientific solutions to human problems.

Regrettably, however, science and religion do not see eye-to-eye. In recent years, a strong rivalry has opened up between the scientific community and the representatives of organized religion, a rivalry that could provide an obstacle to the global consensus necessary to create truly civilized societies. If humans wish to live in diverse, free societies and attain self-government through the elimination of state coercion, they must agree to a common global law. This requires a change in attitude from the adherents of both science and religion.

The Biological Significance of Religion

Scientists should bear in mind that religious adherents tend to live in small, family-oriented communities with face-to-face relationships and high trust levels, based on strong moral traditions. From a scientific point of view, this represents an adaptive preference that is inherited from the evolutionary period when all communities had these attributes. Thus, it might be surmised that the remarkable persistence of religious practices in the modern age is partly due to the adaptive preference of adherents for community life that is more natural than that of the industrialized society in general. The tendency of a majority of humans to form small, more natural, communities should be no surprise to anthropologists in the light of their knowledge of pre-agricultural hunter-gatherers.

Nearly all scientists consider that the supernatural aspects of religion may be an obstacle to attaining a global consensus on the moral obligations of humans. But scientists should applaud the persistence of religious groups in rejecting the amoral, industrialized mass society in favor of communities more like those that evolved from nature. Religious communities surely attest to the human need for the community and morality that are essential constituents of an adaptive civilization.

With regard to the widespread criticism of religious "fundamentalism", and the political conflict and violence associated with it, religious authority is clearly just one type of illegitimate coercion present in the modern world. I have consistently enunciated throughout this book that the solution to group violence is to criminalize all coercive practices, including those of nation states, by the creation of global law to enforce "living by contract," which is the scientifically consistent definition of civilized conduct.

Religious Adherents Must Accommodate Scientific Truth

Those who embrace a religious way of life should also come to terms with science. Humans are intelligent and have an inbuilt need to decode the natural laws that govern the world around them. For several hundred years, patient, disciplined men and women have investigated and revealed the scientific knowledge on which modern civilization is now based. Living in that modern civilization – as most religious people must – implies acceptance that most of the accumulated scientific body of knowledge is irrefutable.

Yet many religious people still reject major components of the scientific view, such as the evolution of the species. Evolutionary theory is now making a major contribution to civilization, especially in medicine, and its principles are proven to hold true in daily laboratory procedures across the world. Whatever truths and values are comprised by the religious way of life, they cannot depend upon teaching children untruths about the world.

In contrast, much of religious theology was written at least one thousand years ago, and presents a view of life seen through the eyes of militant people in pre-industrialist warrior states that were continually subject to warfare. If "holy" books contain elements that are no longer compatible with the morality or needs of present-day religious followers, then perhaps those responsible should consider updating them to fulfill their intended function better?

A 2012 survey of people in 57 countries found that 59 percent of people described themselves as religious, 23 percent as not religious and 13 percent as atheist. That is a 9 percent drop in the religious group in seven years since the last poll. It is also significant that rich countries have more non-believers and atheists than poor ones, and college educated people are 16% less religious than those without secondary education. (WIN-Gallup International 2012)

The writing on the wall must be obvious to religious communities. Some religious institutions obstinately reject scientifically proven knowledge, even when it is essential for human welfare. And therefore, as people become wealthier and better educated, they abandon religion. The lesson for organized religions is clear. If religions are to survive in a scientific age, they must, sooner or later, define their core values without the aggression against non-believers that feeds violent conflict. This process will strengthen what is valuable and admirable about a religion, and reduce what is increasingly treated with suspicious and disdain by much of the world community. Furthermore, the indoctrination of children with incitement to violence, or with untruths that originated in primitive tribal cultures, may one day become illegal everywhere.

Equally, religious adherents should alter their attitude towards holy scripture, written hundreds of years ago by superstitious, pre-industrial tribespeople when interstate warfare was even more frequent. Those parts of religious theology that relate to tribal hatreds should be regarded as archaic and excluded from the beliefs offered to modern congregations, especially impressionable children. Similarly, all aspects of religious belief that conflict with scientific knowledge or morality should be put aside. There will be resistance, but ultimately we all have to stay up-to-date or become irrelevant.

If religious authorities could manage the massive leap of imagination required to make these changes, the scientific community would have to amend its attitude towards religion, and there would be a foundation for consensus on the moral values of a united human species.

I hope that we can assume that the leading figures in both scientific and religious communities want to move the world towards a more complete civilization – towards, in fact, an adaptive civilization that is integrated with nature. That project is quite impossible within the foreseeable future without a deeper understanding, and some concessions, on the part of both working scientists and religious adherents.

Libertarians Should Advocate Strong Government & Law!

Libertarians believe in optimizing human freedom, and that is certainly part of the healthy aspiration that supports creation of an adaptive civilization. Regrettably, many libertarians see freedom as being the absence of "government" or "laws." But if government and law were removed, chaos would follow, and such a community would once again rapidly regress to a coercive, parasitic state.

Libertarians must learn to value strong government and tough law – the strong, *self-government* of free men and women and their consensual communities, and the tough law essential to protect property rights, contract, and the policing of illicit "harms." Without strong government and tough law, there can be no human freedom; just the jungle.

Libertarians and those who love freedom should be open to the peaceful and orderly emergence of an adaptive, global civilization, based only upon the rule of universal harmonized law, with no state or coercive government. Such a civilization will be governed by millions of local communities, or "bands", each practicing consensual government. Human freedom will be optimized, just as it was in the evolutionary era, before humans were hi-jacked by the coercive state.

For libertarians, an important idea to bear in mind is that human freedom will certainly provide the opportunity for extremely creative and diverse human activities that will often vary greatly from region to region. Nobody can anticipate what other people will desire or accomplish and it is not their business to do so. What we can anticipate, however, is that the members of a free society must comply with the non-aggression principle that evolved in the Paleolithic era in response to natural selection of human intelligence.

We can create a complete civilization by removing the disruptive intervention of the state, but we cannot remove the obligation on free individuals to respect the freedom of their fellows.

The Media and Arts as a Communication Channel

Those who believe in self-governing communities and global peace should evangelize about the subject and create a tradition of active communication through the Internet, the media, and the arts, to establish the concept of a free, civilized world as a goal that can be achieved in the near future.

It is my hope that we can engender sufficient understanding of the topic that it will inspire the writing of plays and popular songs about the adaptive civilization. The creation of an adaptive habitat is the most important transition in human history, as well as being the greatest adventure. The value of creating an adaptive civilization merits celebration by the creation of music, drama, and cinema, perhaps as much as any other event in human history.

The idea of a global civilization is not necessarily attractive to most people, because they cannot easily imagine what changes it would entail. If artists of every kind can understand the need to unite the human species, they can help educate the global public. Below, I discuss some of the changes likely in an adaptive civilization.

Small, Autonomous Communities of the Future

The power of real human communities will transform our societies and the economy. For the first time since the adoption of agriculture, starting about 10,000 years ago, ordinary families will be able to control their own lives and live in more active communities, without any state oppression or coercive taxation. Millions of federated groups, dedicated to the same natural human values, will be able to collaborate for welfare and for social and economic projects of all kinds.

In the economic sphere, individuals and families will decide whether to invest or to participate in any specific project, ranging from international parties and festivals up to the creation of new global infrastructure. Many tiny communities, federated as equals with real-time Internet communications, will have the economic muscle to obtain the best financial and legal advice, protecting group members' interests and therefore eliminating some of the key differences between rich and poor members of society.

A World of Cultural Diversity

The phrase "global civilization" is uncomfortably close to "world government" and we need to explain the difference. Many people sense that global competition between states already results in standardization that reduces cultural differences. Will a global civilization, united by laws that prohibit the initiation of force, reduce diversity and subject people to bland, repetitive experiences? The answer is "no." In fact, the tendency to cultural uniformity that we can see today is mainly a product of the standardization preferred by centralized states.

Governments are locked into economic, and sometimes military, competition and they constantly monitor their rivals and attempt to keep up with economic or military developments. Coercive governments constantly intervene in the economy and retain vast numbers of people as civil servants, military personnel, police forces, and teachers, and it is only natural that large organizations, subject to military-style discipline, should favor standardization and compliance, rather than individual self-expression.

When humans do break free from the parasitic state, the multitude of self-governing communities that replaces the state will generally have an interest in differentiating themselves and retaining strong identities that are attractive to members of other groups, and to social and business partners of all kinds. Human diversity will naturally thrive in an environment of freedom.

Today, we can see a similar trend in manufacturers, which always seek to differentiate their products and services in order to position themselves in unique market segments and to avoid deadly head-on competition and price wars.

When nation states disappear, individual humans will remain competitive in relation to any mutually desired resources. Commercial companies will continue to attempt to create products and services of higher quality and lower price than their rivals. Under the state, many leading corporations, such as telecommunications and software companies, have been regarded as strategic national assets with military implications, and this has greatly limited international collaboration.

In a free world, individuals and companies will be able to travel anywhere and collaborate with people of any nationality in order to achieve overall efficiency. The consequence will be a very high degree of integration between the people, technology, and financial investments, from all parts of the world. Wealth differentials will plummet and technological development will tend to equalize. One result will be the disappearance of the motivation for workers from developing countries to immigrate to rich countries to find work, a phenomenon that has created a large part of the modern world's racial friction.

In Future, Humans May Compete for "Good Genes"

In primitive bands, natural selection was an unconscious process in which those individuals that were well-adapted to the habitat tended to have more offspring than others, and therefore passed on the genes for good adaptation. In a global culture without national barriers, and with universal access to knowledge, men and women may more consciously select the best genes for their children.

In the past, competition between racial subgroups, arising from ignorance of our common genetic heritage, has poisoned the world. In the future, it is likely that parents will continue to search for partners with the best genes to produce children who are healthy, attractive, and intelligent. But science has now established that desirable characteristics are widely distributed through all racial subgroups. Therefore, the resumption of natural selection, freed of the prejudices of state-sponsored nationalism, will create a revolution in racial relationships, making race a benefit, rather than a burden.

Smart women and men will one day perceive the astounding variety of human traits in Africa, India, China, South Asia and Europe as fabulous resources of great human genes. The rush to blend the most appropriate genes and have the "best" babies they can will return to women and men in industrialized societies their lost pride in parenthood and protect the exquisitely beautiful human species from the ever-growing degeneration of the human genome and culture in the evil state "livestock farms" of the early 21st century.

We should never forget that all the admirable qualities of humans,

morality,
creativity,
spontaneity,
problem-solving,
lack of prejudice
Self-actualization   acceptance of facts

self-esteem, confidence,
achievement, respect of others,
Esteem   respect by others

Love/belonging   friendship, family, sexual intimacy

security of body, employment, resources,
Safety   morality, the family, health, property

Physiological   breathing, food, water, sex, sleep, homeostasis, excrete

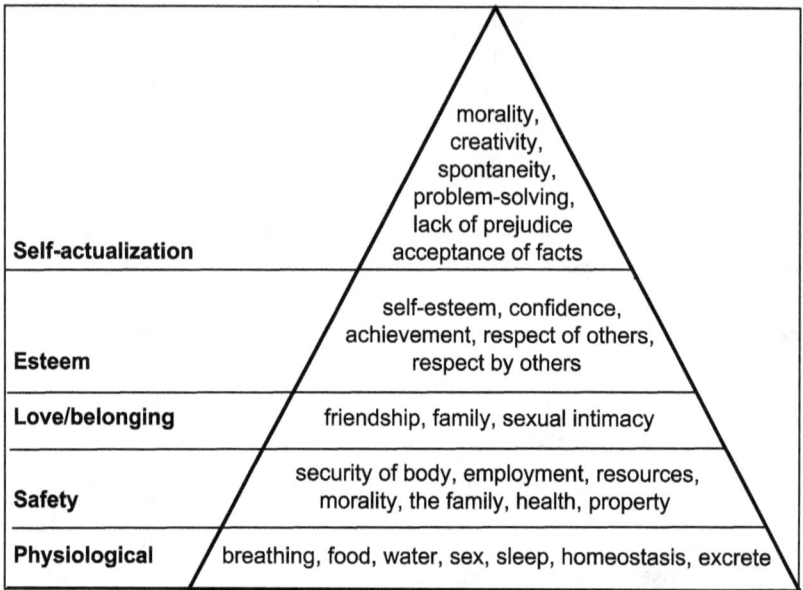

Fig.11. Maslow's Hierarchy of Needs. All humans need autonomy and cultural support to express their genes in the process Maslow called "self-actualization." The state blocks autonomy and the cultural support of the family. Source: CC 3.0.

including intelligence, creativity, sociability, truthfulness, reciprocal altruism, and duty, evolved in the natural habitat and will be fully available in any future society that ceases to abuse human nature.

An Adaptive Society Serves Individual Self-actualization

In the past, few people would waste their time speculating on the "purpose of life." The majority believed in a magical god and was told by religious leaders that these gods had a purpose for each one of us, but that this was mysterious and unknowable. People with a scientific attitude explained that nature had no purpose, and therefore life had no purpose, either.

Today, if you ask college students to define the purpose of life, they will frequently answer: "Self-actualization," see Fig.11. Self-actualization is the fulfillment of the individual's genetic potential, which can only be achieved by a highly developed adaptation to the civilized habitat. This viewpoint expresses the important idea that individuals must not only explore their own needs and priorities, but the needs and priorities of society in general in order to achieve self-actualization.

If individuals need to be free to set their own goals and seek their own fulfillment, then the well-being of society in general must also depend upon individual freedom to act, because society is merely the aggregate sum of all individuals. The idea behind an adaptive society is that the only goal for individuals is to seek self-actualization, and therefore, the only goal for society is to give every individual the opportunity to do just that.

Raising Children to be Civilized

Whatever plans are made for a fully civilized global community, and whatever laws are passed to create the appropriate conditions, the kind of society that results will depend upon the early education of children. Because children are born with immature brains, which complete their development during childhood and adolescence, their early education – or, too often, indoctrination – determines much of the resulting nature of society.

The state controlled education that we have today is clearly the worst possible option, since it builds into each child a loyalty to the arbitrary borders of a nation state. Ideology and propaganda are used to convert the natural human loyalty to family and community into blind service to the state, which can be easily converted into a nationalistic enthusiasm for warfare, whenever the state decides on that policy.

The only legitimate form of education is one based on the truth, which is that all humans belong to a single species, that humans are both intelligent and moral, and that legal equality and autonomy are their birthright.

Children must also have human rights, perhaps modified for practical reasons and their own protection. Among these should be the right to be free of physical violence, including spanking.

Another right is the right to work if they choose. In recent times, people in rich countries have come to regard "child labor" as something horrific, especially when it takes place in foreign countries and helps to undercut the wage levels of wealthy nations. Although it is obviously undesirable for children to be forced to work, or to work in conditions that may cause bodily or mental harm, it is desirable that children learn to do socially useful work at an early age, to habituate them to the reality that adults are expected to earn their place in society. For children, one of the most vital aspects of early education is to learn to be creative and entrepreneurial, so that they can eventually find work that they choose to do with pride and which will enable them to progress along the path to self-actualization.

Preventing the Mutilation of Children

Another area requiring law reform is the global prohibition of any form of bodily mutilation practiced on those who are unable to give their informed consent to it. This should certainly include both male and female circumcision and a long list of mutilations carried out as part of tribal customs in many parts of the world.

Any significant surgical procedures undertaken for cultural reasons should require the formal consent of a subject who is both adult and mentally competent. The age of consent can only be legitimately decided by a direct global vote open to the whole human species. This is a controversial subject as, while children become biologically adult when they reach puberty and can become parents, recent research has shown that the human brain is still developing in the late teenage years. It could be argued that life in a modern technological environment demands more mental maturity than was required for young people to cope in simple rural societies of the past.

Another huge concern is the conservation of nature, because modern industries generate such a wide array of pollutants and potential harms. The scientific and engineering communities are quite capable of delivering technology without pollution or harms, but this requires a fundamental change in the priorities of human government.

The Conservation of Nature

Under the coercive state, we constantly see compromises made in remedying the unintended consequences of technology, whereby some people suffer harms, which the state considers acceptable in view of its desire to dominate in the intense international rivalry between nations. In societies committed to human adaptation, this inter-state rivalry will be ended and the legal system will restore personal and property rights to all persons, thus making illegal the use of technologies that cause any foreseeable harm to persons or their property.

In a fully civilized society, productive industries can have no more right than individuals to harm persons, or their property, because productive industries are directed by individuals who must bear responsibility for their actions.

In a civilized human species, the only legitimate legal restraints are those that prohibit the initiation of force, and thereby deliver to all individuals the opportunity to pursue self-actualization, which encompasses the sole definable purpose of human life.

Glossary of Terms

Adaptive society

The author coined the term "adaptive society" to refer to future human communities that use the law to defend people against all harms instigated by others, including those caused by the maladaptive use of technology, thus ensuring that the artificial habitat of civilization is well adapted to the biological needs of the human species. In industrialized societies, it is essential that scientifically conceived law is introduced to ensure that the artificial habitat (i.e. "civilization," based on many technologies), remains adapted to humans, where necessary remedying any potentially harmful side-effects of those technologies.

In complex societies, adaptive fit between humans and their environment is maintained by cultural evolution, which I describe under the heading "habitat evolution." Evolution of a whole society depends upon the free interchange of all members of that society, and the free expression of their adaptive preferences. This means that the governance of an adaptive society must be consensual, and that it must prohibit the initiation of force by any member, on the basis of what is now known as the non-aggression principle.

Civilization

The word "civilization" has two distinct meanings. The most common meaning refers to any large, complex human society.

Adaptive Society generally employs the second major meaning of "civilized" and "civilization," which refers to human conduct that is regarded as moral rather than barbarous. A moral person "lives by contract", which entails making promises and keeping them, and using force only in self-defense, according to the non-aggression principle.

If a society conformed absolutely to the non-aggression principle, its government would have to be consensual, because the use of force

227

for taxation, initiating warfare, or other controversial purposes would not be possible. The borders of such a society would constitute, not the limits of conquest of a nation state, but rather, the limits of the private property rights of its individual members.

The complete civilization of a society is only possible if the non-aggression principle is fully implemented. But since any society that complied would be vulnerable to predation from societies that retained the use of force, then complete civilization is apparently possible only for the whole human species, not for any part of it.

Collective domain

In a society based exclusively on free markets and private owner-ship, there will still be a requirement to construct major infrastructure such as roads and airports that will displace residential and commercial landowners. Current methods of removing private landowners from the path of infrastructure rely on government coercion (such as "compulsory purchase" or "eminent domain"), which invites arbitrary government and corruption. As an alternative, I propose "collective domain," in which multiple real estate owners approached by buyers wishing to dis-place them in favor of a major infrastructure project must negotiate col-lectively. This would mean that, if the price offered by the developer were sufficiently above market values, then a majority of owners would agree to sell out, and the minority of owners who were dissatisfied by the offer would still have to accept it.

Collective Domain is designed to eliminate arbitrary government, the corruption of officials, and "holdout" landowners who try to make windfall profits. See more details in Chapter 7.

Communo-Fascism

I coined this expression to emphasize that communism and fas-cism, once regarded as being based on opposed political creeds, are ac-tually both expressions of totalitarian statism. In all modern states, in-cluding democracies, governments create hierarchies to facilitate cen-tralized control. Communist states use their illegitimate power to incor-porate enforced equality of remuneration and conditions for part of the population. Fascist states use the same sovereign power to incorporate enforced inequality for parts of the population. In practice, all states em-ploy coercion to create both these distortions when convenient, and therefore can be said to incorporate elements of "communo-fascism."

Cultural evolution

In anthropology, the term "culture" describes a particular form of society, or a stage of civilization achieved by a tribe or a nation of people. So the change over time in societies is often called "cultural evolution", or "sociocultural evolution." In *Adaptive Society*, I have found it desirable to distinguish between the part of culture that evolves slowly, by biotic, or Darwinian evolution, and the part that evolves very rapidly, according to non-Darwinian evolution. Therefore, I have introduced the term "habitat evolution," to describe the accelerated rate of development that results from human intelligence and the science and technology enabled by it. In my account, the civilized habitat of humans comprises three elements: tangible and intangible artifacts; accumulated scientific knowledge; and learned behaviors relating to technology.

Fitness (Darwinian)

The ability of individuals or populations to survive and reproduce in a given environment so as to propagate their genes.

Government

The word "government" means the management of society, which is indispensable, but it does not necessarily include the sovereign state that gives current governments their power to coerce their subjects. In a truly free society, including the foraging bands in which all humans evolved, the law prevented leaders from using force, and therefore individuals practiced "self-government," and communities employed consensual self-government.

Most current governments take their power from the sovereign state, and consequently have a monopoly of force, and the right to utilize warfare as a tool of policy without being punished for it; we need to abolish this type of government.

Perhaps a better word to describe the management of society is "governance," a word used to describe some collaborative business partnerships. The expression "voluntary governance" is used by some libertarians, especially Michael McConkey, to refer to the consensual management of free societies in the future.

Habitat components

Humans have used technology to construct an artificial habitat that evolves and exhibits emergent order. The human habitat comprises learned technical knowledge, learned technical behaviors, and artifacts, and I have described these three elements as "components" of the evolving habitat.

Habitat evolution

Habitat evolution is the process by which civilization tends to evolve so as to provide consistently adaptive habitat conditions for humans as technologies generate rapid change. Evolving habitats can also be seen in other species, such as the social insects, and beavers.

The habitats created by non-human species are ultimately controlled by DNA, as part of the "extended phenotype" explained by Richard Dawkins. In contrast, the human habitat comprises artifacts, learned behaviors related to the creation, maintenance and use of artifacts, and learned knowledge related to science, technology, or artifacts: all things that are outside of direct control by DNA. This means that the evolution of human civilization (e.g. "culture" in the language of anthropology) is based on a non-Darwinian mechanism.

Habitat evolution is distinguished from biotic evolution, firstly, because DNA cannot encode or represent the incremental changes that constitute the evolution of technology and artifacts. Second, because the components of the human habitat – artifacts, technical knowledge and technical behaviors – are subject to individual and social human selection rather than natural selection. Charles Darwin stressed the central importance of natural selection to the evolution of the species.

Hunter-gatherers

Hunter-gatherers are bands of people who subsist by hunting, fishing, or foraging for plant foods in the wild. All humans were hunter-gatherers during most of the evolutionary period, until the invention of agriculture approximately 10-15,000 years ago. Scientific knowledge of the way of life of hunter-gatherers has been accumulated through archeology, genetics, and the study of human groups that retained the hunter-gatherer lifestyle in the modern era.

Law, parasitical and natural

Laws are the rules of a society that are implemented by using sanctions against those who contravene them. At the heart of all legal systems is the law against the initiation of force that originally evolved in implicit form, as a consequence of human intelligence, and is today known as the "non-aggression principle."

It is arguable that, if the non-aggression principle were implemented effectively, then all other social regulation could be consensual, since all harms that are not self-inflicted result either from the initiation or force, or from pure accident.

Natural and unnatural phenomena

Science has little to say about what is "natural," because everything that ever happens is subject to immutable, natural laws. From this extreme perspective, it is logical to say that "everything is natural," but that removes all meaning from the words.

In practice, however, when we classify things as natural or unnatural, we are distinguishing between the evolved ecological conditions on earth, that incorporate numerous cycles in which some organisms utilize the output of other species to create a sustainable biosphere and, in contrast, human technologies which rapidly deplete natural resources and produce damaging waste, and are therefore unsustainable.

Thus, when we see a human artifact such as an urban landscape, a large factory, a petrochemical works, or a transport highway, we recognize that it is a product of technology, based upon human intelligence and we describe it as "unnatural."

It is vital to realize that although technology is unnatural, its primary purpose is generally adaptive for humans, although it may have maladaptive side-effects. The burning of fossil fuels, for example, provides the energy that it essential to sustain human life and the infrastructure of civilization. However, its harmful side-effects include pollution that damages human health and the ecology.

Proper human governance should ensure that the harmful side-effects of every technology are systematically remedied or alleviated. It is equally important to ensure that technologies can be sustained without ecological damage.

Non-aggression principle

The non-aggression principle refers to the widely-supported moral principle that individuals should not initiate force, although they may use force against attackers to defend themselves or other innocent parties. The use of force includes any kind of theft, fraud or rape. Even if merely threats of violence are used by a potential assailant, rather than actual force, the result is still that resources are taken from the victim involuntarily.

Note that the general public in virtually all societies accepts the non-aggression principle, but that governments of states routinely claim sovereign power and initiate force, just as criminals do.

Paleolithic period

The Paleolithic period is the "Stone Age," during which humans used stone tools and weapons. The Paleolithic is divided into three periods, approximately as indicated below, with "kbp" representing thousands of years before the present time:

Lower Paleolithic: 2.5 million – 200,000 kbp (years before present). This period includes the first tool-using ancestors of humans.

Middle Paleolithic: 200 kbp – 45 kbp. This period included the first anatomically modern humans, classified as Homo sapiens.

Upper Paleolithic: 45 kbp – 10 kbp. This period included the emergence from Africa of people with all modern human characteristics, able to make efficient stone tools and create complex culture, including rituals and art.

These dates are approximate because different human societies progressed through the use of stone tools at different rates, and therefore the term "Paleolithic" does not describe a precise period of time.

Rent-seeking

Rent-seeking activities are ways of profiting from power over the market, without having to contribute goods or services of value to others. Many kinds of state legislation and monopolistic licensing practice provide politicians with arbitrary power over the community that can generate opportunities for rent-seeking.

Medieval guilds had monopoly rights to certain crafts, that reduced competition and therefore increased the prices to customers. Modern governments license a wide variety of occupations, providing the same unfair benefit to those in the monopoly. The biggest example of rent-seeking is warfare and the arms industry, which generate trillions of dollars of revenue that state officials can tap in ways too numerous to conceive. The war on drugs, and the state welfare system also generate astronomical opportunities for "easy money" for the parasitical machinery of the state.

Technology

In *Adaptive Society*, technology is defined very broadly, as any sustained change to the human habitat resulting from human learned behavior. For example, when humans use their intelligence to create a new way of doing something that changes their habitat in the long term, such as making stone tools, wearing clothes, or cooking, the process of changing the habitat can be described as a "technology."

The state

A state is a particular area of the Earth's land surface, together with all the people living within its borders, that is subject to the monopolistic power of a sovereign government. States were created either by military conquest, or the arbitrary decisions of existing states. States are governed by individuals or groups who can obtain the power to do so, either by armed force, or by popularity, e.g. through electoral success.

The social organization of states therefore contrasts with the social organization that evolved with human groups, which was based on individual autonomy and consensual decision-making.

Voluntarism

The principle that social institutions such as those for education, healthcare, or welfare, should be supported by private finance and organization, rather than by state agencies. Humans evolved in societies that were entirely voluntaryist and therefore human intelligence and morality must be optimally adapted for such social relationships. In *Adaptive Society*, the author argues that retrieving the natural, entirely voluntaryist, social organization is the only way in which humans can create a peaceful and just civilization.

Acknowledgements

I began to think about social organization and government when I was very young, thanks in part to being born in WWII, when the damage done to humans by the nation state system was probably at its historical peak. I must also acknowledge the influence of my Scottish father, William Henry Milburn, who passed on to me his free-thinking humanist views well before I was of school age. The influence of my rational and moral father highlighted the grotesque nature of warfare between nation states, the utter amorality of all political systems, and the powerlessness of millions of people whose lives were thrown away for nothing.

Writers today are able to "stand on the shoulders of giants" more easily than ever before, and I have endeavored to utilize the most relevant information available to me from scientific resources, heavily using the superb facilities of the Hong Kong University of Science & Technology. I have also learned from great thinkers about liberty, past and present including, for example, the admirable and hyperactive US-based Future of Freedom Foundation, under founder and president Jacob G. Hornberger, and vice president Sheldon Richman.

I am a commercial technology writer by profession and my book is essentially a solo act, so I have no collaborators to thank or to share the blame for my writing errors. I must, however, acknowledge a practical debt to my scientific, medical and academic editor, Gillian Kew, for her patience, especially in reducing my unsubstantiated claims, hyperbole and gender bias. Also for her superhuman patience as I ground through repeated edits. Gillian can be found at WWW.GillianKew.org.

My graphic designer, Wong Ka Po, who works for the IT publishing industry in Hong Kong, is as rapid and creative in turning design work around as I am slow, and I appreciate how the relative clarity of the finished book has emerged from my inchoate sketches and ideas.

My family, including Lorna, Rebecca, and Scott Milburn, and my son-in-law, Bofu Xue, have contributed valuable encouragement and feedback. They also provided a sounding board for new ideas and the optimistic viewpoint of a new generation.

I owe most gratitude to my wife, Caroline Lo Sin Ming Milburn, whose hard work and loyalty have made it possible for me to spend years developing my original tentative ideas on adaptation into what I hope is a strong hypothesis on both the failure of human adaptation and the means at our disposal to fully accommodate the biological needs of humans in modern societies.

Bibliography

Barkow (1992). *The Adapted Mind: Evolutionary Psychology and the Generation of Culture.* Ed. by Jerome H. Barkow, Leda Cosmides, John Tooby. NY: Oxford University Press.

Bastiat, *Frédéric* (2007). The Law. Auburn, AL.: Ludwig von Mises Institute.

Belfer-Cohen, Anna and Bar-Yosef, Ofer. (1989) The Origins of Sedentism and Farming Communities in the Levant. Journal of World Prehistory, Vol. 3, No. 4 (December 1989), pp. 447-498

Biddulph, Steven (2006). *Raising Babies – Why your love is best.* London: Thorsons (HCOL).

Boehm, Christopher (2001). *Hierarchy in the Forest: the evolution of egalitarian behavior.* Boston MA: Harvard University Press.

Boldrin, Michele & Levine, David K. (2008). Against Intellectual Monopoly. Cambridge: Cambridge University Press.

Boyd, S. Eaton, Melvin Konner, Marjorie Shostak (1988). Stone Agers in the Fast Lane: Chronic Degenerative Diseases in Evolutionary Perspective. *The American Journal of Medicine,* Volume 84, April 1988.

Bracha, Oren (2005). *Owning Ideas: A History of Anglo-American Intellectual Property.* Cambridge MA: Harvard Law School.

Breggin, Peter R. (2000). *Dr Breggin testifies before US Congress.* http://www.breggin.com

Campbell, T. Donald (1965). Variation and Selective Retention in Sociocultural Systems. A chapter in: *Social Change in Developing Areas,* edited: Herbert R. Barringer, George I. Blanksten and Raymond W. Mack. Rochester, USA, VT: Schenkman Books Inc.

CFR (2013). *Same-Sex Marriage: Global Comparisons.* Council on Foreign Relations website, July 2013. http://www.cfr.org

CIA (2013). *The World Factbook.* Country Comparison: Birth Rates. *https://www.cia.gov/library/publications/the-world-factbook/*

Coase, Ronald, H. The Nature of the Firm, in *Economica,* Vol. 4, No. 16, pp. 386-405, (November 1937)

Coase, Ronald, H., The Problem of Social Cost, *Journal of Law and Economics* 3, 1-44 (1960).

Coyle, Joseph T. (2000). Editorial comment in: Trends in the prescribing of psychotropic medications to preschoolers. *Journal of the American Medical Association*, 283, 1025-1030.

Cviklová, Lucie (2012). Advancement of human rights standards for LGBT people through the perspective of international human rights. *Law Journal of Comparative Research in Anthropology and Sociology, 2012, Vol3, No 2.*

Cziko, Gary, (1995). *Without Miracles: Universal Selection Theory and the Second Darwinian Revolution.* Cambridge, MA: The MIT Press.

Darwin, Charles (1999). *On the Origin of the Species.* NY: Bantam Dell.

Davies, Stephen (1983). Against the Professions. *Political Note no.19.* London: The Libertarian Alliance.

Dawkins, Richard (1976). *The Selfish Gene.* Oxford: Oxford University Press.

Dawkins, Richard (1982). *The Extended Phenotype: the Long Reach of the Gene.* Oxford: Oxford University Press.

De Duve, Christian. (2010). *Genetics of Original Sin: the Impact of Natural Selection on the Future of Humanity.* New Haven CT: Yale University Press.

Dunbar, R. I. M. (1992). "Neocortex size as a constraint on group size in primates." *Journal of Human Evolution* 22 (6): 469–984.

Eaton SB, Konner M, Shostak M. (1988) Stone agers in the fast lane: chronic degenerative diseases in evolutionary perspective. *American Journal of Medicine.* 1988 Apr; 84(4):739-49.

EU (2010). *Citizens' Attitudes Towards Alcohol.* Brussels: EU.

FAO (2005). *The State of Food Insecurity in the World.* Rome: FAO.

FAO (2012). *The State of Food Insecurity in the World.* Rome: FAO.

Friedman, David D. (2009) *The Machinery of Freedom: Guide to a Radical Capitalism.* NY: Harper & Row.

Friedman, Milton, (1978). *Free to Choose.* A US television series based on a 15-part public lecture program.

Hamilton, M., Milne, B., Walker, R., & Brown, J. (2007). Nonlinear scaling of space use in human hunter-gatherers. *Proceedings of the National Academy of Sciences*,104 (11), 4765-4769.

Hayek, Friedrich A. (1945). The Use of Knowledge in Society. *American Economic Review 35: 519- 30.*

Hodgson, Geoffrey M., & Knudsen, Thorbjorn (2010). *Darwin's conjecture: the search for general principles of social and economic evolution.* Chicago: The University of Chicago Press.

Hont, Istvan (2010). *The Jealously of Trade: International Trade and the Nation-State in Historical Perspective.* Cambridge, MA: Harvard University Press.

Kaplan, Hillard (1997). The Evolution of the Human Life Course. Chapter 10 in: *Between Zeus and the Salmon: The Biodemography of Longevity.* Washington DC: National Academies Press.

Kelly, Raymond C. (2000). *Warless Societies and the Origins of War.* Ann Arbor: The University of Michigan Press.

Kendall, Henry (1992). *Warning to Humanity.* Cambridge, MA: Union of Concerned Scientists.

Kokesh, Adam (2012) *Freedom is inevitable.* Video at Youtube website: http://www.youtube.com/watch?v=Wdxa-TZn4Uw

Lazarou, Jason, Pomeranz, Bruce H., Corey, Paul N. Incidence of Adverse Drug Reactions in Hospitalized Patients. *JAMA, April 15, 1998-vol 279, No.15.*

LeBlanc, Steven, with Register, E. Katherine, (2003). *Constant Battles.* New York: St. Martin's Press.

Lee, Richard B. (1968). What Hunters Do for a Living, or How to Make Out on Scarce Resources. In: *Man the Hunter* (Eds., Richard B. Lee & Irwin DeVore). Chicago: Aldine de Gruyter.

Lee, Richard B. (1979). *The !Kung San: men, women, and work in a foraging society.* Cambridge, Mass.: Cambridge University Press

Leitenberg, Milton (2006). *Deaths in Wars and Conflicts in the 20th Century.* Cornell University Peace Studies Program Occasional Paper, # 29.

Lindsey, Brink (2002). *Against the Dead Hand: The Uncertain Struggle for Global Capitalism.* New York: John Wiley & Sons, Inc.

Locke, John (2007). *Two Treatises on Government.* Minneapolis, MN: Filiquarian Publishing.

Malthus, Thomas (1993). An Essay on the Principles of Population. New York: Oxford University Press.

Manning, Richard (2004). *Against the Grain – how agriculture hijacked civilization.* New York: Farrar, Straus and Giroux.

Martin P. S. (1967). Prehistoric Overkill. In: Pleistocene extinctions: The Search for a Cause. (ed. P.S. Martin and H.E. Wright). New Haven: Yale University Press.

McConkey, Michael (2011). *Whither Regulation.* Ludwig von Mises Institute of Canada, Dec 14.

McConkey, Michael (2013). *Anarchy, Sovereignty, and the State of Exception: Schmitt's Challenge.* The Independent Review, Winter 2013.

Meadows, Donella H., Meadows, Dennis L., Randers, Jørgen, and Behrens, William W. III. (1972). The Limits to Growth. New York: Universe Books.

Mises, Ludwig von (1935). *Economic calculation in the Socialist Commonwealth.* In:

Mohler Jr., Albert, Lesbians raising sons; got a problem with that? *Baptist Press*, December 30, 2004.   http://www.sbcbaptistpress.org/bpnews.asp?ID=19814

Molyneux, Stefan (2012). *The Handbook of Human Ownership – a Manual for New Tax Farmers.* E-book: http://board.freedomainradio.com

Morgan, Patricia M. (2008). *The War Between the State and the Family: How Government Divides and Impoverishes.* New Brunswick NJ: Transaction Publishers.

Morris, Desmond (1996).*The Human Zoo.* New York: Kodansha America Inc.

Morse, Jennifer R., (2008). The Empty European Village. *Mercatornet,* 6 June 2008. www.mercatornet.com

Mosher, Steven W (2008). *Population Control: Real Costs, Illusory benefits.* Transaction Publishers: Piscataway, NJ.

Mummert, Amanda, Emily Esche, Joshua Robinson, George J. Armelagos. (2011) Stature and robusticity during the agricultural transition: Evidence from the bioarchaeological record. *Economics & Human Biology, Volume 9, Issue 3, July 2011, Pages 284-301.*

Peltzman, S. (1975). The Effects of Automobile Safety Regulations. *Journal of Political Economy* 83, no. 4.

Pinker, Steven (2002). *The Blank Slate: The Modern Denial of Human Nature.* New York: Viking Penguin.

Pritchett, Lant (2010). The Cliff at the Border. Chapter in *Equity and Growth in a Globalizing World,* by the Commission on Growth and Development. Washington DC: World Bank.

Richerson, P. J., & Boyd, R. (2005). *Not by Genes Alone: How Culture Transformed Human Evolution.* Chicago: University of Chicago Press.

Richman, Sheldon (2010). "Capitalism and the Free Market, Part 1." *The Freeman, magazine of the Future of Freedom Foundation* (August 2010).

Rothbard, Murray N. (1963). War, Peace, and the State. In: *Egalitarianism as a Revolt against Nature and Other Essays.* Auburn, AL: Ludwig von Mises Institute.

Rothbard, Murray N. (2006). *For a new Liberty: The Libertarian Manifesto.* Auburn, AL: Ludwig von Mises Institute.

Sahlins, Marshall (1972). *Stone Age Economics.* New York: Aldine de Gruyter.

Schmitt, Carl (2005). *Political Theology: Four Chapters on the Concept of Sovereignty.* Translated by G. Schwab. Chicago: University of Chicago Press.

Smith, Adam (2000). *The Theory of Moral Sentiments.* Prometheus Books. NY Prometheus Books.

Tocqueville, Alexis de, (2003). *Democracy in America.* London: Penquin Group (and public domain).

Thornton, Mark (1991). *The Economics of Prohibition.* Salt Lake City, UT: University of Utah Press.

UNU-WIDER (2006). *The World Distribution of Household Wealth.* Helsinki, Finland: UNU-WIDER.

US Census Bureau (2009). *Custodial Mothers and Fathers and Their Child Support: 2007.*

WHO (2005). *Inequalities in Young People's Health: HBSC International Report from the 2005/2006 Survey.* Copenhagen: WHO.

WHO (2012). *Alcohol in the European Union: consumption, harm and policy approaches.* Copenhagen: WHO.

WHO (2009). *Global Health Risks: Mortality & Burden of Disease Attributable to Selected Major Risks.* Copenhagen: WHO.

Wilson, Edward O., (2004), *On Human Nature.* Cambridge, Massachusetts: Harvard University Press.

Wilson, Timothy D. (2004). *Strangers to Ourselves: Discovering the Adaptive Unconscious.* Cambridge MA: Belknap Press of Harvard University Press.

WIN-Gallup International (2012). *Global Index of Religiosity and Atheism 2012.*

Woodburn, James (1982). Egalitarian Societies. *Man, Sep. 1982, Vol 17, No. 3.* London: Royal Anthropological Institute of Gt. Britain and Ireland.

World Bank (2011). Gender equality and development. In: *World Development Report 2012.* Washington DC: The International Bank for Reconstruction and Development/The World Bank.

Yunus, Mohammad (2006). *Nobel Peace Prize Lecture.* Available at website: www.mohammadyunus.org

Zerzan John, (1999). Elements of Refusal (1988), in: *Against Civilization: Readings and Reflections.* Los Angeles: Feral House.

Index

www.ingramcontent.com/pod-product-compliance
Lightning Source LLC
Chambersburg PA
CBHW050111280326
41933CB00010B/1056